GETTING THE GOODS

Getting the Goods

Ports, Labor, and the Logistics Revolution

EDNA BONACICH
AND JAKE B. WILSON

CORNELL UNIVERSITY PRESS

Ithaca and London

This book is dedicated to the loving memory of Vici Adams and Liberty Jaswal.

First published 2008 by Cornell University Press

First printing, Cornell Paperbacks, 2008

Printed in the United States of America

Library of Congress Cataloging-in-Publication Data
Bonacich, Edna.
    Getting the goods : ports, labor, and the logistics revolution / Edna Bonacich and Jake B. Wilson.
       p. cm.
    Includes bibliographical references and index.
    ISBN 978-0-8014-4572-9 (cloth : alk. paper)
    ISBN 978-0-8014-7425-5 (pbk. : alk. paper)
  1. Container terminals—California—Los Angeles. 2. Container terminals—California—Long Beach. 3. Cargo handling—California—Los Angeles. 4. Cargo handling—California—Long Beach. 5. Transport workers—California—Los Angeles. 6. Transport workers—California—Long Beach. 7. Shipping—California—Los Angeles. 8. Shipping—California—Long Beach. 9. Business logistics—California—Los Angeles. 10. Business logistics—California—Long Beach. I. Wilson, Jake B. II. Title.

HE554.L7B66 2007
387.1'53—dc22   2007028874

Contents

Preface

 This book tells the story of global logistics—how goods are distributed in the global economy—from the point of view of one of the major nodes of global distribution, the twin ports of Los Angeles and Long Beach in Southern California. These ports are an important gateway to the entire United States for goods produced in Asia. Through their piers pass 40 percent of the large containers in which manufactured goods are now shipped and 80 percent of the imports from Asian manufacturing countries such as China. Together, they constitute the fifth-largest container port in the world, having fallen recently from third place because of the rapid growth of a number of Chinese ports. We use this location to illustrate how globally produced imports move from other countries, particularly in Asia, to U.S. consumers.

 We will show you how goods get to the ports; what happens to them when they arrive; where they go; and how they are distributed, stored, and delivered. You will meet many of the key actors in this system and learn who exercises power over logistics and how they use it.

 It is common knowledge that conditions for workers in many global factories, especially in less developed countries, have come to resemble the sweatshops of the late nineteenth- and early twentieth-century United States. Underage workers—often teenage girls—slave for long hours at boring, repetitive tasks in factories where health and safety conditions are ignored. While a great deal has been written about the conditions the production workers face, less attention has been paid to the important workers who move the goods that eventually end up at the stores where you shop. This book tells the story of those workers and the work they do to get us the goods we all depend upon. In particular, we are concerned with how logistics workers have fared in the logistics revolution. The relevant workers here include seafarers, longshore workers, truckers (especially port truckers), railroad workers, and warehouse and distribution center workers. We are interested not only in what is happening to these people but also in their potential for organizing to protect their rights as workers.

We want to note that we have chosen to focus exclusively on imports rather than exports, containerized ocean transportation rather than air freight. Our emphasis is on manufactured consumer goods that are imported to the United States from Asia in containers. (Increasingly, agricultural products are moving into containers, as are automobiles. We have not tried to disaggregate them from the totals—we simply treat containerized imports as our object of study, based on the assumption that the vast majority fit within our topic of interest.) We have not conducted an in-depth study of the third-party logistics firms that serve as specialized intermediaries for the industry. Despite the size and range of some of these firms, we see them as secondary actors who are essentially service providers to the importing and exporting community.

Our approach to this study has been eclectic. We have sought every source of information available. In general, however, the approach has been more qualitative than quantitative. We have not conducted a survey or created a data set that allows for multivariate analysis. Rather, we have attended meetings, conducted in-depth interviews, visited facilities, read reports, followed the newspapers and trade magazines, joined list-serves, and the like. Our approach has been one of immersion in the social reality we are studying, and we have used all available means. In a sense, we did what historians would do to investigate a topic in the past, except that we were doing it in the present.

What we offer here is a look at supply chains and marine freight distribution from a sociological perspective. We are interested in the underlying social relationships of power, inequality, and exploitation that shape global production and distribution. It is a perspective that is often lost on the economists and scholars of business and public policy who study the industry. In that sense we come as sociologists of the industry, to examine how it is socially constructed and the consequences it has for people and society as a whole.

This book is the product of collaboration between Edna Bonacich and Jake B. Wilson. Before going further, let us describe how each of us was attracted to this project.

EDNA'S STATEMENT

I began this project in 2001 or so, and I had been thinking about it for a number of years prior. Jake joined me in 2005 to participate in the writeup. At that point, we coauthored a couple of articles (Bonacich and Wilson 2005; Bonacich and Wilson, 2006). Although I had spent more time with the topic and several years in the field, Jake quickly grasped the significance and scope of the project and brought skills and interests to it that I do not have. Without his partnership, this volume would never have been completed.

After I state my history and relationship to the project, Jake presents his own history and connections. I am deeply grateful to him for joining me in this work and have learned and grown from our collaboration. Jake brings a political sensibility, especially around the issue of race and racialization, that has strengthened our work. He also is much more comfortable on the computer than I am and has a facility with the Web and with graphics that I lack. Once Jake joined the project, we consulted about everything. This book is truly a product of both of us.

Here is my story: I was drawn to the ports of Los Angeles/Long Beach (LA/LB) long before I started serious research on them. My fascination may have stemmed from my commute from West Los Angeles to the University of California, Riverdale (UCR), where I teach, along Route 60 (the Pomona Freeway). Every year there seemed to be more and more trucks hauling containers, with the names of various steamship lines emblazoned on their sides, names like Evergreen, OOCL, China Shipping, APL, Hanjin, Hyundai, and Maersk. Seeing these multi-ton leviathans rumbling down the road made me aware of the flood of imports that were coming into our country through the ports. In addition, I passed a complex of giant warehouses as I drove past the intersection of Route 15, in the Ontario area of southern California. These buildings bore the names of some major U.S. manufacturers and retailers. I imagined a connection between the container trucks and the warehouses: the ports belched forth containers, the trucks drove them up to Ontario, and the warehouses unloaded them and sent them on to the rest of the country. This was my somewhat faulty picture.

Another source of interest came from my long-term involvement with the garment industry. Not only had I studied and written about the industry, but I had also worked on a volunteer basis with the union—first with the International Ladies Garment Workers Union (ILGWU) and later with UNITE (the Union of Needletrades, Industrial, and Textile Employees), which was formed by the merger of the ILGWU and the Amalgamated Clothing and Textile Workers Union (ACTWU)—and had also participated in various anti-sweatshop activities. Although the Los Angeles apparel industry is still substantial, it was evident that swaths of garment production had moved offshore—and were continuing to move. Although the clothing was produced abroad, much of it was being sewn for the U.S. market. It had to be re-imported, and the ports must play a critical role in that process. In a way, as local production moved away, I followed the industry down to the ports.

In looking across the Pacific Ocean at apparel production in Asia, I became aware that lots of organizing was going on there. Giant factories—global sweatshops—had emerged in countries like Indonesia, China, Thailand, and Vietnam, producing garments at a fraction of the U.S. cost, often under onerous conditions, including low pay, long hours, and few basic rights. In some instances workers were on the march, demanding improvements. Was there anything that we, on this side of the ocean, could do to support them? That the goods generally had to pass through the ports seemed to afford an unusual opportunity for solidarity. What, I wondered, were the possibilities for local workers involved in the international distribution (or logistics) system joining together with Asian production workers to insist on changes in the progression of global capitalism? I consulted with some friends—Katie Quan and Jill Esbenshade at Berkeley; Peter Olney, organizing director for the International Longshore and Warehouse Union; Fernando Gapasin at UCLA. All thought it a good idea, but we needed to know a lot more about how the logistics systems work.

With this encouragement, Goetz Wolff, then research director for the L.A. County Federation of Labor, and I applied for and received a small grant from the University of California's Institute for Labor and Employment (ILE). Goetz and I had worked together on a previous ILE grant on organizing manufacturing workers in Los Angeles. We developed a division of labor, whereby he took responsibility for the manufacturing project and I took responsibility for the logistics study; I later received another small ILE grant of my own to pursue it further. Goetz and Peter Olney of the ILWU have continued to work on logistics, developing and overseeing research on the subject. Goetz now runs the Global Logistics Institute, which brings together scholars from around the world who are interested in this subject, and I participate in it. I have benefited tremendously from these relationships, but this work, including its flaws, is Jake's and mine.

And so I launched this project in the summer of 2001. The impulse behind it was political. It seemed to me that the ports, especially the LA/LB ports, and their surrounding transportation and distribution systems were an important and vulnerable node in the global system. If the transportation and warehouse workers in Southern California could organize with a view to supporting the struggles of workers in Asia (and the rest of the world), they had the potential to insist on real changes in the workings of global capitalism. Of course, given the state of the U.S. labor movement, this was mainly a flight of fancy. Nevertheless, I decided that I wanted to learn about how the system works, and at least open up the opportunity for workers and their organizations to use the information in their struggles.

I like to try to connect my research with an ongoing struggle, and the one that seemed most promising was the Teamsters' port trucker campaign. I became friends with Gary Smith, the LA/LB organizer for this campaign, and tried, futilely it turned out, to involve myself in this effort. More important, Gary and I shared what was going on in the larger industry, trying to figure out what it all meant and how it might be useful to workers' struggles. Goetz, Gary, and I eventually approached Teamster regional leader Manny Valenzuela about organizing in the distribution centers (DCs) of Ontario, and a group was formed, including members of the ILWU organizing department, that tried to move this idea forward—with very limited results.

Conducting this research has been an adventure. First, the ports themselves are amazing places. I find myself in awe of their scale. As you drive down the 710 (Long Beach Freeway) or the 110 (Harbor Freeway), surrounded on all sides by container trucks, you begin to see in the distance giant cranes towering over the landscape. And you see containers piled up high in every direction. The stacks of containers allow for vistas with perspectives that fade into a distant vanishing point. I am not a photographer, but I found myself compelled to drag a camera with me, to try to capture the sights. Of course, others have noticed the photogenic quality of the scenery, and every port-related office and publication has splendid pictures that capture the scope of the thing.

The adventure lay not only in the ports themselves but in driving to sections of the city, my city, where I have lived for around forty years, that I had never dreamed existed. As most people know by now, despite its Tinseltown reputation, Los Angeles is an industrial city. (When we speak of the "city of Los Angeles," we do not mean the technical jurisdiction of the City of Los Angeles, which is a peculiarly gerrymandered slice of the County of Los Angeles. Rather, we mean the metropolitan area, namely the County of Los Angeles, which includes eighty-seven other city entities along with other unincorporated areas. Indeed, the urban area can be thought of as consisting of five counties, namely: Los Angeles, Orange, San Bernardino, Riverside, and Ventura. As will become evident, our project also certainly involved the Inland Empire counties of San Bernardino and Riverside.) Large sectors are composed of factories, warehouses, rail yards, and so forth, with little or no residential or commercial presence. These areas are off the beaten path, part of the underbelly of the city, and no one ever goes there without a clear purpose. I certainly had never seen them. So this research has opened up aspects of the city to me that most people know little about and have never seen.

I am not someone with a good sense of direction, and I have a fear of getting lost (probably linked to a couple of getting-lost traumas at the age of four), so I prefer to stick to paths I know well. But this research forced me to get out my Thomas Guide and figure out how to get to all kinds of unknown places. Along the way, I actually shed some of my fear of disorientation. I amazed myself as I set off on untraveled roads through the industrial wasteland, searching for buildings where an interviewee was located.

Another adventurous aspect of this research concerns the fact that the world of logistics and transportation is overwhelmingly masculine. Here I was, a woman of advanced years, entering a foreign country of male concerns: big machinery, giant corporations, huge entrepreneurial schemes, the movement of millions of tons of goods. Often I would enter situations where I was the only woman in sight. Young men would refer to me as "ma'am," a term that captured all the dimensions of my uncomfortable presence. And yet seeing a "man's world" also opened unfamiliar views of the world. I was indeed a stranger in a strange land.

Although I received some research assistance from Rebecca Giem, who helped with the study of distribution centers in the Ontario area, and Manuel Barrajas, who helped me interview Ernesto Nevarez, a man who had years of experience with the port truckers' movements, the bulk of the field research was a single-woman operation. I felt I needed to go out and see for myself, to talk to people, to attend events, even to read reports myself. I had to immerse myself in the research, and I could not delegate that. I don't like applying for big grants. I certainly would not like administering them. I feel that having money can be more of a burden than a benefit. So my research approach is small, almost intimate, yet I want to understand "the big picture."

The big picture, in this case, involved trying to understand the entire logistics system surrounding the ports. This included shippers (as the companies that import and export goods are called in the industry), the steamship companies and port terminals, the ports themselves, port trucking companies, the railroads, warehouses and distribution centers, and various intermediaries that can be lumped together in the general category of third-party logistics firms, or 3PLs. I wanted to know how cargo moves, who exercises control, and how power is wielded. I also wanted to know about labor throughout this complex industry. How have labor standards fared? What are the unions doing? I found myself bouncing from one topic to another, circling around the whole complex of issues, occasionally alighting on one subject for a brief period. I gave this approach a philosophical, or at least aesthetic, rationale. Having taken some drawing classes in my youth, I remember a teacher telling us that the biggest mistake that people new to drawing make is to focus on the details instead of the larger patterns of light and shade. The details, he said, emerge from the whole, while the pasting together of the details rarely captures the complex of interrelationships. This is what I have striven for in this study. Some details may be fuzzy (or even, heaven forbid, inaccurate), but I hope that the whole, and the way the parts relate to the whole, is basically correct.

Part of the methodology of this study involved interviewing industry people in depth. I like talking to people and learning about their world. I believe I am a good listener. And the truth is I found myself liking almost everyone I talked with during the course of this research. This poses a major dilemma for me. I consider myself to be a Marxist, at least in the loose sense of the term. By this I mean that I believe that capitalism is based fundamentally on the exploitation of labor and that the social inequality that is a noteworthy characteristic of the system is not ephemeral but endemic. I also believe that global capitalism is like an out-of-control train hurtling down the tracks, careening from side to side, and threatening to overturn and destroy everything at any moment. The environmental devastation that we are causing is one horrible symptom of the problem; we cannot continue to rape the earth at the current rate without committing species suicide and bringing down many other species, if not the entire planet, with us. I see consumerism, the value system driving the train, as a barren social philosophy that leaves us empty and without meaning in our lives. Moreover, I believe that the people who are oppressed by the system, based on class, race, nationality, or gender, will eventually rise up and demand fundamental change. As I have already indicated, I hope that our work will contribute in some small way to that process.

Now, most of the informants in this study, especially those on the management side, would be horrified by these views. Most of the corporate people that I interviewed are not what you would call capitalists. They are, for the most part, employees—professionals and managers who work for corporations or organizations that represent corporate interests. They are typically salaried, and they do not make obscene amounts of money. But their interests are closely aligned with global, corporate, capitalist interests, and most of them are firm believers in the system. They accept a world view that says that the free market and private ownership of productive property are the best way to organize human society. While there was variety among them, a goodly number had negative views of labor unions, which they saw as obstacles to progress.

I listened carefully and, I hope, respectfully to their points of view but did not reveal my own, knowing that if I did, conversation and exchange would become impossible. Nevertheless, I want to do them justice. I want to include in this volume a fair description of the world as they experience it. I definitely do not want to demonize them. In fact, they were almost all helpful, friendly, sensible people. Some of their criticisms of the unions were well-founded. And some were decidedly sympathetic to the most oppressed workers—the port truckers. The important point is that, within their own world and its frame of reference, they are decent people. I don't question their integrity as human beings. But I do have serious questions about the world in which they participate. I know that they will be offended by this book and will probably feel that I have betrayed them. But I want to underscore that my critique is *not* personal. It is systemic.

During the course of this research, all hell broke loose on the docks. The ILWU's contract with their employer, the PMA (Pacific Maritime Association), a group of steamship companies, terminal operators, and stevedoring firms, expired on July 1, 2002. Negotiations began before this date, of course, but they became more acrimonious until the PMA locked the union out on September 29, 2002, claiming that workers were engaged in an unannounced slowdown. On October 9, 2002, President Bush intervened by invoking the Taft-Hartley Act, calling for an eighty-day cooling-off period and federal mediation.

This series of events, along with the process of talking with friends and colleagues about our project and of making a few presentations about it at conferences, deepened my understanding of the project's political significance. The basic reality is that the logistics system is the Achilles' heel of globalization. The West Coast ports lockout is estimated by some to have cost the U.S. economy a billion dollars a day. But the ports are only one small part of a complex and far-flung network of transportation and distribution that depends on a constant flow of goods in a predictable and timely fashion. Any glitches in the system anywhere along the supply chain can cause major losses to the corporations involved in global production and trade. The implications are staggering, not just for trade unionists but also for the working class as a whole. Here lies a source of real economic power, one exploited by the giant corporations, which seem to be ruling the world without any serious challenge (backed, of course, by the U.S. government and military).

The realization that this project had major political implications led some others to want to collaborate in some aspects of it, notably, two of my colleagues at UCR, Christopher Chase-Dunn and Tom Reifer. We received a year-long grant from the U.C. Institute for Labor and Employment (ILE) and exchanged some stimulating ideas. I kept in contact with Peter Olney, organizing director of the ILWU, and Jeff Hermanson, at the time a senior advisor at the AFL-CIO's Solidarity Center, in the hope that the ideas and information presented here would be useful to them in their efforts to bring about progressive change. Most recently, some strategic researchers in the International Brotherhood of Teamsters (IBT) and the new Change to Win (CTW) labor federation reviewed a manuscript version of this book and appear to find it useful for their planning.

Despite the political concerns that drove this research, we have tried to present our findings in an objective manner. We hope that this study of the ports and their surrounding logistics system is valid in its own right, apart from its potential political uses. In other words, we hope that this book presents a truthful and accurate analysis of the relations surrounding the ports, regardless of anyone's political assumptions and goals. In a sense, its main purpose is theoretical—to help us understand the forces that are driving our world today.

JAKE'S STATEMENT

For many years I have been fascinated by the world's oceans. Growing up in Diamond Bar, about thirty miles east of Los Angeles in Southern California's dry desert habitat, I always loved to visit the ocean with my family. The cool, aromatic ocean winds to this day remain my favorite thing about the coastal shores of California. My passion for the ocean flourished as I immersed myself in radical environmental activism in my teens and early twenties. During these years, I interned with the Sea Shepherd Conservation Society, where I got the chance to embark on an oceanic direct-action campaign on the high seas. The voyage started on the East Coast of the United States, and we would eventually sail thousands of nautical miles through the waters of Belize, Honduras, Panama (via the Canal), the Cocos Islands of Costa Rica, and Mexico. The voyage ended in Long Beach Harbor. I remember my awe as we slowly moved past the Port of Long Beach. For me at the time, the image of the huge transport vessels overflowing with containers visually depicted capitalism in motion. Little did I know that years later I would embark on yet another journey; this time, however, my journey would not end at the Port of Long Beach but rather begin there.

When I began working with Edna in the summer of 2004, I immediately became excited about her work on the Southern California ports. Much of my free time would be spent reading (and re-reading) the preliminary drafts she shared with me. I would always look forward to our conversations about the topic during our regular meetings. During this time, I began doing various research reports for a grant that Edna had received: I studied everything from neoliberalism, Wal-Mart, and consumption to contract manufacturing, sweatshops, and production in China. Eventually Edna and I would produce a couple of articles on Wal-Mart. The more research I conducted with Edna, the more I became immersed in the project.

In 2005, Edna graciously asked me if I would be interested in coauthoring the book. I was honored and thrilled to be on board. Working with Edna on this project has been an amazing experience. For me, the project's scope and potential are immense, as are the political implications of the work. Since immersing myself in this book project, I decided to continue my connection with the ports by choosing the ports of Long Beach/Los

Angeles as the sites of study for my doctoral dissertation, which focuses on race, gender, and conflict among workers at the ports. Collecting data for my dissertation, especially talking with longshore workers, has allowed me to hone my understanding of the complex relationship between labor and capital on the waterfront, and to bring in a personal connection with the people who make the ports function.

Acknowledgments

As usual, we received considerable help from lots of people in working on this project. In trying to list them, there is always the danger of forgetting someone; if we have, please forgive us.

We start with our editor, Peter Wissoker, who encouraged us to do this project when it was merely a thought-germ and who gave us valuable feedback all along the way. His thoughtful support and help in rewriting and reorganizing whole sections of the manuscript have been invaluable. Without his oversight, this book would never have been published.

Various people connected with labor in one form or another have contributed to this work. We have already mentioned some of them. Peter Olney and Goetz Wolff have shared our interest in logistics. Ruth Milkman, Kent Wong, and Katie Quan have been generous in sharing information and ideas. On the ground, Gary Smith proved to be a buddy in working on the port truckers, and Craig Bagdasar, an ILWU foreman, was generous with his time and help beyond anything one could ask. He has become a lifelong friend as a result. Jeff Hermanson, who used to be the international director of organizing for the ILGWU and who later worked for the AFL-CIO's Solidarity Center and is a major innovator in international labor organizing, has taken an interest in this project and given us helpful feedback. Finally, David Young, former organizing director of the ILGWU on the West Coast and currently executive director of the Writers Guild, has been a continuing source of inspiration regarding organizing strategy.

Friends, colleagues, students, and former students in the university world have also been both helpful and encouraging. Especially noteworthy is Chris Chase-Dunn. We obtained another ILE grant together, along with Tom Reifer, and exchanged ideas about this project for a year. More important, Chris assigned the first draft of our manuscript to a graduate class of his, and we received wonderful suggestions for revision from him and the class. Students who played a role as research assistants for parts of the project include Rebecca Giem, Tony Juge, and Khaleelah Hardie. Ex-students Ralph Ambruster Sandoval, Carolina Bank-Muñoz, Ted Levine, and Jill Esbenshade have all provided encouragement and feedback.

Another group to thank are the people whom we interviewed. We have listed them at the end of the book. Some, maybe most, were incredibly helpful, and we hope we have acknowledged them properly in the text. Needless to say, without their wholehearted cooperation, this study could not have been conducted.

Finally, we come to our family and friends. Jake wants to thank and acknowledge his parents, Mary and Jay Wilson, for their uncompromising support and continual life lessons, which helped him though this process. He and Edna both thank Jake's partner and fellow student, Sabrina Alimahomed. Edna thanks her husband Phil, her beloved partner for over forty years, and her wonderful children and their partners: Emma and Stephanie, Jane and Jessie, and Cory and John, and now the magical grandchildren, Ruby and Alexander. In their own way, each of these people—and probably others—exchanged ideas with us and gave us support for the effort. We are grateful for your presence in our lives.

Acronyms

AB	Able-bodied Seaman
ACD	Automated Cross Docking
ACE	Alameda Corridor East
ACTWU	Amalgamated Clothing and Textile Workers Union
AFL-CIO	American Federation of Labor–Congress of Industrial Organizations
AISA	American Institute of Shippers Associations
AQMD	Air Quality Management District
APL	American Presidents Line
ASN	Advanced Shipment Notification
BCO	Beneficial Cargo Owner
BLE	Brotherhood of Locomotive Engineers
BNSF	Burlington Northern Santa Fe
BOC	Beneficial Owner of Cargo
CAFTA	Central American Free Trade Agreement
CFS	Container Freight Stations
CITT	Center for International Trade and Transportation
CLM	Council of Logistics Management
CPFR	Collaborative Planning, Forecasting, and Replenishment
CSCMP	Council of Supply Chain Management Professionals
CTW	Change to Win
CWA	Communications Workers of America
DLSE	Division of Labor Standards Enforcement (of California)
DMA	Distribution Management Association of Southern California
EDD	Employment Development Department

EDI	Electronic Data Interchange
EPZ	Export Processing Zone
ERP	Enterprise Resource Planning
ESOP	Employee Stock Ownership Plan
FEUs	Forty-Foot Equivalent Units
FICA	Federal Insurance Contributions Act (Social Security)
FOB	Free on Board
FOC	Flag of Convenience
FTZ	Free Trade Zone
GOH	Garment on Hanger
IBT	International Brotherhood of Teamsters
ICA	Interstate Commerce Act
ICC	Interstate Commerce Commission
ICTF	Intermodal Container Transfer Facility
IEEP	Inland Empire Economic Partnership
ILA	International Longshoremen's Association
ILE	Institute for Labor and Employment
ILGWU	International Ladies' Garment Workers' Union (also ILG)
ILO	International Labor Organization
ILWA	International Logistics and Warehouse Association
ILWU	International Longshore and Warehousing Union
INS	Immigration and Naturalization Service
IMC	Intermodal Marketing Company
IMO	International Maritime Organization
IMRA	International Mass Retailers Association
ITF	International Transport Workers Federation
ITGLWF	International Textile, Garment, and Leather Workers Federation
ITO	International Trade Organization
JIT	Just In Time
KCS	Kansas City Southern Railroad
LA/LB	Los Angeles/Long Beach
LACD	Los Angeles Customs District
LATA	Latin American Truckers Association
LCL	Less Than Carload (for railroads) or Less Than Containerload
LTL	Less Than Truckload
M&M	Mechanization and Modernization Agreement
MARAD	Maritime Administration
MCA	Motor Carrier Act
MCD	Manual Cross Docking
MFA	Multi-Fiber Arrangement
MLB	Mini-landbridge

MTA	Metropolitan Transit Authority
NAIOP	National Association of Industrial and Office Properties
NCCC	National Carriers Conference Committee
NITL	National Industrial Transportation League
NMFA	National Master Freight Agreement
NRF	National Retail Federation
NVOCC	Non-Vessel-Operating Common Carrier
OCW	Overseas Contract Workers
OSRA	Ocean Shipping and Reform Act
OTI	Ocean Transportation Intermediary
OTR	Over the Road (trucking)
PEB	Presidential Emergency Board
PEWS	Political Economy of the World System
PIERS	Port Import Export Reporting Service
PMA	Pacific Maritime Association
PMSA	Pacific Merchant Steamship Association
POLA	Port of Los Angeles
POLB	Port of Long Beach
POS	Point of Sale
PSS	Peak Season Surcharge
RFID	Radio Frequency Identification
ROCE	Return on Capital Employed
SANBAG	San Bernardino Association of Governments
SAP	Structural Adjustment Program
SASC	Steamship Association of Southern California
SCM	Shipping Container Marking
SEIU	Service Employees International Union
SIC	Standard Industrial Classification
SKU	Stock Keeping Unit
SP	Southern Pacific Railroad
SSA	Stevedoring Services of America
STB	Surface Transportation Board
SV	Surplus Value
TDU	Teamsters for a Democratic Union
TEUs	Twenty-Foot Equivalent Units
3PL	Third-Party Logistics (Provider)
TIRRA	Trucking Industry Regulatory Reform Act
TL	Truckload
TMA	Transport Maritime Association
TNC	Transnational Corporation
TOFC	Trailers on Flat Cars
TSA	Transpacific Stabilization Agreement

Acronyms

TUTA	Troqueros Unidos de Transporte Asociados
TWC	The Waterfront Coalition
UFCW	United Food and Commercial Workers Union
UNCTAD	United Nations Conference on Trade and Development
UNITE	Union of Needletrades, Industrial and Textile Employees
UP	Union Pacific Railroad
UTU	United Transportation Union
VICS	Voluntary Interindustry Commerce Standards
VMI	Vendor Managed Inventory
WCWC	West Coast Waterfront Coalition
WERC	Warehousing Education Research Council
WRTU	Waterfront Rail Truckers Union

GETTING THE GOODS

PART ONE

THE LOGISTICS REVOLUTION
AND ITS CONSEQUENCES

CHAPTER I

The Logistics Revolution

A quiet change has been occurring in the way consumer goods are being produced and delivered. It has not received much public attention, but it has had a sizeable impact on society and the way it is organized. We call this change the logistics revolution.

A military term, *logistics* refers to a system that continually supplies an army in the field with both the means of living and the means of effectively waging war. Keeping an army adequately supplied, especially during the chaos of a distant war, is a huge and complex undertaking, as one can imagine. The concept of logistics was borrowed by commercial enterprises to describe their own challenges in keeping customers properly supplied. Until recently, the term was generally limited to the transportation and warehousing functions that any company needs to fulfill.

But the idea of logistics has undergone a metamorphosis. Its meaning has been expanded to refer to the management of the entire supply chain, encompassing design and ordering, production, transportation and warehousing, sales, redesign and reordering. This entire cycle of production and distribution is now viewed as a single integrated unit that requires its own specialists for analysis and implementation. It is this shift in perspective that we refer to as the logistics revolution.

The logistics revolution is a new phenomenon, demonstrated by the flurry of textbooks that have been published on the topic in the last decade (e.g. Bolstorff and Rosenbaum 2003; Bowersox, Closs, and Cooper 2002; Handfield and Nichols 2002; Hugos 2003; Schechter 2002; Seifert 2003; Wood et al. 2002). One book, published in 2005, starts by saying that the authors wanted to write such a book ten years earlier, but "we merely would have been speculating about the future of supply chain management as a core management discipline" (Cohen and Roussel 2005, ix). However, the groundwork for the logistics revolution was being laid as early as the 1970s. Before developing this historical context, let us consider the underlying systemic impulse behind it.

Underlying Causes of the Logistics Revolution

Following the lead of British critical geographers (Ducatel and Blomley 1990; Harvey 1999; Wrigley and Lowe 1996, 2002), we view the logistics revolution as having arisen in response to a chronic problem of the capitalist system, namely, the disjuncture between production and distribution, or supply and demand. The system is given to overproduction, or to producing goods that consumers do not want, or will not buy, and the challenge is to sell all the goods that are produced. Producers have devised various methods to cope with this problem, including increased advertising, market research, product proliferation, branding, and consumer credit.

The logistics revolution is an attempt to bridge the gap between supply and demand more effectively. The purpose is to link supply to demand. The goal is to have exactly the inventory one needs, in terms of both quantity and mix of goods. That way a company can avoid the twin dangers of overstocks (goods that are not moving and must be sold below cost or disposed of entirely) and understocks (not having enough of the products that consumers wish to purchase at a given moment).

Logistics analysts treat the entire supply chain as a single continually flowing system. By doing so, they seek to control costs, to limit inventory pileups at any stage of the chain, to speed up the time it takes to cycle through the system, and to provide better service to consumers.

At the heart of the change in the concept of logistics is a change in the balance of power between manufacturers and retail stores, often referred to as a movement from "push" to "pull" production and distribution (WERC 1994, 7–9; Seifert 2003, 5–7). Under the "push" system, production was dominated by large consumer goods manufacturers. They had long production runs in order to gain efficiencies of scale and minimize unit costs. While the manufacturer's product costs were shaved, higher costs accrued at other stages of the supply chain. Manufacturers used deals and promotions to get retailers to make large advance purchases, while retail buyers increased the volume of purchase orders to take advantage of these discounts. Retailers would carry excess inventory and would have to depend on promotions to get the accumulated goods to move. Meanwhile, they were ill equipped to deal with a sudden surge in consumer demand for a "hit" product, like an unexpectedly popular toy for Christmas (WERC 1994, 7–8; Seifert 2003, 5).

Under the "pull" system, consumer behavior is tracked by the retailers, who then transmit these preferences up the supply chain to the producers. Manufacturers try to coordinate production with actual sales, minimizing inventory buildup anywhere in the chain by collecting data from retailers at the point of sale (POS). Retailers share POS information with their vendors, who can then rapidly replenish the retailers' stock. The result is a reduction of inventory throughout the supply chain, which cuts costs for both manufacturers and retailers.

Implementation of the pull system has led to efforts to integrate processes along the entire supply chain, across the various businesses that make it up—businesses that usually operate as independent, competitive, and often secretive entities. For example, manufacturers and retailers have historically viewed each other with caution, reluctant to reveal their costs to each other. Such barriers to information-sharing are breaking down, making the whole system more efficient, minimizing total cost, and maximizing speed and turnover. Firms try to move beyond the functional excellence of one part of the supply chain (for instance, warehousing) toward integrated solutions that serve the whole system. Protective channel walls between functions are broken down as the members of the supply chain realize their common goals.

The result of this change in orientation is that the competition has shifted, to some extent, from the firm level to the supply chain level. The basic unit of competition has become the supply chain—or rather the supply network, since firms at different levels have multiple and constantly shifting relations with any number of companies at any given time. For example, a retailer buys from multiple and changing suppliers, who in turn deal with multiple and changing contractors. Those contractors are being supplied by multiple and changing manufacturers, who produce goods for multiple and changing retailers. All this makes for a very complex network of overlapping relationships.

Thus retailers and their suppliers and transportation providers ideally form strategic alliances, sharing information so that all partners are able to respond rapidly to shifts in demand. New technology, such as EDI (electronic data interchange) and a number of other integrated programs, enhances communications between supply chain partners (WERC 1994, 9). Making this happen is the job of logistics specialists or analysts (Cohen and Roussel 2005). Needless to say, there has been a huge growth in logistics specialists both within companies and as independent firms that provide logistics services, known as third-party logistics firms, or 3PLs.

The logistics revolution grew out of a particular political context including attacks on the welfare state, deregulation, and increased international free trade that began in the 1970s. It truly came into its own with the elections of Ronald Reagan in the United States and Margaret Thatcher in Britain in 1980. The key idea that marked that time was to allow the market, both domestically and internationally, to operate with a minimum of interference by governments. Called neoliberalism outside of the United States, the model also came to be known as the "Washington consensus" because the United States pushed it so hard.

The minimization or elimination of government regulation in certain sectors of the economy played a critical role in shaping the logistics revolution. For example, fair trade rules, which protected manufacturers against discounting at the retail level by letting the manufacturer set the retail price of its products and compelling retailers to abide by it, were removed, allowing for the emergence of the giant discount retailers like Wal-Mart (Petrovic and Hamilton 2005). The deregulation of transportation, especially of the trucking industry, permitted greater cooperation among the segments of the supply chain. At an international level, the imposition of a neoliberal, free market ideology on developing countries led to the increased investment of U.S. (and other developed countries) capital in these countries. All these changes were vital preconditions for the full flowering of global production and the logistics revolution.

Much has been written on this shift in policy and the reasons for the changes (e.g. Armstrong, Glyn, and Harrison 1991; Brenner 2002; Pollin 2003), and we will not develop the topic here. Our main concern is with the impact of these changes on logistics, and the effects, in turn, of changes in logistics on economy and society. But let us start first with the central changes that comprise the logistics revolution.

CHARACTERISTICS OF THE LOGISTICS REVOLUTION

The logistics revolution is correlated with a number of important shifts in the current stage of capitalist development. They include a shift in power from producers and manufacturers to retailers, in other words a rise in retailer power; changes in the character of production; changes in the distribution of freight; and changes for workers and their unions in production and distribution. Throughout this section we use Wal-Mart Stores, Inc., as a prominent example of some of these changes.

The Rise of Retailer Power

Having POS data as the driver of production puts power in the hands of retailers, especially the big ones, because they are at the end of the supply chain. They are in the position of telling manufacturers what consumers are actually buying and therefore what the manufacturers should produce, when they should produce it, and, sometimes, at what price (Bonacich and Wilson 2006). This is a significant change from thirty years ago.

This power shift has been led by Wal-Mart and is marked by its rise to the position of biggest company both in the United States and in the world (when measured in terms of revenue and employees). In 2001 Wal-Mart became the first retailer to achieve the top position in the Fortune 500, surpassing General Motors and Exxon. Wal-Mart's revenues in 2006 were $350 billion, or over a third of a *trillion* dollars. The company made $11 billion in profits, accounted for 2.3 percent of the U.S. GDP, and continued to be the largest employer in the world.

The "Wal-Mart effect" has become a phenomenon. Singlehandedly, it is said, Wal-Mart has forced its suppliers to cut costs, made it more difficult for companies to compete on any terms other than price, and made it close to impossible for manufacturers and service providers to pass on the cost of improvements in products and services to consumers in the form of price increases (Fishman 2006; Lichtenstein 2006). Not only does Wal-Mart engage in these practices itself, it has also compelled its competitors to follow its model. Whether general merchandisers like Target or specialty stores like Toys "R" Us, most large retailers have been forced to change their practices.

The size of the giant retailers adds to their power, and the bigger they are, the more power they are able to exert. They can offer take-it-or-leave-it deals to their vendors, who often have no option but to take it because of the volume involved, because of the dominance of a handful of retailers over whole industries.

Retailers are placing ever more stringent requirements on their suppliers. They insist on speed and perfection in deliveries, fining their vendors for the tiniest error or delay. For example, they will specify that goods are "store-ready," with labels and packaging meeting the retailer's detailed specifications. They insist on short lead times (ten days or fewer, in many cases) so that a steady flow of merchandise is brought to the store. This means that deliveries are much more frequent than they used to be. Packaging must be precise, with bar codes placed exactly where the retailer wants, and the vendor must provide advance shipment notification (ASN; see WERC 1994, 5).

This shift in dominance from manufacturers to retailers marks one of the major and largely neglected features of globalization. Some authors argue that the key to globalization is the opening up of financial markets, leading to the dominance of finance capital. While finance capital has undoubtedly gained in power, so has commercial capital, with giant retailers helping to shape the development policies of entire countries as well as hindering the development of some countries as they exit for other markets.

It was the logistics revolution that turned this kind of power relationship on its head. The collection of POS data put power into the hands of the giant retailers. They knew what consumers were buying, which prices were

7

most effectively maximizing sales, which products were gaining and losing popularity, and how buying patterns were differing demographically and regionally.

Yet despite considerable concentration and accumulation of power in the retail sector, retailing remains a very competitive industry. There are far too many retail stores in the United States, yet the chains continue to move into oversaturated markets. Southern California is a good example. Already there is more square footage per consumer in this region than anywhere else in the country, yet Wal-Mart, Kohl's, Dillard's, and Walgreens are all trying to penetrate the market. This seemingly irrational behavior is driven by the need to avoid conceding any territory to one's major competitors, to meet them head-on in all markets. One might describe this as an irrationality of capitalism as a system, despite the rationality in the calculation of individual firms.

Yet even though competition for consumers is fierce, each of the "big box" stores represents a substantial order for the products of manufacturers and this gives them quite a bit of negotiating power with their suppliers. Taking Wal-Mart as the epitome of a giant discount retailer, we should recognize that the company is certainly not a monopoly and does not exercise monopoly power to drive prices up. But in many industries, it comes close to being a monopsony—that is, a single buyer instead of a single seller. Wal-Mart dominates certain commodities, especially those that fit its model of "low margin, high turn." The company controls 10 percent of the U.S. apparel market, 13 percent of consumer electronics, 16 percent of food and drugs, and 21 percent of toys, while in home improvement and automotive it has a smaller but rising share (according to a Morgan Stanley report on the company dated 2/12/04).

Many vendors find the company hard to avoid. Procter and Gamble sells 17 percent of its goods to Wal-Mart, according to an article in *Fortune* (11/26/03) by Matthew Boyle. Dial Corporation, maker of Dial soap, does 28 percent of its business with Wal-Mart. If it were to lose that account, it would have to double its sales with its next nine largest customers in order to maintain the same level of business (Fishman 2003, 73). Suppliers find themselves too dependent on Wal-Mart, with no other outlet offering them remotely the same volume. In the words of former Wal-Mart manager Jon Lehman, who was interviewed on the *Frontline* show "Is Wal-Mart Good for America?" on PBS, suppliers reason: "We can't get out of bed with Wal-Mart now. We've been in bed too long. We have nobody else to sell our merchandise to that matters anymore."

The U.S. government is very concerned about monopoly power in relation to the consumer, but not with the exercise of monopsony power over suppliers. The supreme value of lowering consumer prices is enshrined in U.S. antitrust law, which sees the primary purpose of the law to be the protection of consumers from anticompetitive behavior, but there is hardly any concern over the problem of monopsony. For this reason, the tremendous power of the giant retailers is overlooked, or at least not seen as violating any antitrust laws. As long as the consumer interest is being served, the U.S. government takes little interest in any other fallout of rising retailer power.

Apart from its power in relation to manufacturers, Wal-Mart has played a leading role in developing the logistics revolution. As Jon DeCesare, a logistics consultant, told us: "Wal-Mart wrote the book, and it keeps rewriting it every day." In the article in *Fortune* by Matthew Boyle (11/26/03), Wal-Mart is described as "the company that almost singlehandedly made the bar code ubiquitous by demanding 20 years ago that suppliers use it." Numerous authors have deemed its mastery of logistics to be the cause of its success. According to Peter Tirschwell, editor of the *Journal of Commerce*, in a column entitled "Demanding, Exacting, Uncompromising" (1/19/04), "Wal-Mart has set the pace by expanding the definition of logistics practices." He points out that, because Wal-Mart and the other big box chains compete so aggressively on price, margins in the retail sector are razor-thin, which forces the industry to cut costs to the bone and give top priority to logistics.

Wal-Mart has streamlined logistics by sharing data electronically with its suppliers and by driving out unnecessary middlemen, all for the purpose of offering rock-bottom prices to its customers. The importance the company attaches to logistics is shown in its leadership: both David Glass and Lee Scott, the previous and present CEOs, came out of logistics (Slater 2003). For example, Scott was elevated by Glass from the transportation department. This mindset has enabled Wal-Mart to maintain lower inventory levels than its competitors. It can reorder quickly and be sure when the goods will arrive. By 1983 it was spending less than 2 cents per dollar on distribution, the lowest rate in the retail industry (Ortega 1998, ch. 8).

Wal-Mart decided to own and control its own trucks and computer systems, treating these as core competencies of the company. The company invested heavily in information technology and bought a fleet of trucks (Hugos 2003, 38–39). It bought a satellite system for $24 million in the early 1980s. By 1988 it had the largest privately owned communications network in the country (Ortega 1998).

The techniques that Wal-Mart developed are now being copied by its competitors and by others in unrelated industries. Wal-Mart introduced at least four key concepts: the strategy of expanding around distribution centers (DCs), using electronic data interchange (EDI) with suppliers, the big box store format, and "everyday low prices" (Hugos 2003). Almost every logistics textbook, and there are many of them, uses Wal-Mart as a prime example of cutting-edge logistics practices.

The advantages of these four innovations are as follows: First, Wal-Mart enters a region by building a new DC in a central location and opening a group of new stores around it. This enables the company to add new stores at little additional cost. Second, the use of EDI with suppliers cuts the transaction costs of ordering products and paying invoices, since these functions are handled electronically. In addition, Wal-Mart gains control over the scheduling and receiving of products, ensuring a steady and accurate flow of products to its stores. Third, the big box format allows Wal-Mart to combine a store with a warehouse in a single facility. The big box holds large amounts of inventory and saves on the shipment of goods from a warehouse to the store. And fourth, the stability of "everyday low prices" enables Wal-Mart to forecast sales more accurately and smooth out demand swings associated with special sales events.

Wal-Mart also developed a system of replenishing its stores twice a week, while its competitors were replenishing twice a month. This limited the time in which store managers had to forecast sales, increasing their accuracy. More frequent replenishments led the company to pioneer the cross-docking system as a means of reducing the cost of small lot replenishments. Cross-docking is a system where truckloads from a particular producer arrive at the DC and are unloaded; their contents are then broken down into smaller lots and combined with the smaller lots of other trucks bound for the same destination. DCs that cross-dock enable products to flow faster through the supply chain. Moreover, the costs of handling are reduced, since storage and retrieval are no longer necessary (Hugos 2003, 41, 94).

Another Wal-Mart initiative, begun in the fall of 2005, is a program called Remix. According to an article in *American Shipper* by Eric Kulisch (December 2005), it will significantly change the way Wal-Mart's supply chain operates. The purpose is to keep high-demand items in stock by segmenting its 117 DCs into low- and high-velocity facilities that will supply stores with certain items, such as diapers, paper towels, and health and beauty items, on a more frequent basis than normal store deliveries. The goods will be delivered on floor-ready pallets. The old system divided DCs into dry grocery goods, general merchandise, cold storage, and apparel. Apparently the high-velocity DCs will deliver more than once a night and more frequently during the day.

Wal-Mart is also leading the retail sector in the implementation of other logistics innovations outside the firm, including greatly increasing the demands that retailers place upon their suppliers. These retailers, Wal-Mart included, are pushing activities that they used to perform back onto their suppliers. These include such requirements as: putting the final price labels on goods, placing garments on hangers before they are shipped to the retailer, ensuring that labels are placed in the exact spot on the box that the retailer requires, and packing boxes to the retailer's precise specifications.

Wal-Mart and other giant retailers have the power to impose these and other requirements on an "accept-the-terms-or-you-will-be-dropped-as-a-vendor" basis. In addition, they can impose costly consequences for the tiniest of errors, such as charging a $25 per box fine if a label is crooked. The specificity of the requirements and the financial penalties have been intensifying.

In previous research on the apparel industry in Los Angeles, Bonacich and Appelbaum (2000) found that apparel manufacturers in Los Angeles complained bitterly about these retailer practices. Called "chargebacks," these continual fines, they felt, were set at levels way out of proportion to the offense. The manufacturers would state sarcastically that the retailers were "making their profits at the loading dock instead of on the sales floor" by looking for the smallest error to charge back to the vendor. Given that most manufacturers are producing for multiple retailers, they are left with the headache of meeting each one's specific requirements.

An example of a Wal-Mart initiative that is being imposed on suppliers is RFID (radio frequency identification). Wal-Mart is pushing for its top suppliers to move beyond conventional bar-coding to this new (and unproven) technology. RFID tags and readers are very expensive to install, and a standardized form of the technology has yet to emerge from the pack of those who are producing it, so a heavy investment in the wrong form may end up as a costly mistake. Moreover, in interviewing one of Wal-Mart's suppliers, the firm's logistics manager pointed out that his company cannot see any benefits to them from installing it—only Wal-Mart will be in a better position to track its products more thoroughly. Boyle of *Fortune* (11/26/03) reported that one analyst estimated that Wal-Mart would save about $8 billion a year by using RFID, while a typical consumer products supplier would have to spend between $13 and $23 million to install it. Says Peter Leach, a reporter for the *Journal of Commerce* (10/18/04): "Suppliers will not see any return on the investment they'll have to make in order to comply with Wal-Mart's requirements, beyond the fact that they will keep Wal-Mart as a big customer."

A good overview of the way large retailers seek to work with manufacturers can be seen in the relationship between Wal-Mart and Procter and Gamble. P&G was known as a tough company that was able to dominate its market and its retailers. It used its own research on consumer buying to argue with retailers for increased shelf space. P&G was widely viewed as a self-aggrandizing bully (Kumar 1996).

At first the relationship between Wal-Mart and P&G was difficult. "P&G would dictate to Wal-Mart how much P&G would sell, at what prices, and under what terms. In turn, Wal-Mart would threaten to drop P&G merchandise or give it poorer shelf locations" (Kumar 1996, 121). The relationship began to change in the mid-1980s, and they managed to work out a partnership based on sharing information to increase sales and lower costs for both companies (Kumar 1996, 121–22).

The two companies developed a sophisticated EDI link, which gave P&G the responsibility for managing its Wal-Mart inventory. P&G received continuous data via satellite on sales, inventory, and prices, enabling it to replenish goods rapidly, often directly from the factory to individual stores. The two firms use electronic invoicing and electronic transfer of funds. The order-to-delivery cycle has been speeded up, and stock-outs have been almost entirely eliminated. Meanwhile, various costly processes, such as order processing and billing, have been rendered unnecessary, and errors have been reduced (Kumar 1996, 122–23).

Changes in Production

Accompanying the logistics revolution, and an essential part of it, has been a shift from what has been called Fordism, or mass production, to flexible specialization or flexible production (Castells 1996; Harrison 1994; Harvey 1990; Piore and Sabel 1986). Flexible production is, in turn, linked to product proliferation. Basic, mass-produced items have been transformed into "fashion basics." Minor variations are introduced to a basic product, giving the consumer many more choices. This greater variety is then produced in response to an ever-changing demand (Abernathy et al. 1999). This means that manufacturers have many more specific products to produce. Alternatively, different combinations can be put together in warehouses so as to meet the requirements for variety.

Some of the concepts of the logistics revolution were derived from the competitors of U.S. companies. For example, the concept of "lean production" was pioneered by Toyota. Toyota analyzed its entire production system and was able to create a continuous production flow by creating teams of workers who performed different functions. The company was able to cut the cost and time of production drastically and to become much more flexible in responding to the varieties of consumer demand (Womack and Jones 2000, 222). Toyota's innovations forced U.S. automobile companies to introduce similar changes.

Flexibility appears to have two related meanings. First, it means the ability to respond to shifting demand, in other words, to produce and deliver a much greater variety of fashion basics than was possible under a system of mass production with long runs of the same products. Second, it refers to flexible production schedules or the growth in contingency. In this meaning, goods are only produced on an as-needed basis. Contingent production takes the place of predictable production runs.

Flexible production is linked to outsourcing, or contracting out. A core firm (let us term it the *parent company*) contracts out much of its production, rather than having it done in-house. It uses multiple contractors that each produce only part of its wide array of products. These contractors can be employed, or not, as the need arises, and generally cannot count on a steady, predictable set of orders. The parent employs a changing network of contractors, depending on shifting demand, with whom it works with varying levels of regularity. This network can be in constant flux, as some contractors are dropped from the roster and others are added. The contractors themselves may produce for several parent companies. The result is a set of overlapping and continually changing relationships. The degree of contingency varies among contractors. Some have long-standing, stable relationships with particular parent firms. They are surrounded by concentric circles of less connected, less stable contractors, some of whom may be their own subcontractors.

Despite the fact that we have used the term *parent company* to designate the firm that sits at the top of the network, its outsourced producers are typically not subsidiaries. The parent usually has no ownership stake in its contractors (though there may be exceptions). The typical relationship is arm's-length, allowing the parent the supreme flexibility of terminating the relationship at any time with minimal cost.

Flexible production is connected with offshore production. Once firms began to outsource their production, there was no need to keep it close by. Contracting out freed them to scour the world for the best deals they could find. They could seek out the cheapest labor and have them work under the most oppressed conditions. Globalization became a partner of flexible production. This pattern has been associated with the rise of global sweatshops (Varley 1998) and what has been called "the race to the bottom" in terms of labor standards, as poor developing countries have vied for production contracts by promising foreign companies low-cost, compliant labor. Needless to say, the rise in offshore production is linked to the decline of manufacturing jobs in the United States.

Retailers are playing an important role in the shift to offshore production. They set up buying offices around the developing world and purchase goods made to their specifications. The producers of these goods may be "independent" companies, but they are fully dependent on the merchandising of retailers from the United States and the rest of the developed world. They exist in response to retailer demand. Sometimes it may be possible for them to break out of this dependent role, but a huge amount of production occurs on these terms. Buying offices are another type of arm's-length arrangement, along with contracting and subcontracting (Petrovic and Hamilton 2005).

The giant retailers also help to drive domestic production offshore by insisting on the constant lowering of prices to the point where the goods can no longer be made legally in the United States. When manufacturers complain, the retailers symbolically shrug their shoulders, implying: "Do what you have to do to cut your prices."

Changes in Logistics

Production networks, with contracted-out factories, require more efficient logistics (meaning production planning and freight transportation). With globalization, it is necessary to coordinate complex, sprawling, ever-changing supply networks. Goods need to be moved quickly and accurately, at low cost, over great distances. This kind of coordination has depended upon evolving information and communications technology (IT).

A very important innovation was the development of containerization (Levinson 2006). Containers allow for intermodal transportation, that is, the movement of goods across ship, rail, and truck without having to unload and reload the cargo (Müller 1999). A container can be packed at a factory in Asia and unpacked only when it arrives at a warehouse in Chicago.

The development of intermodalism is a critical element in the emergence of Southern California as a major global gateway to Asia. Before containers, freight bound from Asia to the East and Midwest, still the most important economic regions of the country, had to pass through the Panama Canal to be unloaded at East Coast ports. Intermodalism allowed containers to be unloaded on the West Coast and sent by rail to the East. This was quicker than the canal and opened the possibility of almost limitless growth in trade. The shift to containers and intermodalism started in the 1970s and kept growing. The process is not complete for all markets, but it is for the Pacific trade.

Intermodalism depended on a change in the regulatory regime governing transportation (Peoples 1998; Teske, Best, and Mintrom 1995). The old system had separate governance structures for each mode of transportation and had set up barriers to their cooperation. Deregulation also played an important role in lowering freight transportation costs, making the system more attractive. The deregulation process began in the late 1970s and became full-blown throughout the decade of the 1980s.

Logistics, as we have said, has emerged as a specialty area, with individuals and firms dedicated to developing and operating more efficient logistics systems. Sometimes companies have their own logistics specialists. But increasingly a legion of third-party logistics companies (3PLs) has emerged; in other words, logistics itself is being outsourced. These companies vary in their focus. Some run warehouses, some are affiliates of the steamship lines, some are global companies that plan and operate the entire supply chain for a company, and some are mainly IT firms that provide computer programs for improving the efficiency of the supply chain.

One of the key purposes of a focus on logistics is to limit the accumulation of inventory anywhere in the network. Logistics analysts tend to be global thinkers who focus on the integrated system as a whole, rather than its parts, making sure that everything moves smoothly through the entire network. They are continually devising methods to improve the flows of information and goods up and down the supply chain and to cut out any unnecessary steps.

In effect, logistics experts operate on the principle that capital not in motion ceases to be capital. They look at ships as floating warehouses. Ideally, there should be no point, from production to final sale, when goods sit around waiting for further processing. The flow from sale to ordering to production to shipping and to the next sale should occur in one smooth motion. This is the idea behind the logistics revolution.

Changes for Labor

The logistics revolution, the rise of retailer power, and the changes in production and logistics have all had a major impact on labor in both production and distribution. Setting aside the sales labor force, let us focus on production and logistics labor, both local and global. Each group of workers in each particular industry has its own unique story, but there are some general impacts that seem to apply to most. These are: increased contingency, weakened unions, racialization, and lowered labor standards. Let us look at each of them more closely.

Increased Contingency. The rise of outsourcing and contracting out means that there are layers of intermediaries between the parent company and its "employees." Although the workers of these outsourced entities are not strictly employees of the parent, in reality their fate is often a direct product of the parent's actions. Not only can the parent cause them to lose their jobs by shifting production away from their direct employer, but the parent can also set the terms of their employment. In the face of the anti-sweatshop movement's fierce criticisms of conditions in these contracted factories, some parent companies have passed codes of conduct and have implemented inspections. These efforts demonstrate both the depth of the sweatshop problem and the power of big parent companies to intervene. Underlying the codes, however, is the ability of the parent companies to impose low prices on their suppliers (for both goods and services), creating the very conditions that the codes are now trying to repair.

Flexible production creates shifting networks of outsourced companies, of contractors and subcontractors who are faced with instability and unpredictability. They only get work when there is work to be had. They cannot count on a steady stream. In the old days, mass-production factory work was stable, and risk was pushed out to the retailer. With the pull system, the retailer minimizes its risk and pushes it back to the manufacturer. The bigger manufacturers can, in turn, push it out to their contractors and on down the chain. Manufacturing and contracting for a manufacturer become more contingent operations that cannot count on their next contract but must be continually scrounging.

In sum, flexibility (contingency) works well for the retailer but makes life more difficult for the outsourced producers and service providers. In turn, this makes life more difficult for the employees of these entities, who sometimes push contingency onto the workers themselves in the form of piece-rate, temporary, and part-time positions, independent contracting, and the like. These irregular forms of employment have grown enormously in the United States as a concomitant of the logistics revolution (Carre et al. 2000). Contingent workers often suffer from a host of ills, including not only irregular work but also low pay and the absence of benefits.

We should recognize that the picture of unstable and shifting contract relations is not absolute. Parent firms typically surround themselves with concentric circles of contractors who are more or less central to them. The "nearer" companies are those with whom they may have developed strategic partnerships and on whom they rely for steady supplies and services. The further one moves out in the contracting system, the more contingent the relations are. So, while flexible production does create an increased ability on the part of the parent to shift production around the world, this mobility is not infinite.

Weakened Unions. Big, stable companies lend themselves to unionization. Contingent relations make it much more difficult. (The apparel industry has a long history of contracting and subcontracting, and the apparel unions have long struggled with this problem; see Bonacich 2000 and Bonacich and Appelbaum 2000.) With contingent connections, the parent can effectively shut out unionization.

Consider what happens if the workers in a subcontracting firm demand a union or demand increased pay or better working conditions. The parent, faced with increased costs from that particular firm, is likely to simply drop it from its roster and find another who pays what the parent generally pays and not a penny more. The efforts of the workers are doomed. Perhaps they can gain small improvements, such as cleaner bathrooms or an enforced lunch-hour, but they cannot make a significant dent in the price of their labor. Moreover, the parent company can push the price of labor down by seeking to undercut the price of labor of its contractors with even lower labor costs elsewhere in the world. When the world is accessible to a retailer or large manufacturer, they can set an ever lower standard for everyone to meet. This race to the bottom lies at the heart of the resurgence of sweatshops.

The contracting-out system causes both the direct employer (the contractor) and the geographical jurisdictions that house contractors to become fiercely anti-union. The contractor knows that if a union manages to establish itself in his factory (or among his transportation workers), the parent companies that he works for will shun him; he will be driven out of business. Therefore he is highly motivated to keep unions out by legal or illegal methods. Similarly, export-processing zones (EPZs), regions, and entire countries face the same basic logic: if organized labor becomes a force that can improve wages, benefits, and working conditions, industry will flee the territory. Workers will have won hollow rights without jobs. Some countries, such as Mexico, China, and South Korea, have state-recognized unions, which participate in curbing the rise in labor standards and set another layer of constraint on worker protest and demand for change. Others set up legal and political restraints on unionism, including tolerating the murder of labor leaders.

The weakening of unions is also clearly linked to a change in regulatory regime in the developed world, from the welfare state of the post–World War II period to the neo-liberalism that began to take over in the mid-1970s and that has been imposed on most of the developing world. The welfare state fits well with the push production model, whereas neo-liberalism and its promotion of the free market as the primary regulatory mechanism fits well with flexible production and distribution. Which came first may be hard to determine—they grew in tandem.

An important part of the free market ideology involves seeing unions as an impediment to the free flow of the market. Instead of viewing unions as helping to bolster consumer demand by putting money into the hands of workers (the Keynesian model), they are seen as obstructionists who put up rigid rules in the face of the need for increased flexibility. Worse still, they are sometimes viewed as a kind of protection racket that stalks the economy seeing where it can extort some money from capitalists and pocket most of it without benefiting most of the workers they claim to help.

Weaker unions have a direct relationship to increasing social, economic, and political inequality. Increased inequality is patently evident throughout the world, not only within developed and developing countries but also between countries. Capital is able to act in its own interests without much serious opposition. While unions are not the only important opposition to the unchecked growth of capitalist power, they are certainly an essential part of any oppositional coalition. Their decline hurts the entire society.

Racialization. The shift toward contingent relations has been accompanied by the employment of workers with fewer rights and less power.

Companies are now free to search the world for the most rightless and disempowered workers. Typically these are workers in the early stages of proletarianization. They are peasants who are being forced off the land and into wage labor. They are in a position of having to accept bargains of desperation. They also often live under regimes that are trying to lure foreign capital in an effort to develop their countries and who, overtly or covertly, offer the promise of workers who will work for low wages and not demand more. While some may want to blame this on corruption and the desire to support an emerging bourgeoisie, at least some of the time there appears to be no other choice. Governments either join this game or their people will starve.

It has often been noted that many of these new workers of the global economy are women (see, for example, Lee 1998; Ngai 2005; Salzinger 2003). We want to emphasize that they are also racialized. By this we mean that they are viewed as the "undeserving other" and suffer from the absence of basic citizenship rights. In other words, a stratum of workers is created who lack the basic rights and respect received by Western workers. They often have dark skin, don't speak the dominant language, lack access to basic education, and serve as undifferentiated, "unskilled" labor. Their lack of citizenship rights, the "right" language skills, and sufficient formal education, as well as their "difference," are used as justification for their less than humane treatment. Although overt racism may be absent from upon racial understandings—that the lives of some people, some workers, are less important than those of the dominant group, typically white and Western (Glenn 2002).

The absence of citizenship rights arises at both the local and the global level. At the local level, it can take the form of authoritarian regimes that deny full political participation to their own populations. Under these circumstances, workers may be formal citizens, but they lack the right to protest, to form unions, or to put in power a regime that protects their interests.

Another form of local lack of citizenship rights concerns immigrant workers, especially undocumented immigrants. Of course, until they gain formal citizenship rights, all immigrants must go through a waiting period of enhanced vulnerability to deportation should they express any demands. Undocumented immigrants face an even bleaker political landscape, making them especially vulnerable to bargains of desperation. Immigrants in Southern California, for example, are racialized as Mexican or "Hispanic" and seen as simple, inferior peoples whose needs are limited. The fact that so many workers in the region lack the right to vote and can easily be deported helps to create a stratum of low-wage workers who have a very hard time fighting for basic rights in the workplace. (This does not mean it cannot happen; see Milkman 2000.)

The main point is that the border serves as an important dividing line, regarding the rights of workers (Bank Muñoz 2004). Whereas capital, and the governments that stand behind it, is determined to eliminate border limitations to the free movement of capital, it has no intention of providing the same rights to labor. Capital is free to find the best deal it can anywhere in the world. Labor is afforded no such equivalent right. The result is the strengthening of the position of capital in relation to labor. Racialization helps to justify the inevitable increased inequality. The workers themselves, their characteristics, their lack of sophistication, their helplessness, their lack of skills, their great need, their inferior culture, their sexism, their corrupt political institutions, and so on are to blame for their poor treatment.

More complex is the issue of the citizenship rights of workers who work for the contractors of the transnational corporations (TNCs), what we have been calling the parent companies. If citizenship includes the right to have some say over one's employment situation (by being able to elect governments that provide some regulation of employers, for example), then global workers have none in relation to their ultimate employers. When a company such as Wal-Mart puts pressure on a supplier in China to make some commodity for a price that does not allow workers to live at a decent standard, what recourse do those workers have against Wal-Mart? They certainly have no political rights over a foreign company like this. Again, this is not to say that nothing can be done to embarrass and pressure TNCs. We are simply making the point that global production serves to deny certain kinds of basic citizenship rights to workers in relation to the "employers" who ultimately determine their fate.

Gender dynamics compound these forms of oppression, so that women of color are often the ideal global workforce. However, we want to emphasize that the gendering occurs within a context of racialization and the denial of citizenship rights. Women of color are especially vulnerable not only because they are women but also because they are rightless people of color. In some industries, such as transportation and warehousing, male workers still predominate, though they still suffer from racialization.

Lowered Labor Standards. The rise in contingent employment relations, the weakening of unions, and the racialization (and gendering) of large and growing segments of the workforce lead to the lowering of labor standards. Workers in the TNC-dominated consumer goods industries find themselves generally working for long hours with low pay and poor health and safety protections. They lack the basic right to form or join unions that can protect them.

In the West, globalization has meant both the loss of production jobs and the deterioration of those that remain, including their transference to racialized immigrant workers. In the United States, for example, hours of work have lengthened, benefits have shrunk, unions have lost power, and conditions have generally deteriorated. We cannot claim that conditions have worsened from some preexisting state in the developing countries, but it is fair to say that conditions for workers are poor on multiple fronts. The promise is held out that this is a short-term sacrifice that must be made for the country to develop, after which everyone will see an improvement in their situation. But does this day ever come? Mexico, which provides low-wage labor to a number of U.S. industries, is finding that no matter how poor its conditions, it can be undercut by China. The promise of ultimate rise seems empty.

Who is responsible for deteriorating labor standards in much of the world? The beauty of contingent relations is that the ultimate perpetrator, the parent company, the TNCs who engage in arm's-length relations with their suppliers and contractors, can deny responsibility for labor conditions in their supply chain. Their defense is simple: "They are separate companies. We don't run their businesses for them. If they oppress their workers, it is not our fault." This position tends to racialize the contractors and suppliers, who are defined as sleazy businessmen who would steal from their own grandmothers if they could make a fast buck. Absent from their model of the world is any acknowledgment of the *power* that the TNCs exercise to create lowered or bottom-level labor standards.

Indeed, ignoring the role of power in global capitalism is a chronic problem. The corporations, and the economists and governments who support them, see the world as driven by markets and free choice, and they have no room for the exercise of power in their models. Their criterion is simple: if no-one is holding a gun to your head, you are free to choose. If you work in a job where the pay is low and conditions are terrible, it is because you choose to do so. Short of outright slavery, the bargain between employer and employee is freely undertaken, as a contract between equals. This portrait completely ignores the role that a multi-billion-dollar U.S. retailer can play in setting the terms of employment all over the world.

Focusing on logistics labor (transportation and warehousing), in particular, statistics show that U.S. logistics costs have declined significantly since the early 1980s. They have dropped from around 19 percent of GDP to around 10 percent. The industry prides itself that the reason for this shift lies in all the efficiency gains of the logistics revolution. Inventory costs have been cut, and so have the costs connected with most of the modes of freight transportation. Yet questions can be asked—questions that lie at the heart of this book: How much have these gains been made at the cost of workers? How much of the reduction is a product of the shift to contingent employment relations, to the weakening of unions, and to the racialization of the workforce? How have labor standards fared as a result of the logistics revolution? Can it be claimed that logistics workers are better off today as a result of these shifts, or are they worse off? And if they are worse off, what does this mean for the touted benefits of this change?

In short, then, the logistics revolution leads to a rise in retailer power, a shift to flexible (contingent) production relations including increased off-shore production, and a change in logistics to containerization, intermodalism, and JIT transportation and warehousing. These changes in turn impact labor in the form of increased contingency for workers, weakened unions, and racialization, all of which contribute to a decline in labor standards. This decline is notable in all aspects of industry, namely, retail sales, production, and distribution (logistics). While the return of sweatshops in production has received considerable attention at both the global and local levels and critiques are emerging about the labor practices regarding their sales workers by the giant retailers, deteriorating conditions for logistics workers have mainly gone unnoticed (there are exceptions, of course; see Belzer 2000; Peoples 1998). However, that gap will be remedied in the chapters that follow as we show both how the logistics revolution really works and how various groups of logistics workers have fared as their world changed.

We believe it is necessary for unions and working class leaders, in general, to acknowledge in full the changes that are occurring in the global economy. They need to absorb the implications of the logistics revolution. They need to use it to their advantage, instead of trying to move backwards in time to some golden era that never was and that never can be achieved. There is a need for an equivalent paradigm shift in social struggle—one that fully encompasses the implications of the logistics revolution.

The fact is that the economy has changed dramatically, and worker organizing needs to change along with it. In most industries it has become almost impossible to organize one plant or firm, because it will simply disappear. Parents will shift their business away, and the company will go out of business.

This reality has led U.S. unions (for example) to move away from manufacturing and to focus on services, including public sector functions, that clearly cannot leave the country. It is no accident that SEIU is the largest and most powerful union in the United States today. While this approach may be practical in the short run, it avoids a confrontation with the most vital and powerful sectors of the capitalist class. To the extent that organizing is occurring, it is at the periphery of the economy and not in its heart.

We realize that organizing under conditions created by the logistics revolution is not easy. It may require campaigns of scale that we have never seen, and it may demand a consolidation of resources and of inter-union cooperation and coordination that has never been tried before. The labor movement may also have to abandon its standard approach of trying to win a contract with a single large employer. "Flexible organizing," in which, for example, membership in the union does not depend on stable employment in one location—may need to be considered. And unions may have to develop their own form of JIT strategies—where they have the flexibility to take advantage of vulnerabilities that show up unexpectedly, by acting rapidly to take advantage of the weakness.

Another clear implication of this analysis is the central significance of the transportation and warehousing unions. They cover workers who serve as the circulatory system of global capitalism. Global production and distribution thrusts them into prominence as strategically vital actors. The challenge for them is not only to get their own unions in order and to struggle for gains for their membership, their challenge also lies in recognizing the role they could play in gaining the power necessary for the working class to place serious demands on global capital. They have the potential power to change a corrupt and unsustainable system that is increasing human inequality and misery for millions of people. This is the opportunity that the logistics revolution affords.

CHAPTER 2

Importers

In the trade and transportation industry, importers and exporters are called shippers. Confusingly, the owners of ships are not called shippers but carriers. Shippers are the companies that own the cargo that needs to be moved or shipped, while carriers are transportation providers, including the steamship lines, railroads, and trucking companies that the shippers employ to move the cargo. Shippers sit at the top of the system of production and transportation of imports, serving as the instigators of the import trade and ultimately footing the bill for it. They employ carriers to do the actual work of shipping, but they determine what will be imported and to where.

In 2005, according to *Journal of Commerce* (*JoC*) investigations (5/29/06, 4A, 16A-24A), the United States imported 17,377,965 TEUs (twenty-foot equivalent units, the standard measure of ocean containers). Of these, 695,000 TEUs (4 percent) were imported by Wal-Mart. The next biggest importer was Target, with 371,000 TEUs, and the third was Home Depot, with 335,000. Thirty-three of the top hundred importers were retailers, as were six of the top seven, including Sears, Lowe's, and Costco. Among the top hundred were also manufacturers (especially of electronic goods), automotive companies, and appliance manufacturers, but giant retailers stand out as the major importers via ocean transportation to this country.[1]

---

[1]Not all imports come to this country via ocean transportation. About 17 percent of the value of the goods that enter the United States through the Los Angeles Customs District are shipped by air. These tend to be higher-value, lower-weight items because air freight is so much more expensive than ocean shipping; if you measure imports by volume or tonnage, air freight accounts for an even smaller percentage (Kyser 2006).

The exporting picture is very different. The top exporter was a waste-paper company that exported 244,400 TEUs. Prominent among exporters were makers of forest products and chemicals, like Weyerhaeuser, DuPont, and Cargill. The total number of exported TEUs was a fraction of the total imports, and the value of exported goods was generally much lower than the value of the imports, reflecting the well-recognized trade imbalance of the United States, especially with Asian countries (JoC 5/29/06, 4A).

Wal-Mart's dominance of the importers' list is not new, and its lead has been widening. The *Journal of Commerce* develops lists of the top hundred importers (and exporters) of containerized products every year. Wal-Mart's growth as an importer can readily be traced. In 2001 the company brought in 260,000 TEUs. In 2002 the number grew a small amount, to 291,900. Then in 2003 it took a major leap, to 471,600 TEUs, again in 2004 to 576,000 TEUs, and, as we have seen, to 695,000 TEUs in 2005. This rise reflects the tremendous growth in trade in recent years and particularly the growth of manufactured imports to the United States. Target's imports grew from 121,000 to 371,000 TEUs over the same period, and Home Depot's rose from 80,000 to 335,000 TEUs. So we see that this is not simply a Wal-Mart phenomenon.

Not all importers to the United States are U.S. companies. Transnational corporations (TNCs) with U.S. operations or subsidiaries can also be major importers. For example, among the top twenty importers of containerized goods to the United States is the Korean conglomerate LG Group, which imports chemicals, electronics, and telecommunications products; Philips Electronics, a subsidiary of a Dutch company; Ikea, a Swedish furniture retailer; Dutch beer maker Heineken; and the U.S. subsidiary of the Japanese tire manufacturer, Bridgestone (JoC 5/29/06, 16A).

Importers can be divided into senders versus receivers, called shippers versus consignees. Thus, a shipper can be an Asian producer who sends goods to a consignee, for example, a U.S. retailer. When we are talking about small importers, this distinction can make sense because the consignee in this case plays no role on the exporting side and simply awaits the delivery of his goods. But when it comes to large importers, like giant U.S. retailers or manufacturers, the distinction is blurred, since big importers are often involved in sending the goods from Asia. For this reason, the industry uses the term *shipper* as the more general designation, often dropping the distinction between shipper and consignee.

Shippers can hire a number of types of intermediaries to handle their freight transportation needs. These include freight forwarders, non-vessel-operating common carriers (NVOCCs or NVOs), or companies that do not own ships but arrange for shipping by buying space on the steamship lines, consolidators, and various other types of logistics companies. Some of them are termed ocean transportation intermediaries (OTIs) by U.S. law.

The general term for all of these logistics service providers is "third party logistics company," or 3PL. Some of the steamship lines operate their own 3PL subsidiaries.

When people talk about logistics as a topic of study, they frequently mean the study of 3PLs, some of which are giant, powerful companies, like UPS and Excel. We have chosen not to place special focus upon them, since we see the shippers as the primary powers behind the logistics companies. The 3PLs are essentially middlemen who provide business services to the importers and exporters.

Importers vary tremendously in size. They can consist of individuals, tiny companies, small and medium-sized firms, and giant multinational corporations. They are probably roughly distributed according to the commonly known Pareto principle, also called the 80–20 rule, which says that in many distributions, the best-endowed 20 percent will possess about 80 percent of the resources and vice versa—the vast majority will only account for a small percentage of the resources. In this case, the vast majority of importers are small, so even though there are many of them (say, 80 percent of the total), they only account for a small proportion of total imports (say, 20 percent). Meanwhile, a few large shippers (about 20 percent of the total) account for the bulk of imports (something like 80 percent).

Unfortunately, we do not have the total number of companies (and individuals) that import to the United States, which we assume is in the hundreds of thousands if not millions, but we do have the total number of TEUs that were imported in 2005, namely 17,377,965. The top 100 importers, a tiny fraction of the total, brought in 5,157,400 TEUs, or about 30 percent. The top ten importers accounted for 2,498,100 TEUs, or 14 percent of the total. Thus the top ten accounted for almost half of the imports brought in by the top hundred shippers, all of whom are substantial importers. On top of that, Wal-Mart alone accounted for 28 percent of the imports of the top ten companies. So the curve is steep at the top of the distribution and quickly flattens out to a gentle slope.

Just to give us a sense of the amounts that are involved, consider the fact that the one-hundredth importer, according to the *Journal of Commerce*, brought in 12,000 TEUs in 2005. Twelve thousand TEUs a year, or 6,000 FEUs (forty-foot equivalent units), which are far more common, may not seem that much, especially when compared with the volumes of the top three importers, but it means 33 TEUs for every day of the year, or 16 to 17 standard containers, each filled with about 30 tons of goods. That is a huge amount of commodities to sort and deliver. Now consider Wal-Mart's volume in 2005. With 695,000 TEUs per year, Wal-Mart has to import over 1900 TEUs, or 950 standard containers (FEUs) a day on average—a potential logistical nightmare of major proportions. In any case, it is safe to say that even the smallest of the top hundred importers is a major importer indeed.

As one can imagine, size is related to power, including bargaining power in relation to carriers. The big shippers can use their huge volume to push down the cost of transportation and to gain other types of preferential treatment. Deregulation by the Ocean Shipping Reform Act (OSRA) of 1998 allowed shippers and ocean carriers to engage in confidential rate agreements. Before OSRA, shipping rates were published. With the passage of the law, the big shippers could hide their special deals more effectively. Of course, word gets around about the rates, and the big shippers' rates become the standard to which smaller shippers aspire but can never attain. This advantage fosters the concentration of wealth and power, as the small are, in a sense, taxed to the benefit of the bigger, richer companies. As a consequence, smaller shippers seek to consolidate their cargo by joining together in shipper associations (described below) and by using OTIs and 3PLs to get a better rate from the carriers.

This chapter deals with the activities of importers, especially retailers, in offshore production as part of their logistics programs. The movement of manufacturing to the world's poorer countries is a critical element in globalization. Here we consider the companies that are actually driving this move and that end up importing the products back to the United States.

OFFSHORE PRODUCTION, RETAILERS, AND SWEATSHOPS

Almost by definition, importers are entities that are linked to offshore production, whether they are foreign or U.S. companies. They are the entities that arrange for the shipping and entry of goods made abroad. The bigger importers are generally TNCs with footholds in a number of countries. TNCs can engage in offshore production for the local markets in which they are located. For example, Wal-Mart arranges for production in China, some of which will be sold in the newly expanded Wal-Mart chain there. Our focus is on those TNCs that import goods primarily from Asia to the United States. In this capacity they become global shippers.

As we have pointed out, TNCs can engage in foreign direct investment (FDI) or arms'-length transactions—international contracting and licensing—where they do not own the companies in which their goods are produced. Global shippers, in other words, often own nothing except, perhaps, buying offices and the offices of their various types of agents. They invest nothing in the production facilities but have a profound effect on them anyway through their buying activities as well as direct intervention in what is made, how it is produced, in what time frame, under what conditions, and, most important, for what price.[2]

[2]Most research on the development of Asia as a production center for the global economy focuses on the economic development of the exporting countries and their capacity to

Retailers started to play a role in shaping global production after 1965, when they began to send buyers to Asia and to set up buying offices there. The impetus came from the internal restructuring of the retail industry in the United States, which led to a search for offshore products. By providing a guaranteed market for Asian products, retailers stimulated Asian manufacturing development. They also helped to create the suppliers themselves. With the support of governments (in the construction of logistics and financial infrastructure) and Asian trading companies (sometimes also facilitated by governments), they set up a system of contract manufacturing whereby retailers would specify their requirements to Asian suppliers on an arm's-length contracting basis that required no direct investments by the retailers. The retailers were joined by branded producers, like the Gap and Nike, which also owned no factories but engaged in contract manufacturing in Asia for the U.S. market (Petrovic and Hamilton 2006).

The non-ownership by U.S. shippers of global production facilities affords them tremendous flexibility. If embarrassing revelations arise in connection with a particular supplier, the shippers can claim no responsibility, since they have no overt legal involvement in the company (even though in practice they may determine the conditions there by setting the prices and standards of production). They can use a particular supplier on an as-needed basis and can drop it if they are not satisfied, for any reason. Without owning significant assets in a particular location, the shipper can fairly easily shift production location from one factory to another, sometimes changing countries in the process.

This system of offshore production and contracting is associated with the rise of global sweatshops or factories that pay close to or below subsistence wages, where typically young, female employees work long hours under harsh and sometimes dangerous conditions. Countries in the Global South that are trying to establish programs in manufacturing for export, as a first step towards economic development, compete with one another to offer the most attractive package of incentives, including the lowest-cost labor, to TNCs, in a race to the bottom. Sweatshops in the developing world are not a product of preexisting labor conditions in those countries. Rather, factory managers lower wages and working conditions in order to survive in the highly competitive system of outsourcing and the disparity of power among the various actors (Varley 1998, 83).

Outsourcing in developing countries is a complex business, often involving various intermediaries. These middlemen arise because local manufacturers

---

produce exports. However, there is another way of looking at it. Petrovic and Hamilton (2006) have developed the concept of "market makers" to describe the role that giant Western retailers have played in creating a demand for these products and in shaping the capacity of Asian countries to meet this demand.

27

lack the information, language skills, communications infrastructure, or experience with complex legal and documentation requirements and are sometimes located in outlying areas. Usually only those U.S. companies that are able to maintain an office or agent in Asia can make direct arrangements with overseas manufacturers, and only the largest and most sophisticated offshore manufacturers are able to deal directly with U.S. companies. Otherwise, contractors, agents, or trading companies step into the breach. These intermediaries charge a commission based on a percentage of the value of the goods. They also hide information from both sides of their transactions, making it difficult for both buyers and producers to know what the other is doing or sometimes even who their contractors are (Varley 1998, 90–94).

The competitive character of U.S. retailing, especially among the discounters, is forcing retailers to seek out ever cheaper goods. "In turn, retailers pressure contractors, agents and trading companies for lower-cost goods. Large buyers may offer extremely low prices to their suppliers on a take-it-or-leave-it basis" (Varley, 95). Meanwhile, more and more developing countries are trying to establish an export sector, allowing U.S. firms to search for those suppliers that will give them the lowest prices for the best quality. As a result, U.S. companies are able to dictate the prices they are willing to pay. A director of international trade for the American Textile Manufacturing Institute stated, "You don't tell Wal-Mart your price. Wal-Mart tells you" (cited in Varley 1998, 95).

Competing middlemen contribute to the problem by offering the lowest prices and then squeezing local manufacturers. Local manufacturers often accept deals where they are paid less than the cost of manufacturing the goods, hoping they can find a way to make it work. Few contractors are willing to turn down an order, fearing they may lose the customer forever. The result is sweatshop-style production, including failure to pay workers on time (sometimes, at all), forced and unpaid overtime, speed-ups, lack of attention to health and safety issues, and so on (Varley 1998, 95).

As Neil Kearney of the ITGLWF (International Textiles, Garment and Leathers Workers Federation—a federation of trade unions in these industries from around the world) stated: "These [multinational] companies adopt codes of conduct, some of them in very nice language, but then they negotiate deals which make it impossible for their contractors to honor the codes. The companies say to the contractor, 'Please allow for freedom of association, pay a decent wage,' but then they say, 'We will pay you 87 cents to produce each shirt. This includes the wage, fabric, everything'" (cited in Varley 1998, 95–98).

Other aspects of the system lead down the road to sweatshops. Subcontracting is common, leading to tiny, hidden workshops and work at home. There can be what Varley calls "dicey payment arrangements" (1998, 98).

Instead of using letters of credit through banks, more informal arrangements are negotiated where the producers cannot ensure that they will be paid the agreed-upon amount, if at all. The system also shifts risk from large U.S. retailers to factories in developing countries. For example, a producer may invest in expensive equipment to produce free samples in the hopes that a buyer will place an order (Varley 1998, 98–102). Whether they intend to or not, U.S. shippers can play a critical role in the reproduction of sweatshops. The sheer size of their ordering power coupled with huge competitive pressures among contractors and intermediaries to win the work create a breeding pool for sweatshop proliferation.

As an example, let us briefly consider Wal-Mart's relations with its suppliers in China, the country where most of its offshore production is located. The home office of Wal-Mart Global Procurement is in Shenzhen, China. By locating there, the company can exercise greater oversight over its suppliers and over the factories they use, according to *Fortune* reporter, Jerry Useem, in an article entitled, "Should We Admire Wal-Mart?" (2/23/04).

Wal-Mart is not just a passive recipient of Chinese-produced goods but an active producer of those goods. The company is a major actor in China not only as an expanding retailer power but also, perhaps more importantly, as a shaper of production. Ex–store manager Lehman, interviewed for the *Frontline* television program, "Is Wal-Mart Good for America?" (available at www.pbs.org) reported that the company's pressure to cut production and shipping costs is just as intense in China as in the United States. The "natural" cheapness of Chinese production is not enough for Wal-Mart. The company puts pressure to lower the already poor conditions still further.

Wal-Mart's procurement staff members are constantly making deals with hundreds of Chinese manufacturers on a daily basis in order to produce goods tailored to Wal-Mart's own stringent specifications; these include pricing, quality assurance, efficiency, and delivery. Wal-Mart is also known to demand that its suppliers change their bookkeeping systems and improve their logistics to meet rigid delivery schedules while maintaining the lowest price margins. In exchange for Wal-Mart contracts, Chinese companies are often required to open up their books to Wal-Mart and cut prices where necessary, if Wal-Mart decides the supplier's profit margins are too large. Wal-Mart demands rock-bottom prices and forces its clients to cut costs in order to remain in contention for export orders (See "3 big threats to China's economic miracle," Jim Jubak, MSN Money, 5/7/04).

This is neatly illustrated in a *Wall Street Journal* article (11/13/03) about Ching Hai, a contract manufacturer that produces juicers, fans, and toasters for some of the largest retailers, with Wal-Mart as its largest client. Over the last decade, the average wholesale price for Ching Hai's products has almost been cut in half, from $7 to $4, in order to continue doing business with the stringent cost demands of Wal-Mart. Wal-Mart's Chinese producers have to find ways to lower their costs, which often leads to further exploiting their labor force. Ching Hai was forced to cut its labor force in half while maintaining the same level of order. The company had a starting wage of $32 a month, which was lower than the local minimum wage, and many employees had to work eighteen-hour days. In spite of all the cost-cutting efforts, the company was barely profitable. Furthermore, Ching Hai has been investigated for its high rate of workplace accidents, presumably because of the intense pressure placed on the supplier to increase production output.

In sum, Wal-Mart is far from a passive recipient of Chinese-produced goods merely taking advantage of the low wages that are prevalent in a newly developing country with a large, untapped, labor supply. Rather, it is playing a role in keeping labor standards in China as low as they can be pushed.[3] Wal-Mart is not alone in this endeavor; all the giant TNCs play a part in trying to cut labor costs even in poor countries. When China proposed to revise its labor law to improve the power of workers and unions in October 2006, the American Chamber of Commerce in Shanghai, with companies like Wal-Mart and Nike as members, recorded its fierce objections.

GROWTH OF GIANT CONTRACTORS

U.S. retailers and manufacturers who engage in offshore production make much larger profits than their suppliers, a fact that has led large manufacturers in Hong Kong, Taiwan, South Korea, and now China to engage in more independent production, including developing their own labels (So, Nin, and Poston 2001) and establishing branches in other countries. These contractors are becoming competitors of the firms they formerly supplied and shippers as well. For example, Payless Shoes, the largest U.S. importer of footwear, stocks goods from such a contractor. A Taiwanese bicycle manufacturer, Giant Manufacturing Corp., used to be a supplier of Schwinn but now produces its own bicycles. Fang Brothers is another example, a giant Hong Kong–based apparel producer that opened its own retail chain (Varley 1998, 102; Appelbaum and Lichtenstein 2007).

Gabriel Kahn, a reporter for the *Wall Street Journal,* has conducted some research on the new giant contractors, finding them continually expanding their role in global production. One of his articles, "Made to

---

[3]We should recognize that not all of the pressure exerted by Wal-Mart on Chinese producers is negative. The company also provides training to Chinese companies on how to prepare for and compete in the U.S. market. In so doing, it is helping Chinese firms to "modernize."

measure: Invisible supplier has Penney's shirts all buttoned up—From Hong Kong it tracks sales, restocks shelves, ships right to the store—Inside a 'radical' power shift" (9/11/03) describes a Hong Kong–based shirt maker named TAL Apparel Ltd., which has developed a close relationship with J. C. Penney: "TAL collects point-of-sale data for Penney's shirts directly from its stores in North America, then runs the numbers through a computer model it designed. The Hong Kong company then decides how many shirts to make, and in what styles, colors and sizes. The manufacturer sends the shirts directly to each Penney store, bypassing the retailer's warehouses—and corporate decision makers" (A1).

Kahn calls this a "radical power shift" in the relations between retailers and their contract manufacturers, increasing the power of the latter. TAL is a giant contractor that produces about 12.5 percent of the dress shirts sold in the United States. "As retailers strive to cut costs and keep pace with consumer tastes, they are coming to depend more on suppliers that can respond swiftly to their changing needs," Kahn observes. "This opens opportunities for savvy manufacturers, and TAL has rushed in, even starting to take over such critical areas as sales forecasting and inventory management."

TAL was negotiating a similar deal with Brooks Brothers in 2003, and it produced pants in Malaysia for Lands' End that it shipped straight to U.S. customers. For J. C. Penney, TAL has reduced the six months' worth of inventory it used to carry in its warehouses and reduced the three months' worth it carried in its stores to zero. Essentially, Penney's has outsourced its inventory management to TAL. The Hong Kong firm also maintains shirt design teams in New York and Dallas, which tests products in Penney stores, and then makes the decisions about which to produce, how many, and with what variations.

As of 2003, TAL did not produce in China but located its factories in countries with higher wages, such as Thailand, Malaysia, Taiwan, and Hong Kong. The company made up for higher labor costs with greatly improved supply-chain efficiency. This example illustrates how the most advanced features of the logistics revolution are appearing in Asia.

The other example described by Kahn concerns a Chinese garment producer named Luen Thai Holdings Ltd., which is creating a "supply-chain city" in the city of Dongguan in South China ("Making Labels for Less," *Wall Street Journal,* 8/13/04, B1). The goal of this project is to work with U.S. brand-name companies, like Liz Claiborne, to concentrate their production in China more, now that the country quotas under the Multi-Fiber Arrangement (MFA) have been terminated.[4]

---

[4]See UNCTAD (2005), a report that was authored by Richard Appelbaum. The MFA was gradually phased out; it was terminated at the beginning of 2005.

The supply-chain city of Luen Thai saves on both time and cost, writes Kahn: "'Right now, there is a lot of duplication,' says Chris Chan, Liz Claiborne's vice president for Asia. When prototypes come out of the factory they are sent back to New York to be inspected and possibly modified, then shipped back again to the factory in China. 'When it's all finished, it gets checked again,' Mr. Chan says. The process sucks up precious time and requires additional staff."

The new system will bring together the New York and Chinese staff at the Dongguan campus, enabling Luen Thai and Claiborne to cut their staffs from one hundred to sixty. And they save precious time by not having to send goods back and forth. Luen Thai hopes to attract other U.S. apparel manufacturers to the Dongguan site, such as Polo Ralph Lauren Corp. In the supply-chain city, the same scan-and-track inventory system is used by everyone from the textile producer to the retail stores, and the goods get shipped straight from the factory to a specific store that needs them. This reduces the unit cost drastically, to as low as 20 cents. So here we see an example showing that China is starting to enter the logistics revolution.

Gabe Kahn told us about the giant Asian contractors: "The giant contractors want to handle all of the logistics in Asia, including the warehousing, and ship directly to the store. A lot of functions are migrating to Asia. It is better if they are closer to the point of production versus the point of sale. Then they can make decisions as they arise. If a company's personnel move to Asia, they can get the goods in three days instead of ten."

Another major example of a giant multinational contractor is Li and Fung, a garment producer based in Hong Kong. Li and Fung is the model company, according to Kahn. According to its website (www.lifung.com), the firm has sourcing offices in forty countries. It promises its customers global supply chain management, one-stop-shopping service, quick response, and social responsibility. In other words, Li and Fung can take over the role of arranging for the production and timely delivery of apparel for Western manufacturers and retailers.

According to Kahn, Victor Fung talks about "the soft three dollars." This means that the vendor sells the goods to the retailer for one dollar and the retailer sells for four dollars. The Asian producer has to beat his head to lower his costs to 90 cents. But another approach is to get some of the three dollars. To do this, you buy the brand. This is what some of the giant contractors are doing. For example, Li and Fung licensed Levi's Signature brand, which sells in Wal-Mart. They design, produce, ship, everything.

Still another example is the vacuum cleaner producer Dirt Devil. The Asian supplier bought the brand and moved production out of Ohio. By locating everything near the production site, they were able to be more innovative and respond more quickly. They could lower their research and development costs and save time on decision-making. This practice, Kahn believes, will become more frequent.

SHIPPER LOGISTICS PRACTICES

How do the major retailers and brands actually organize their offshore procurement? Do they use agents or intermediaries? Do they have any direct relationship with their suppliers? And if so, how much control do they exercise over them, given the arm's-length character of the relationship? In the case of retailers, are they more actively engaged with those suppliers who are producing private label for them? These are the kinds of questions we sought answers to. Since companies are typically very secretive about such matters, it was difficult to get people to talk about it, but we made some progress into this world.

We interviewed an important executive of one of the giant retailers by phone. This person was extremely helpful but wished to remain anonymous. The executive laid out the approach of the giant retailers to offshore sourcing in Asia. We wondered whether the retailers are involved in Asian production primarily when they are producing their stores' private label. The executive disabused us of this notion:

> We are involved in all production in Asia, not just private label. We engage in the direct importing of both private label and branded goods. We work with the producers, oversee the production of our goods, and set up specifications for our products. It makes no difference whether the products are branded or private label. In neither case do we own any factories, so we are always dealing with someone else's factories. But we may rethink this with regard to certain products.

The retailer has a private label program, which it began about a dozen years ago. If it was able to get 20 percent better value than the brand and better quality at the same time, then it would switch to private label. It would benchmark private label against the brand. Sometimes it would sell the brand right next to the private label items. "Essentially this was saying to the brand that its prices were too high." This drove down some prices—for example, on diapers. "Private label has played a role in bringing down industry prices," the executive said.

> We had some phenomenal successes with private label. One example is our private label batteries. In this case, we pushed the brand price down, but ended up going back to private label. In the case of film, we got Kodak to bring down the price, and ended up going back to the brand.

When this retailer started outsourcing in Asia, it used a broker in the United States that worked with a trading company in Asia. Our informant thought there might have been another broker for the factory. But now the retailer's policy is to try to get as close to the factory as possible and to limit the role of brokers: "We don't have our own offices in Asia, but some Asian companies are big enough that they serve as their own broker, so we can buy directly from them." In contrast, Wal-Mart has its own offices in Asia. In our informant's experience, it is the department stores that especially use buying agents. They form consortia for group purchasing. The big box retailers are generally trying to get rid of unnecessary middlemen.

We tried to get a better understanding of the retailer's logistics practices. It uses POS data only for replenishment. When it decides to try a new item, it uses its sales history to determine the size of the order. EDI (electronic data interchange) is still in its infancy in Asia, according to our informant. There is a lack of a common standard. So this retailer does not use EDI (or VMI, vendor managed inventory) in importing from Asia. They are used in the United States, and they are coming to Asia: "Eventually the vendor and retailer community will develop a communications network to standardize ordering at an international level." Our informant continued:

> Part of the problem is that, in dealing with Asia, you can't control the firewall, which we can do in the U.S. Possibly it is happening in some countries where the retailer and vendor use the same communications network. Maybe this happens in Taiwan in certain cases. I imagine that Procter and Gamble in China would sell to a Chinese retailer using EDI. But everyone is struggling with communications from one country to the next. EDI and VMI are only being used in North America, especially Canada and the U.S., and to some extent in Mexico.

This retailer uses JIT practices for anything manufactured locally. It has daily and sometimes twice-daily deliveries. There is a command from the company president that there should always be one day's worth of sales on the floor. This has allowed the company to reduce its number of SKUs. Imports, in contrast, are planned inventories. They are rotated into the stores by SKU. They can be seasonal, like furniture, which is not replenished and involves a one-time buy. Because of these practices, the lockout of the longshore workers at the West Coast ports in 2002 created serious havoc for this retailer.

Of course, our informant did not know exactly how Wal-Mart operates in Asia, since it is a competitor and very secretive, but the executive guessed that it does more automated purchasing there than the executive's own retailer. This is because Wal-Mart sells lower-end goods and owns communications systems. It may use EDI to order and deliver goods to its own offices in Asia.

The question of whether logistics revolution practices can be used in Asia, and especially China, intrigued us, and we tried to answer it. An article in *American Shipper,* a trade journal, reports that China is still way behind in its logistics development (Philip Damas, "Solving China's Logistics Paradox," 7/05, 10–16). Logistics costs there are high: China spends 19 percent of GDP on logistics, compared to 10 percent in Europe and the United States. The reasons for this are numerous: poor infrastructure development, regulatory burdens with requirements varying from one province to the next, difficulties in tracing shipments, and huge inventory levels. One logistics executive estimated that there were ten thousand logistics professionals in China in 2005, when they need about a million. Of course, all of this is in the process of transformation, and no doubt China will catch up in logistics proficiency. Still, we wanted to find out if any U.S. shippers were able to use the latest logistics techniques there now.

We spoke briefly over the phone with Rick Jackson, a logistics expert at The Limited, on 9/8/04. The Limited, an apparel retailer, does not own any factories in China but does source there. They use two methods: they have an internal sourcing arm called Mast Industries, which sources all of their apparel and lingerie, and they have agents with whom they contract all non-apparel goods. The agents arrange for the production of goods designed by The Limited and produced to their specifications.

The Limited collects POS data and uses it for JIT production and delivery. They use it for initial launches and to react quickly to hot items. However, they do not use EDI with their Asian vendors. How quickly can product be delivered?

> If the goods are in inventory, they can be delivered in seventy-two hours. This means air shipment. Air costs $1.25 to $1.45 a pound, compared to 20 to 30 cents by ocean, so there is a difference of one dollar. We use air transport for high fashion and lingerie. Ocean transportation from Hong Kong takes 19 to 20 days door-to-door, to our DCs in Columbus, Ohio. Once at the DC it takes 5 to 10 days to get to the stores, so if we need a hot item we don't use ocean.

The Limited maintains several DCs in Columbus but does not have one on the West Coast, even though 65 percent of their imports come through LA/LB and Seattle. (The rest come via air freight.) The goods are "hot hatched" off the ship, meaning that they are the first to be taken off. This preference is accorded them because the company uses a small group of transportation providers and has long-term relationships with them.

Another set of phone interviews was conducted with a logistics expert at a U.S.-based electronics manufacturer, who also did not want to be identified. We asked whether it was possible to do EDI in Asia; the source replied that the company for whom the source works does not. It trades a lot of data electronically, but very few purchase orders are automated. It gets its orders from the retailers as EDI (Wal-Mart, Target, office supply companies like Staples and Home Depot) but cannot replenish that way.

It has to place regular orders. The company uses ERP—Enterprise Resource Planning. It collects huge amounts of data (by satellite) and tries to figure out supply and demand. It asks its Asian suppliers to produce a certain amount. The suppliers get back to the company with a counter offer of an amount and commit to it. They schedule dates and quantities.

The biggest user of electronic information is the company's forwarder, a U.S.-based firm that operates worldwide and has an office in Asia. The forwarder serves as the company's agent. They go and pick up the freight and take it to the carriers, which provide either ocean or air service. They take physical possession of the goods, and then our manufacturer gets into the forwarder's system to see what is happening and where things are. According to our informant:

> The retailer wants JIT delivery. They give us 14 to 20 days for delivery, but we have a lead time of sometimes 100 days. We have to use modeling to make predictions. We have to order in January to get it in April. We can't use air freight very much, because it cuts into our margins. So 90 percent of the inbound goods from the Far East come by ocean. If it drops to 70 to 80 percent, it impacts our margins. We have to create an artificial inventory. Our product [a consumer electronics item] has a peculiar seasonality. We don't have a Christmas push. We are now [July] right in the middle of our peak season, which is back-to-school. So our season runs from May to September. We sell to the big box retailers and sellers of office supplies and home equipment, some of which treat our products as loss leaders. They make their margins on other products, like backpacks. We have to have goods in stock here, so that the retailer can get a JIT order from us when they need it. We artificially inflate inventories at the beginning of the second quarter, and gradually bleed them down to the fourth quarter.

In other words, this manufacturer provides warehouses that the retailers' DCs can draw upon for JIT purposes. The retailer does not need to maintain inventory and pushes that requirement back onto the manufacturer. Meanwhile, the U.S. manufacturer is not in a position to ensure JIT production in Asia for itself so that it can avoid inventory buildup in U.S. warehouses. Just-in-time principles serve the needs of the retailers, but do not reverberate all the way up the supply chain in this case. The retailers maximize their flexibility at the manufacturer's expense.

The Asian suppliers make corrections during the season. The U.S. manufacturer sometimes has to go back to the supplier to say it needs more. The supplier usually stockpiles pieces so that it can respond to these kinds of requests. In January, the company makes an estimate of how much is likely to sell. Then it makes course corrections as the season progresses. The model may be doing better or worse than expected, so the company can make changes as the year goes by. But by the third quarter it has very little time to react. There is little room for miscalculations. The company's goal is to end the year with as little inventory as possible.

Here is what our informant said about production in China:

> It's getting easier. We were trailblazers in getting goods produced in China. We partner with folks who are international companies who produce for many different companies. We have been moving production from Shenzen to Shanghai. Shanghai is cheaper. There is availability of labor from rural areas nearby, and they have the infrastructure to transport them. The workers are plentiful, skilled, and trainable. First our goods were produced in Taiwan, then Shenzen [near Hong Kong], and now Shanghai. These companies are multi-billion dollar contractors. Some are Taiwanese, and others are Chinese. We do multiple sourcing. Getting piece parts is an issue. We have to compete with producers of cell phones, digital cameras, and other popular consumer goods. We want to avoid shortages. We go to the contractor with an engineer and tell them precisely what we want, and they produce it. We started with one company twenty years ago. We were one of the first Fortune 500 companies to do this, even though our production isn't the biggest. But they value the length of our relationship, and we each have loyalty to each other. Loyalty matters more in Eastern cultures than in the U.S. They will make concessions for us if we need them, even though we are a small buyer. There is mutual respect.

Finally, we contacted Jon DeCesare, a logistics expert to see what he thought about the use of advanced logistics practices by the big box retailers in Asia. Here is what he said:

> The big box retailers vary a great deal in their sophistication, so you can't generalize. They make general forecasts and then fill in the details using POS. In terms of sophistication, Wal-Mart wrote the book—and rewrites it every day. Target is trying to keep up, as is Best Buy and Home Depot. For example, Target will budget shelf space for a certain product, and they lose money if it isn't there on time. They reckon they save one hundred million dollars for every day they can take out of the transit time. So the supply chain is incredibly important to them. But what they mainly seek seems to be visibility, not replenishment orders. They want to make sure that goods are moving as planned. They want a glass pipeline. They want to be able to see where their SKUs are.

He thinks they do not have direct EDI connections, where POS data are sent out. Rather, their inventory control departments get the data, make adjustments to orders, and then send them out.

An example is Huffy bicycles, made in China. Wal-Mart may order fifty thousand units, which are then delivered to a Huffy warehouse in the United States. Wal-Mart then asks for them on a JIT basis—in smaller lots, like five thousand. But they also have the power and flexibility to tell them that they don't need any more after they have received thirty thousand. So then Huffy is stuck with twenty thousand, which it has to figure out how to unload. "This is a common scenario," says DeCesare. He says there is a movement by retailers to pick up FOB in Asia. They deal directly with the steamship line. This gives them greater visibility in terms of the location of their cargo and the flexibility to set up alternative routings if needed.

If we can generalize from this limited research, it appears that the most advanced features of the logistics revolution have not fully penetrated Asia, especially in the arena of the outsourcing of manufactured goods in countries like China. Offshore production and importing, especially when ocean transportation is involved, apparently does not operate on JIT principles—yet. Part of the reason lies with the relatively intractable length of the ocean voyage, but some of the problem lies with the insufficient development of Asian/Chinese logistics. This latter will undoubtedly be remedied in the next few years, and we can expect more efficient replenishment programs there soon.

SHIPPER ORGANIZATIONS

Shippers are organized in a number of ways. Smaller shippers (and larger on occasion) sometimes form shippers' associations for the purpose of gaining strength in numbers. They are nonprofit organizations that band together around various points of commonality, such as region or commodity, but some are open to anyone. By combining in this way, they can get better rates for transportation (see Joseph Bonney, "Strength in Numbers: Shippers Associations Add Services, Gain Acceptance by Carriers," *Journal of Commerce*, 8/13/01, 10–14).

Among the biggest are the Streamline Shippers Association, which specializes in imports from China, Japan, Korea and Southeast Asia, and the Wine and Spirits Shippers Association. They are among the dozen largest importers to the United States. There is an American Institute of Shippers Associations (AISA) that brings them together. The *Journal of Commerce* also has printed a list of them (8/13/01, 16–19). To give a flavor of the kinds of commodity importers that combine in this manner, here are a few examples: automotive, food, bicycles, chemicals, fashion accessories, footwear retailers, gloves, and toys. There are also associations that specialize in a region, like the Caribbean, Western New York, Southern Ontario, the Pacific Northwest, and so on.

At another level is the National Industrial Transportation League (NIT League). This is an organization, primarily of domestic manufacturers, that has been around for decades. It is the nation's oldest and largest shippers' organization, and it has played an important role in shaping U.S. transportation policy. The NIT League has primarily focused on domestic freight transportation, but it now has formed a sub-group called the Global Shippers Network which, as the name implies, involves the international trade and production community.

Retailers have also formed their own organizations. There are two major ones: the National Retail Federation (NRF) and the Retail Industry Leaders Association (RILA), formerly the International Mass Retailers Association (IMRA). RILA has retailer, manufacturer, and logistics company members and tries to coordinate relations between the two types of companies as well as represent their mutual interests. It has a Supply Chain Leaders Council. It puts on an annual Logistics Conference. Here are some of the companies whose logistics managers sit on the steering committee for the conference: Family Dollar Stores, Maersk Logistics USA, Target Corporation, Dollar General Corporation, Wal-Mart Stores, FedEx Services, Lowe's Companies, United Parcel Service, Best Buy Co., The Home Depot USA, Exel, and Sears Holding Co. (see www.retail-leaders.org). So we see that some of the biggest mass retailer importers are among its members.

One of the most important shipper organizations, which focuses especially on the ports, is the Waterfront Coalition (TWC). It began as the West Coast Waterfront Coalition (WCWC). Formed in 2001 to deal with the contract negotiations with the ILWU in 2002, it has since expanded into an organization that deals with shipper concerns regarding port issues around the country. The key person who pulled it together is Robin Lanier, who used to work for IMRA. She started the WCWC by calling on her friends and associates, leading to a heavy representation of big box retailers including, importantly, Wal-Mart.

Here is the way TWC defines its mission:

> The Waterfront Coalition is a group of concerned business interests representing shippers, transportation providers, and others in the transportation supply chain committed to educate policy makers and the public about the economic importance of U.S. ports and foreign trade, and to promote the most efficient and technologically advanced ports for the 21st century. (www.portmod.org)

The goals of TWC are fourfold: to be the unified voice supporting the implementation of available technology and infrastructure at the ports; to be the main source of information for supply chain stakeholders, especially shippers, about the importance of cooperative efforts to increase port efficiency and security; to be an agent for change through education, pilot projects, and advocacy; and to educate and communicate with the public, the media, and the government about the importance of the ports.

In sum, TWC is an effort to develop a strong and unified voice, mainly for shippers, to express their concerns and needs regarding the ports. The organization played an important role, for example, in advocating for keeping terminal gates open 24/7 in the face of severe congestion at the ports and also served to rally shippers to make use of these extended gate hours. TWC, specifically in its earlier incarnation as the WCWC, also played an important role in the West Coast ports lockout of 2002, a topic to which we shall return in chapter 7. In other words, they are far from neutral with respect to labor. In a sense, TWC epitomizes the class conflict between the giant retailers and logistics workers. But this is a story for another chapter.

SHIPPER INFLUENCE OVER LOGISTICS

As we said at the beginning of this chapter, shippers, particularly the giant retailers, are the actors with most power in the supply chain. They dictate terms both for their suppliers and their transportation providers. Let us briefly consider the ways that the big shipper-retailers exercise control over ocean transportation and its connected logistics systems.

Helen Atkinson, writing in the *Journal of Commerce,* describes the mass retailers as the "king of the jungle" (Helen Atkinson, "King of the Jungle," *JoC* 2/4/02, 9–12). Speaking of their power as top importers, she notes, "With that kind of clout, retailers can tell even the biggest manufacturers and transportation providers when to jump, and how high. . . . They have used their ever-increasing volume to reduce unit costs for distribution." This is seconded by reporter Peter Tirschwell, who describes the relationship between big retailers and ocean carriers: "Though they use 3PLs for many activities such as preparing goods for the store shelf, retailers negotiate directly with ocean carriers, ensuring that the relationship with an essential vendor industry is unencumbered by third parties. With imported goods now a staple of large retailers' offerings, ocean carriers are critical" ("Demanding, Exacting, Uncompromising," *JoC,* 1/19/04, 14–17).

We will be examining these negotiations in more detail in chapter 4. Here we mainly want to point out that the rates negotiated between shippers and ocean carriers greatly affect the earnings throughout the rest of the freight movement system. They set limits on the price for railroad and truck transportation, because those movements are often covered by the steamship lines.

There is a mutual dependence between the shippers and the ocean carriers. In the negotiations, importers allocate an amount of cargo to a carrier, that is, they promise to provide and pay for a certain volume of freight. In exchange, the carriers guarantee them space on the scheduled vessel, promising that their cargo will not be rolled over to a later trip. But this means that the shipper has to live up to its side of the commitment.

According *JoC* reporter Bill Mongelluzzo, the large retailers dominate ocean shipping rates ("Clout Counts," *JoC*, 2/4/02, 12). For example, in the footwear industry, four major retailers, Wal-Mart, Payless Shoe Source, Target, and Sears, accounted for about two-thirds of all footwear imports to the United States. Smaller footwear shippers band together in a footwear shippers association, but it is the retailers who set the standards. Writes Mongelluzzo, "When a Wal-Mart or a Target meets with an ocean carrier, they expect their volume to command the lowest freight rates. Usually they are right. . . . Since volume is so important . . . a natural pecking order develops." Smaller importers watch the rates achieved by the big ones and use those rates as a benchmark, but they do not expect to pay as little.

Conclusion

Shippers are critical actors in global logistics. They are the reason for the growth in imports. It is their money that pays for global transportation. They sit at the pinnacle of global logistics, determining what will be made, where it will be produced, how it will be shipped, and to where. As we have seen, the giant discount retailers are among the most important importers, so in the hierarchy of power in international logistics, they tend to be dominant. The power of these actors sets a context for understanding the logistics system, which we examine in the next section.

PART TWO

MOVING THE FREIGHT

CHAPTER 3

Containerization, Intermodalism, and the Rise of Los Angeles and Long Beach

In Southern California, two gigantic ports lie adjacent to each other near the San Pedro Bay. Physically, they appear to be a single entity, and it is hard to tell where one ends and the other begins, but they operate as separate jurisdictions under two different city governments. The port of Los Angeles (POLA) is run by the much bigger city of Los Angeles, while the port of Long Beach (POLB) is run by the coastal city of Long Beach. The two ports both cooperate and compete with each other, but together they serve as a major gateway for imported manufactured products from Asia.

Taken separately, they are the two largest individual container ports in the United States. Taken together, until 2004, they were the third largest container port in the world, behind Hong Kong and Singapore. In 2004, they dropped to fifth place behind Shanghai and Shenzhen, reflecting the rapid rise of China as an exporting powerhouse. In 2005, according to tabulations of the top 50 world container ports by the *Journal of Commerce*, the port that handled the most containers was Singapore, with 23.19 million TEUs (7/31/06, 24–31). Second was Hong Kong, with 22.6 million TEUs, followed by Shanghai (18.08 million TEUs) and Shenzhen (16.02 million). Ranked fifth was Busan, in South Korea (11.84 million). Los Angeles ranked tenth, with 7.48 million TEUs and Long Beach eleventh, with 6.71 million. Together they handled 14.19 million TEUs, placing them well above Busan in fifth place. The second U.S. port was New York–New Jersey, with 4.79 million TEUs, putting it in seventeenth place in the world. Five other U.S. ports make the top 50: Oakland (37),

Seattle (44), Tacoma (46), Hampton Roads (48), and Charleston (49). Treating LA and LB as two separate ports, we see that, of the eight U.S. ports that make the top 50, five are on the West Coast.

Almost all of the top 50 world container ports experienced growth in the number of containers they handled from 2004 to 2005. Especially stunning is the growth of the top China ports. Shanghai jumped 24.3 percent in one year, and Shenzhen grew 18.6 percent. The *Journal of Commerce* notes that Wal-Mart maintains its Asian headquarters and global procurement center in Shenzhen, presumably helping to account for its phenomenal growth (7/31/06, 24). Of the top 50, twenty experienced double-digit percentage growth, while only three showed very small declines over the year. Clearly, ocean-borne cargo is being shipped at rapidly rising rates, reflecting the growth in world trade, particularly in the Pacific.

RISING TRADE

Global trade has been growing rapidly since the 1970s, accelerating in each decade. Trade growth exceeds output, especially for manufactured products.[1] World trade reached a value of $8.9 trillion in 2004, in part because of the rising price of oil and other mining products but also because of gains in trade in manufactured goods. Of the $8.9 trillion in total merchandise trade in 2004, $6.57 trillion involved manufactured products (WTO 2005, 1–3).

Asia has become especially important as a source of manufactured exports. In the five years from 2000 to 2004, Asian manufactured exports have expanded by 40 percent and now account for 30 percent of world trade in manufactured goods. Over the same period, while starting from a higher base, European manufactured exports grew 13 percent, and North America suffered a decline until 2004 (WTO 2005, 2).

The two most populous countries in the world, China and India, both showed impressive economic and trade growth in 2004. China's economy grew 9.5 percent and India's grew 7.3 percent. China, in particular, has become an exporting power, especially of manufactured goods. For a number of manufactured products, it has become the largest supplier in the world. This has had an impact on some of its competitors, particularly those engaged in the production of textile and electronic products, where China's increasing exports have led to the lowering of prices (WTO 2005, 1–2).

Despite the rise of these Asian producers, the United States remained the world's leading trader in terms of imports, and second in terms of

---

[1]This section is coauthored with Sabrina Alimahomed.

exports. In 2004, the value of U.S. merchandise exports reached $818.8 billion, accounting for 8.9 percent of global exports, ranking second in the world, behind Germany. Also in the top 10 exporters were China, which attained third rank in 2004, followed by, in order, Japan, France, Netherlands, Italy, the United Kingdom, Canada, and Belgium. Together they accounted for 54.8 percent of world exports. On the import side in 2004, the United States, the world's number one importer, imported $1,525.5 billion in merchandise imports, 16.1 percent of the world's total. The next nine importers following the United States in 2004 were, in order, Germany, China, France, the United Kingdom, Japan, Italy, Netherlands, Belgium, and Canada. The top 10 importers accounted for 57.2 percent of world imports (WTO 2005, 21). If we exclude intra–European Union trade and treat the EU as a single market, Asian exporters rise in importance. The top 10 exporters then become: the EU, the United States, China, Japan, Canada, Hong Kong, Korea, Mexico, the Russian Federation, and Taiwan (WTO 2005, 22).

At one point, both Asia and Latin America appeared to be on a trajectory toward becoming major exporters of manufactured goods, but while several Asian countries have grown, Latin America appears to have fallen behind. In 2004, South and Central America accounted for 3.1 percent of world merchandise exports, far behind Asia, at 26.8 percent. The Latin American proportion has dropped from 11.4 percent in 1948, whereas the Asian percentage has grown from 13.6 in the same year (WTO 2005, 32). Only Mexico appears in the top 20 exporters, with a ranking of 13, exporting 2.1 percent of the world's total. Meanwhile, from Asia, China, Japan, Hong Kong, Korea, Taiwan, Singapore, and Malaysia all appear in the top 20 (WTO 2005, 21).

The United States used to be the leading producer and exporter of manufactured products. In 1970, the United States exported $43.8 billion worth of goods and imported $40.4 billion, for a positive trade balance. In terms of manufactured goods, the country also had a positive trade balance of $4.4 billion. The balance of trade overall fluctuated for a few years but became consistently negative in 1976, but the trade balance in manufactured goods remained positive through 1982. In 1983 that became negative too, with a $22.7 billion deficit (U.S. Census Bureau, Statistical Abstract 2006, Table 1293). Since then, imports to the United States have grown enormously, especially in recent decades, and the country's trade deficit has become vast—and is expanding. In 1970, manufactured imports were valued at $27.3 billion. In 1980 this figure had risen to $133 billion. By 1990 it reached $388.8 billion and, by 2004, $1.175 trillion. In 1970, manufactured goods accounted for 68 percent of total imports. By 2000 they were 83 percent of the total. In 2004 the U.S. trade deficit in manufactured goods was $464.4 billion, accounting for 71 percent of the country's total trade deficit.

Some would argue that despite the tremendous growth in manufactured imports, offshore production remains a minor aspect of the U.S. economy. Nevertheless, there is evidence that, at least for certain manufactured products, global outsourcing has become extensive. According to Gereffi and Sturgeon (2004), in 2001 90 percent of all consumer electronics sold in the United States were produced offshore. Footwear, toys and games, luggage, handbags, and watches and clocks showed import penetration levels of 80 to 85 percent. Seventy percent of bicycles were imported, as were 57 percent of apparel. The widespread belief that manufacturing is fleeing the United States receives some corroboration in these figures.

The U.S. trade deficit keeps growing. In 2005 it reached a record $725.8 billion, increasing by 17.5 percent in that year alone, setting a record in terms of percentage growth for the fourth year in a row. China alone accounted for $202 billion of this deficit: the United States imported $243.5 billion worth of goods from China (about 30 percent of China's total exports of $762 billion). China's trade advantage with the world as a whole, $102 billion, was only half of what it was with the United States. The U.S. trade deficit with China in 2005 is the largest trade deficit between two countries that the world has ever seen (see www.uschina.org/statistics/tradetable.html). It is this rise in trade with Asia, and with China in particular, that helps to account for the rise of the ports of Southern California.

TRADE THROUGH THE LOS ANGELES CUSTOMS DISTRICT

The United States is divided into customs districts, covering all the points of entry in the various regions. The Los Angeles customs district (LACD) includes the ports of Los Angeles and Long Beach, the much smaller port of Hueneme, Los Angeles and Ontario International Airports, the McCarran air field in Las Vegas, and some small oil terminals along the Pacific Coast. Significantly, it excludes San Diego, which serves as a major trade link with Mexico. Obviously, trade information for the LACD is broader than the ports of LA/LB, but they are a very significant component of these data.

The Los Angeles Economic Development Corporation (LAEDC), under the research direction of Jack Kyser, puts out an excellent and thorough annual report entitled *International Trade Trends and Impacts: The Southern California Region,* which examines trade through the Los Angeles Customs District. We rely on the report that was put out in May 2006, covering the results for 2005.

In 2005, the largest customs district in the country, as measured by the value of international trade, was Los Angeles, at $293.9 billion. The U.S. total was $2,575.3 billion, so that the LACD accounted for over 11 percent of the nation's international trade (Kyser 2006, 20). Of imports entering the LACD, 17.2 percent came by air, and 82.5 percent arrived by ship. These figures are based on the value of the products; if we measured by weight or volume, the proportion coming by ship would rise significantly. Since air transport is so much more expensive, it tends to be used only for low-weight, high-value products. For example, 89.4 percent of precious stones and pearls were imported by air to the LACD in 2005, while 99.1 percent of furniture and prefabricated buildings were brought by ships (Kyser 2006, 25).

Three-quarters of the international trade moving through the LACD was imports, and only one-quarter was exports in 2005, reflecting the overall imbalance of trade. In particular, the LACD specializes in imports from Asia. In 2005, Asia accounted for 84.7 percent of imports through the LACD, followed by Europe with 9.1 percent. Central and South America covered 3.2 percent, and Canada and Mexico just 1.2 percent (Kyser 2006, 26). It is clear that Southern California serves primarily as a gateway for Asian imports.

Even greater concentration of function is shown in the imports from China. In 2005, the LACD imported $92.86 billion worth of goods from China (including Hong Kong, which accounted for $2.17 billion). China accounted for 43 percent of all imports through the LACD. The second-ranked import source was Japan, with $34.82 billion (16 percent), followed by South Korea, at $10.86 billion, and Taiwan, with $10.23 billion (5 and 4.7 percent, respectively). The figures per country trail off sharply from there. Imports from China through the LACD have grown dramatically every year over the last decade, typically at a rate of around 20 percent per annum. No other source country comes close to this growth rate for the customs district (Kyser 2006, 27). So we can refine our summary statement: Southern California serves primarily as a gateway for Asian imports, especially from China.

The ports of LA/LB are responsible for a fair share of the imports that are brought into the LACD. Statistics on the West Coast ports are collected by the Pacific Maritime Association (PMA), an organization of steamship lines and terminal operators that serves as the collective employer and implementer of the collective bargaining agreement with the dock workers and their union, the International Longshore and Warehouse Union (ILWU). The PMA puts out an annual report. Their 2006 report, which appeared in March 2007, reports on the tonnage and the container volume of the trade that flows through the ports but, unfortunately, not on the value of the goods. From Kyser, however, we know that $177.8 billion worth of imports were brought in by ship in 2005 and that $40.2 billion were exported by ship, for a total of $218 billion (2006, 24). It seems safe to assume that this figure corresponds to what was handled by the Southern California ports. Unfortunately, Port Hueneme is included in the LACD but it only accounts for 5 percent of total West Coast traffic (as measured by weight), while LA/LB account for 56 percent. The total figure for the two major ports is probably close to $200 billion (Kyser 2006, 22).

The POLB handled 97,291,496 tons of cargo in 2006, while the POLA handled 113,107,896 million tons, for a total of 210.4 million tons. These figures represent tremendous growth over recent years. For example, in 2001, the combined tonnage was 142.4 million tons, representing a 48 percent growth over the six-year period. Tonnage estimates include containers, which are measured by volume rather than weight. The conversion is made by multiplying the number of TEUs by seventeen tons—the average weight of a TEU (PMA 2006, 58).

The ports of LA/LB are not simply container ports. They also deal with general (non-containerized) cargo, lumber and logs, autos and trucks, and bulk cargo, some of which is considerably heavier than containerized goods. In fact, only a little over 5 percent of the total weight carried by the twin ports is in containers. Nevertheless, the containerized portion of their cargo probably covers a high percent of the value of the goods they move. Besides, even viewed strictly in terms of container traffic, the twin ports are by far the largest ports in the United States, as we have seen.

CONTAINERIZATION AND INTERMODALISM

Containerization

The year 2006 marked the fiftieth anniversary of the introduction of containers to ocean transportation (Levinson 2006; Cudahy 2006). Before containerization (also known as a form of unitization), the ocean transportation of freight generally depended on the break-bulk method. Packages were loaded on pallets, which were hoisted in a cargo net by crane onto the ship. Longshore workers in the hold of the ship would carefully stow the cargo to protect it from damage, a lengthy and labor-intensive process. The cargo would have to be unloaded (discharged) in the same manner at the other end of the voyage, making ocean freight transportation a long and costly process (Campbell 1993; Chilcote 1988; DeBoer and Kaufman 2002; Talley 2000).

Containerization has revolutionized this system. It seems safe to say that containerization was a prerequisite to global production and that, without

it, globalization would have been immensely slowed down. Containerization allowed a vast increase in the speed with which cargo could be moved
from one corner of the earth to another. It also greatly reduced the cost
of ocean transportation, making it more cost-effective to produce at ever-
greater distances from the market. Part of the savings was found in the
reduction of labor costs, as we shall see in part 3. But containers also saved
on insurance costs as well as on the cost of maintaining inventory. It made
possible just-in-time production (Levinson 2006, ch. 1). In sum, containerization was an essential ingredient for the logistics revolution that we
discussed in chapter 1. Along with the computer, it helped to change the
world.

Malcolm McLean, owner of a trucking company, is the individual cred-
ited with first developing the concept of containers. He realized that truck
trailers could be filled and shipped without their contents ever having to be
handled between point of origin and point of destination. The wheels of
the trailers could be detachable so that the trailer boxes could be stacked;
the chassis and wheels could be attached or removed as needed. McLean
purchased a small tanker company, which he named Sea-Land, and
adapted it for this purpose. The first voyage, between Newark and Puerto
Rico, took place in 1956. The first international voyage, to Rotterdam,
occurred in 1966, a date that can be viewed as the start of containerization
in international trade (Chilcote 1988, 126–27; Muller 1999, ch. 3; Talley
2000, 933).

Containerization was pushed mainly by the steamship companies rather
than the ports (Campbell 1993, 215). Needless to say, it took some time for
the idea to catch on and for the costly infrastructure that would make containerization practical to be put into place (Erie 2004; Levinson 2006).
Standardizations of various sorts had to be agreed upon. Ports had to
invest billions of dollars in new equipment and terminal designs (DeBoer
and Kaufman 2002, 33). Ships that could carry containers safely needed to
be developed. Railroads had to develop adaptations as well. Nevertheless,
the conversion was fairly rapid, given how much expense was involved.
The truth is that without massive participation by many parties, the transformation could not have occurred, since container ships could only dock
at ports that could handle them, and ports would only invest if they had
sufficient traffic to justify it (Campbell 1993, 218).

Standardized containers are generally 8 feet in width, 8 feet 6 inches
in height, and 20, 40, or 45 feet long. Taller containers, known as high
cubes, are also available, with a height of 9 feet 6 inches. The standard
measure for number of containers is twenty-foot equivalent units (TEUs),
even though forty-foot containers (FEUs) are far more common, presumably to avoid fractions in the counting system. Containers have locking
mechanisms on their corners so that they can be secured to cranes, to truck

chassis, to rail cars, and to each other for stacking (Chilcote 1988, 126; Talley 2000, 933).

Containerization revolutionized ports and the way they handle freight. Large gantry cranes (able to move side to side) now lift the containers from the dock into a ship with slots to hold them in place, and they can also be stacked high on deck. The cranes are designed to carry multi-ton containers. The average weight per TEU is generally estimated at 17 tons, so a forty-foot container would average around 34 tons. Containerization greatly increased the speed with which ships could be loaded and unloaded, dramatically raising the productivity of labor and the ship. It is estimated that productivity increased by a factor of at least ten. Instead of spending half of its time in port, a container vessel could reduce that amount by 10 to 20 percent (Chilcote 1988, 127–30). Whereas it often took a week to unload and load a break-bulk ship, a containership could be in port for one or two days (Talley 2000).

During the break-bulk era, the logic of shipping was to keep ships relatively small, making loading and unloading quicker and easier. To increase service, more ships would be added and more ports visited. By reducing the costs of loading and unloading, containerization changed the logic of shipping. It does not take substantially longer to load and unload a larger container vessel than a smaller one, since additional cranes can be used alongside the ship. It now pays to have bigger and bigger ships. By the end of the 1970s, the largest container ships were already four times larger than the largest break-bulk ships (Chilcote 1988, 131). And the size has continued to climb in each decade, with no end in sight. Now 7,000- and 8,000-TEU vessels are common, and 9,000-TEU vessels are moving on line. Ships like these are longer than four football fields and so wide that they cannot pass through the Panama Canal. Their sheer size is breathtaking to see, as the people that work them scurry around, looking like ants.

Containerization favored large shippers (importers) over smaller ones in comparison with break-bulk shipping. The advantage of shipping full containers was enormous. LCL (less-than-container load) requires consolidation of smaller loads, which in turn requires intermediaries of various types who take their cut (Campbell 1993, 218). Large shippers are able to fill containers, simplifying the shipment enormously.

Intermodalism

The Panama Canal, which was the typical route for goods from Asia headed for the U.S. East Coast, can handle vessels of 3,000 to 3,500 TEUs and possibly, with redesign, a maximum of 4,400 TEUs. Needless to say, this size limitation contradicts the economic advantages of larger container ships, known as post-Panamax vessels. Post-Panamax vessels were made possible by the development of what was called *land-bridge,* the movement of goods from ships to the railroads and across the United States on dry land. *Landbridge* most accurately refers to moving goods across the entire U.S. land mass and on to other ships on the opposite coast for shipment to Europe or elsewhere. *Mini-landbridge* refers to movements where the containers are unloaded from trains on the East Coast and make no further ocean voyages. *Micro-landbridge* refers to rail movements that end somewhere within U.S. territory before reaching the eastern seaboard.

Landbridge was first developed by a company called Seatrain, to move European cargo from New York to California, avoiding the Panama Canal and saving a week in transit time. However, the system works even better from West to East, mainly because of the huge and growing volume of Asian imports. The trans-Pacific shipping lines did not need extra vessels, and they found that their costs were not greatly increased by providing shippers with landbridge service. They led the way in working with the railroads. By the late 1970s, half of the trans-Pacific traffic from Asia to the eastern United States was moving by landbridge (Chilcote 1988, 137–38). The first post-Panamax ship involved in the trans-Pacific trade was developed by the steamship company APL (American Presidents Line) and arrived on the West Coast in 1988.

Landbridge has been a critical component of international intermodal freight transportation (Müller 1999, ch. 6). Containerization allowed boxes to be moved from ships either directly to trains or to be delivered to railheads by port truckers. Although trucking companies also play a critical role in intermodal moves across the nation, the basic units of the port intermodal system are: steamship lines, port truckers (who pick up and deliver containers at the ports and drive them to and from local drop-off points), and railroads. Indeed, in the industry, when people refer to intermodal transportation, they almost invariably mean putting the freight on rail. Of course, the term also has much wider application, including shifts between any two modes of transportation.

Before containers, each mode of transportation and each port had a clearly defined function or "silo mission." For example, steamship companies only had to be concerned about moving goods from one port to another. Containers broke down the silo walls as the modes became more interdependent. Even the ownership of equipment became blurred, as containers, truck tractors, and railcars can belong to any mode (DeBoer and Kaufman 2002, 33).

International intermodalism allowed for the door-to-door movement of cargo on a single bill of lading. One transportation entity could take charge of the entire move, from a factory in Asia to a warehouse anywhere in the United States. This simplified trade enormously, making it much easier for shippers to import goods. The various types of carriers had to cooperate in order to provide continuous, seamless, reliable freight movement. Door-to-door service has sometimes also been used for more sophisticated just-in-time delivery. The evolution of information technology abetted the process (Shashikumar and Schatz 2000).

Today, the term *landbridge* seems to have fallen into disuse. Instead, the industry uses the term *inland point intermodal,* or IPI. This makes sense, since by far the most important kind of move is from a port to an inland center. Using the U.S. land mass as a bridge between Asia and Europe is probably a rare occurrence. Terms like *mini-* and *micro-landbridge* seem to minimize the length and importance of these moves.

The development of intermodalism and IPI was a tremendous boost to all of the West Coast ports, especially those of Southern California. With the rise of trade with Asia, goods were increasingly diverted from the Panama Canal and moved in containers across the United States by rail, a system that shippers found economically beneficial. According to Chilcote: "The combined Ports of Los Angeles and Long Beach subsequently became the largest container load center on the coast . . . partly owing to their enormous local market and partly to intermodalism" (1988, 134).

The Legal Basis of International Intermodalism

The development of international intermodal transportation was held up by the U.S. government for several years for complicated reasons, one being that the steamship lines were unregulated by the government and benefited from antitrust immunity, permitting them to form rate-setting conferences, a topic we cover in the next chapter (Shashikumar and Schatz 2000). At the end of the 1970s, all of the transportation modes were deregulated. The Railroad Revitalization and Regulatory Reform Act was passed in 1976, followed by the Staggers Rail Act in 1980. The Motor Carrier Act of 1980 deregulated the trucking industry. These changes set the stage for permitting international intermodalism to develop. The culmination of this process was the passage of the U.S. Shipping Act in 1984 (Shashikumar and Schatz 2000; Talley 2000).

Prior to the 1984 Shipping Act, the regulation of the railroads by the Interstate Commerce Commission (ICC) and of the steamship lines by the Federal Maritime Commission (FMC) built walls between the two modes of transportation. The 1984 Shipping Act allowed the steamship lines to enter into agreements about rates with the railroads, enabling them to offer customers through-transportation, in other words door-to-door service (DeBoer and Kaufman 2002). Other legislation lifted barriers against trucking companies acquiring railroads and vice versa (Shashikumar and Schatz 2000).

Intermodalism has expanded since 1984. Many steamship lines now offer more services than the basic door-to-door delivery. These include documentation, cargo clearance, warehousing, product assembly, and distribution. Most of the biggest liner companies have their own logistics subsidiaries, which provide a host of such services (Shashikumar and Schatz 2000).

CHANGES TO PORTS

Port Governance

Steven Erie has studied the governance of the ports of LA/LB in some detail. He points out that, unlike most U.S. ports, which are run by regional public authorities, both the city of Los Angeles and, a little bit later, Long Beach, both operating on the municipal level, created a powerful proprietary (semi-autonomous) department to run its harbor. The Southern California port authorities, unlike those of NY/NJ, for example, serve under the nominal control of their mayors and city councils but are, in practice, able to behave as developmental government actors who can pursue a growth agenda with limited interference. The ports act as bureaucratic agencies with considerable "political autonomy and transformative capacity" (Erie 2004, 29–32, 34).

The cities interface with the ports through city-appointed boards of harbor commissioners, who in turn appoint administrations to run the daily affairs of the ports. But the cities have little direct authority over the ports' budgets and capital investments. Their funds are generally shielded from raids by the cities. An important exception occurred for the POLA in the 1990s when the City of Los Angeles laid claim to some port revenues. The city was sued by the Steamship Association of Southern California. The SASC won, and the city had to stop raiding port coffers (Erie 2004, 124–29).

The ports behave more or less like private, profit-making corporations. The ideology of the ports' managers and bureaucrats is consistent with a private enterprise answerable to its stockholders. Of course, one can evaluate this from different perspectives. Erie (2004) sees it in a positive light as providing an opportunity for unimpeded development for the entire region. Gulick (2001) and Hall (2002) both view it more critically, looking more at the costs of such development.

The basic function of the port authorities is to develop the built environment. Gulick (2001, 164–65) describes them as functioning like urban growth machines. That is, their major purpose is to increase the number of TEUs that flow through their facilities by attracting as many shipping

55

companies as possible to use them. In turn, they provide the companies with equipment, infrastructure, and services. The California ports serve primarily as landlords and are described as "landlord ports." They buy cargo-handling equipment, finance the construction of marine terminals, build intermodal facilities, and lease this developed space to the steamship lines, terminal operators, and railroads. They collect rent for the use of these facilities as well as collecting wharfage, which is an assessment per ton of cargo, and dockage, a fee for the amount of time a ship is in berth (Gulick 2001, 169–70).

In a quarterly newsletter called "Re:Port" (Winter 2004), the POLB describes itself this way: "The Port of Long Beach is not responsible for ordering cargo or shipping cargo. We operate as a landlord and lease property to shipping lines from around the world. Shippers—such as manufacturers, large department stores and other retailers—book space with these shipping lines to move imports into the United States. This cargo is then unloaded at the Port of Long Beach to meet the demands of local consumers, as well as consumers throughout the United States."

The newsletter also points out that the port land was transferred to the city by the state of California for the purpose of developing and maintaining a municipal harbor. The port's employees are city employees. However, the port does not depend on tax dollars for its support, generating its own revenues from leases, which pay for employee salaries and benefits, maintenance of the terminals, and repayment of debt for capital improvements. The POLB employs 350 people but is not involved in the employment of longshore workers, who are hired by the terminal operators. The same principles apply to the POLA.

A key feature of ports is that they are fixed in space, whereas their customers are mobile. The mobility of the steamship lines (as well as of the importers and exporters, who can switch ports by switching carriers) puts the ports in competition with each other to lure customers, that is, tenants. LA and LB are in competition with each other, though they have also cooperated over major infrastructure projects.

The Impact of Intermodalism on Competition between Ports

A number of authors (Boschken 1988; Campbell 1993; Chilcote 1988; Corbett 1996; Dowd 1988; Hall 2002; Luberoff and Walder 2000; Slack 1993; Talley 2000) have pointed out that the rise of intermodalism has disempowered ports. Before the takeover of containerization, ports had natural hinterlands, and that ensured the flow of a certain amount of trade through them. With intermodalism, marine containers can be hauled anywhere by truck or train for a reasonable price and do not depend on arrival at a particular port. Even major regions, such as the East Coast versus the West Coast, are placed in competition with each other.

Given the expense of port visits, the steamship lines (like the airlines) prefer to operate on a "hub and spoke" system. Put another way, they want their ever-bigger containerships, which require heavy investment, to maximize their returns by making as many trips across the Pacific as possible. It is more economical to stop at fewer ports—usually two or even only one on the West Coast. This increases the competition between ports, which have invested in very expensive container terminals in the hopes of drawing liner trade. The result has been the development of overcapacity among some of the ports—and investments that may not pay off. Power shifted from the ports to the steamship lines, since the latter could choose which ports they would use based on criteria other than natural hinterland. A tendency toward concentration has developed in the ports system, as the big get bigger and the small lose market share (Chilcote 1988; Gulick 2001, ch. 3). This process does not determine which ports will succeed, but it does determine that some (like LA/LB, as it turns out) will be extraordinarily successful.

Before containerization and intermodalism, the primary customers of the ports used to be the shippers—the importers and exporters. Door-to-door service changed that. It meant that the shippers had less interest in which port was selected. Their major concern was inexpensive and timely delivery and, once door-to-door service was offered, it was up to the steamship lines to decide which were the most efficient ports for discharging cargo. The primary customers of the ports switched to the steamship lines.

Port costs are a small percentage of the total cost of buying and running ships, which means that, in the competition between ports, offering price incentives may not be a viable option. The steamship companies have other priorities in choosing their ports of call. Moreover, with transportation deregulation, public and standardized rates have disappeared, leaving shippers able to introduce such factors as volume into the rates—factors that the ports cannot control. This adds to the vulnerability of the ports, which must compete for steamship liner service (Campbell 1993; Dowd 1988, 230–31).

Intermodalism changes the nature of port investment. Ports used to invest mainly for the benefit of their region. Now they are being asked to invest for the benefit of the entire country (DeBoer and Kaufman 2002, 34), without the security of knowing that the investment will pay off. Even if a port is successful, the regions that are nearby may have to bear additional costs on top of the financial ones, such as congestion and pollution. The contradiction between national benefit and local cost has become a serious problem, a topic to which we shall return (Campbell 1993, 223–25; Erie 2004).

The Ports of LA/LB

Southern California Exceptionalism?

The twin ports of Southern California appear to be an exception to the general pattern of competition between U.S. ports. Dowd, for example, writes that the nation's ports are under tremendous competitive pressure but that a small number of ports can escape it. He gives the ports of LA/LB as an example. Even though they have higher costs than the others, they still are able to attract a lot of cargo. "Long Beach and Los Angeles can set their rates, and have, in fact, set their rates, to provide a very good profit for themselves. This type of situation probably only exists at one other place, and that is the Port of New York/New Jersey" (1988, 26).

Until recently, the ports of LA/LB have been able to avoid the pitfalls of competition. Indeed, the LA/LB ports have had a kind of arrogance about them, feeling that they can get away with almost anything because they have such a hot product. As Dowd notes, these ports are known for being expensive, but it does not matter—the attractions are too strong. Of course, there is no guarantee that this popularity will last (as we shall see below), and undoubtedly there are steamship lines and major shippers who would like to see it changed.

The Size and Importance of the Ports

As we stated at the beginning of this chapter, the ports of LA/LB comprise the largest container port complex in the United States. Our opening statistics looked at overall trade, including both imports and exports. However, if we focus just on imports, the ports of LA/LB stand out even more. According to the U.S. GAO (2003), in the year 2000, the ports of LA/LB accounted for 43.8 percent of imported containers to the top ten U.S container ports. The next largest port complex, New York–New Jersey, was a distant second, with 14.6 percent of total imports to the top ten. The other major West Coast ports, Seattle-Tacoma and Oakland, did not even crack double digits. It is safe to conclude that over 40 percent of the entire nation's containerized import trade passes through the ports of Southern California.

LA/LB was not always the leading port complex of the United States. New York was the most significant port for most of U.S. history. The shift occurred in the mid-1980s. The ports of LA/LB passed NY/NJ in 1986, with 2.719 million versus 2.34 TEUs, and continued growing at a steady clip, whereas NY/NJ dropped and then recouped somewhat in terms of container traffic. By 1992, LA/LB had almost double the container volume of NY/NJ (Rimmer 1998, 443).

In the 1990s, in particular, trade through the ports of LA/LB began to grow at a rapid rate and, despite some recessional blips, has shown a continual upward movement. The ports doubled their volume in the 1990s, and some predict it will double again by 2010 and even treble by 2020, to 24.3 million TEUs per year (Mercer/Standard and Poor's 1998). In 1995, they handled 3.985 million TEUs, a figure that jumped to 6.504 million in 2000 and 9.263 million in 2005 (Kyser 2006, 20). At this rate, the predictions seem to be pretty much on track.

The West Coast Ports

There are twenty-seven ports on the West Coast. The state of Washington has ten, including small ones like Port Angeles and Everett. The major ports of the state are Seattle and Tacoma. Oregon has three ports, with Portland as the most significant. California has fourteen ports, ten of which are in Northern California. For example, Stockton and Redwood City each have small ports. The largest port in the region is Oakland. The four ports in Southern California include LA/LB, San Diego, and Port Hueneme. Six of the ports account for the bulk of the traffic: Seattle, Tacoma, Portland, Oakland, Los Angeles, and Long Beach.

The rise in containerized traffic through the West Coast ports, taken as a whole, is dramatic. In 1970, the West Coast ports moved 8.8 million tons of container traffic. This figure rose to 35 million tons in 1980, 90.3 million tons in 1990, and 174 million tons in 2000. By 2006 it had risen to 361.1 million tons. Containerized cargo also grew as a percentage of total tonnage handled by the ports. In 1970 it accounted for 14.6 percent; in 1980, 30.8 percent; in 1990, 49.7 percent; and in 2000, 67.0 percent. By 2006 the figure had reached 72 percent. All other forms of cargo, including general cargo (break bulk), bulk cargo, lumber and logs, and autos and trucks, either remained stable, declined, or grew a small amount, whereas containerized cargo shows almost a straight line of upward growth (PMA 2006, 61).

The West Coast ports handled 22,086,014 TEUs in 2006. Of these, 6.6 million, or 30 percent, were empties. If we include empty containers, the POLB handled 6,953,564 TEUs, and the POLA handled 8,826,917 TEUs, of which 30–32 percent were empties. Together they totaled 15.8 million TEUs, including empties (PMA 2006, 60). Of course, the principal reason for the rise of the West Coast ports is the rise in U.S. trade with Asia. Prior to 1978, Europe was the primary trading partner of the United States. In that year, Asia took over (Gulick 1998, 62). As Asian countries developed into manufacturing powerhouses with a focus on producing goods for export, the West Coast ports became the nearest points of entry. Most important to this trade is the rise of China. The U.S. economy has experienced a major shift in terms of manufacturing. The eastern and midwestern states used to be industrial centers, and the major flow of manufactured goods was from East to West. Indeed, this created back-flow problems for transportation providers who could not find enough cargo for shipments from West to East. Now, with the rise of manufactured imports from Asia, the flows have been reversed. Manufactured goods arrive at West Coast ports, many of which are shipped East. The back-flow problem has shifted direction, as fewer goods move from East to West than from West to East (Calix 2002, 4).

The importance of the Southern California ports has increased since the mid-1990s. In 1995, the LA/LB ports together accounted for 57.5 percent of container throughput (imports and exports) on the West Coast (Gulick 1998). By 1998 that percent had climbed to 63.7. By 2006 the two ports were accounting for 71.5 percent of West Coast container traffic, up from 69 percent in the previous year (PMA 2006, 58).

The ports of LA/LB are especially popular as points of first discharge for imported goods, according to a report on West Coast ports by Bill Mongelluzzo in the *JoC* (4/10/06, 42–48). In 2005, the POLA accounted for 39.4 percent of first discharged imports on the West Coast (as measured in TEUs), and the POLB accounted for 34.3 percent, for a combined total of 73.7 percent. Seattle was next, with 8.9 percent of the market. Looking at the loading end, we find that 57 percent of the TEUs that arrived at West Coast ports in 2005 were last loaded in mainland China, with an additional 4.5 percent last loaded in Hong Kong, for an aggregate China total of 61.6 percent. Japan was a distant second, with 7.4 percent of the market. China is the biggest exporter and LA/LB the biggest importer, in both cases by far.

Explaining the Rise of the Ports of LA/LB

Why did the ports of LA/LB break away from the pack of West Coast ports? Was this just accidental, or were there compelling reasons? And what is the longevity of these reasons? Can we expect the Southern California ports to continue to maintain their dominance and keep growing, or will other major routes emerge to challenge them? In the next section we examine some of the factors that account for the dominance of LA/LB, followed by a section that considers various alternatives to them.

Size of Local Market. Compared to the other West Coast ports, the ports of LA/LB have the tremendous advantage of being located in a major population center. The Southern California six-county region of Los Angeles,

Orange, Riverside, San Bernardino, Imperial, and Ventura has a population of almost 17 million people (more than the state of Florida) and in 2000 produced goods and services worth over $600 billion, almost half of the state's total of $1.3 trillion. If California were considered as a country, it would rank fifth in the world in terms of GDP, after the United Kingdom and before France, and the six-county Southern California region would rank tenth, just behind Brazil (Calix 2002). A significant proportion of the goods that enter through the ports—some say as high as 50 percent—stays in the region, a point we shall revisit in a later chapter.

Calix points out that the huge local market attracts trade both for final consumption and for adding value to products (2002, 2). In other words, the local economy includes a robust manufacturing sector that is available to interact with imports for assembly, additions, and other value-added services. In fact, Southern California competes with Chicago for the highest number of manufacturing employees in the nation. This double attraction for bringing cargo to Los Angeles in the first place leads to the corollary that it may as well serve as a distribution center (DC) for the country as a whole.

The attraction of the Southern California ports is demonstrated by the tale of one shipper, Hasbro Toys described by Bill Mongelluzzo is an article in the *JoC* entitled "Hasbro Bolts to S. California" (6/17/02, 28–30). Hasbro imports about 17,500 TEUs a year, until recently using Seattle as its main port of entry. The company had a longstanding arrangement with the port of Seattle to occupy a port-owned distribution facility on the waterfront. This was a very advantageous arrangement because it avoided truck hauls to transloading facilities. Also, Hasbro received discounts on ocean freight rates because the steamship lines got the containers back right away and did not have to haul them back from the eastern part of the country. On top of that, Seattle is at least a day closer to Asia than Southern California and is less congested.

But in June 2002, Hasbro opened a DC in Ontario in Southern California's Inland Empire, shifting to the ports of LA/LB as its main port of entry. Why did Hasbro move? The company decided that it could save money if it consolidated all its distribution functions in one facility. And deciding to locate that facility in Southern California rested in large measure on the size of the local market. Not only could Hasbro take advantage of shipping to the closer LA market, but when goods are sent to the East, it is easier to fill domestic containers and trailers for the backhaul because more goods moving from East to West are destined for Southern California.

Geographic Location. The distance between Asian countries and the West Coast of the United States favors the Pacific Northwest ports of Seattle and Tacoma. They are at least one day closer to East and Southeast Asia than

California, especially Southern California. So this again raises the question of why LA/LB became the premier gateway. It is possible that the size of the local market, and infrastructural developments discussed in the next section explain it completely. Yet we believe that another kind of geographic factor plays a role, apart from sheer distance. This is LA/LB's location at the bottom end of the string of major ports on the West Coast. If a ship is only going to stop at two West Coast ports, one will likely be in the North and the other in the South. The most prevalent pattern is for ships from Asia to discharge first in LA/LB, with some loading, and then move up the coast to one other port for further discharging and more loading, and then head back to Asia.

Asian exporting countries can be divided along a North-South axis. The Pacific Northwest ports are all closer to Asia than LA/LB, but the Southern Asian ports, including those of China, are closer to Southern California than the North Asian ports of Japan and Korea. The rise of China and the relative decline of Japan as export powers is therefore linked to the rise of LA/LB relative to Seattle/Tacoma (Gulick 1998). The southward shift of Asian exports benefits LA/LB. Everything points to the continuation of this basic geographic advantage of the Southern California ports.

One port official told us that the preeminent shipping lane in the world is Hong Kong to LA/LB nonstop. Hong Kong, he noted, like Singapore, is a through port. Both of them serve as hubs for production that occurs elsewhere. The steamship line China Shipping was planning to dedicate its largest TEU ships to the Hong Kong–LA/LB lane. "This is the biggest focal point for us," said the port official. "Hong Kong is our Mecca. South China is the heart of our trade." The dominance of Hong Kong in particular may decline as the mainland China ports grow, but the story is basically the same. As Don Wylie, managing director of Maritime Services of the POLB put it at a workshop in Long Beach (8/14/03): "The Southern California ports are perfectly situated between the fastest growing economy in the world (China) and the largest consuming market in the world (U.S.)."

Infrastructure. In terms of infrastructure, the ports of LA/LB benefit from deep water channels and access to roads and railroads that provide good connections to the rest of the country, a topic we shall consider more in chapter 5, when we turn to land-based transportation. Two Class I railroads, the Union Pacific and the Burlington Northern Santa Fe provide service from the ports to the eastern part of the country. In addition, the region is richly endowed with interstate highways, including roads that lead north to cover the Western region as well as roads that lead East.

The state of California has also played a role in the prominence of the ports of LA/LB. California has coastal protection policies that have

prohibited new development along the coastline. These policies have encouraged the expansion of existing ports rather than the creation of new
ones, a point made by Don Wylie at the workshop mentioned above. The
ports of LA/LB have benefited from this forced concentration. However,
critical to the development of the Southern California ports (and the
creation of Los Angeles as the premier gateway for trade with Asia) was
the system of governance of both of the ports and their resulting ability
to invest wholeheartedly in infrastructure without too much interference
(Erie 2004). In other words, the success of these ports is, in part, a product
of entrepreneurship and a government system that allowed public bureaucrats to act as though they were business enterprises while taking advantage
of the public ability to raise the capital to do so. The latest example is the
construction of the Alameda Corridor, based on a public-private partnership, a project that will be considered in chapter 5. The Los Angeles waterfront had few natural advantages. It took human intervention to transform
the ports into the magnificent facilities that they have become.

Gulick (1998) also makes the point that ports can be active in creating
regional development alliances that generate support for port investment
and minimize the likelihood of opposition by social activists, including
environmentalists, who are concerned about the negative local impact
of port expansion—a topic that has recently become a major issue in
Los Angeles. The Southern California port authorities have certainly been
active in pursuing their competitive advantage through investing and
political engagement. Nevertheless, their geographical advantage, given
the changes brought about by containerization and intermodalism, and
the benefits of their large local market provided the ports of LA/LB with a
leg up that almost no investment by other ports could match.

Logistics Services. Once the ports established themselves as key gateways,
various logistics services were attracted to the area. Giant warehouses
are available in the South Bay and in the nearby Inland Empire. Major
corporations have come to Southern California to set up their regional
DCs, in large part in order to have access to the ports. In addition, numerous other companies providing services to the ports and their users
have set themselves up. These include customs brokers, freight forwarders, NVOCCs (non-vessel operating common carriers), container freight
stations, transloading operations, harbor drayage companies, cold storage facilities, export packaging companies, and logistics providers of all
kinds.

A synergy has developed between the growth of the ports and the growth
of these kinds of services. The services have developed because of the ports,
but the customers of the ports are attracted to them in part because of the
ready availability of these services. The interdependence feeds the growth

of both the ports and the services in an interactive spiral of growth. One can describe the ports and their surroundings as a special kind of industrial district, one geared to the process of international trade.

The connection between the ports and available logistics services is evolving. For example, another factor favoring LA/LB is a shift in how Asian imports are being handled. There are good reasons, described by Ted Prince in a *Journal of Commerce* article entitled "Theory of Evolution," that more Asian imports are likely to be transloaded onto domestic carriers rather than shipped back east in ocean containers on double-stacked trains (8/28/06, 16–30). One advantage of transloading ocean containers near the ports and putting the cargo into domestic containers and trailers is the ability to put empty containers back on the ships and send them right back to Asia. If they get sent across the country, it is easy for the maritime containers to get stuck somewhere in the Midwest, without loads to bring back to the West Coast. Repositioning these empties is an expensive proposition.

Another advantage of transloading right away is that some big box retailers and importers of high-value products do not want to decide on the final destination of their imports until the last minute, a practice called "inventory deferral." This provides them with the flexibility to respond to changes in local demand and provide value-added services such as making goods store-ready once they arrive on U.S. soil, which we will look at in more detail in chapter 6.

A shift to transloading benefits the ports of LA/LB because of the density of transloading and logistics services in the area. The more that marine containers are loaded on-dock or near-dock on double-stack trains (trains on which containers can be loaded atop one another in two layers), the more attractive the ports of the Pacific Northwest become, because of their greater closeness to Asia. But when transloading becomes more popular, as it seems to be as of this writing, the more Southern California is the destination of choice.

The Future of the Ports of Los Angeles and Long Beach

The ports of Southern California have continued to grow, despite some important glitches, including the PMA lockout of the ILWU during the 2002 contract negotiations and the severe congestion that held up ships and cargo for weeks during peak season in 2004, both of which will be covered in more detail in other chapters. The trade and transportation community has debated whether the ports of LA/LB will continue to grow at their current sizzling pace and maintain their dominance over Asian imports to the country or not. Of course, change is a constant feature of life, and nothing will last forever. Still, we want to assess the prospects of these ports, at least in the short run.[2]

As of mid 2007, the Southern California ports were showing considerable vitality. In a JoC article entitled "California Bound," Bill Mongelluzzo describes the return of shipments that had been diverted to other ports after the debacle of 2004 (4/24/06, 21–22). For example, in comparing March import figures for 2005 and 2006, the POLA showed a 33.4 percent increase, and the POLB figures jumped 34.4 percent. So in the short run, at least, the future of the ports of LA/LB looks bright.

But there are also threats to this hegemony. One threat comes from the local community, which is not uniformly happy with the continued growth of the ports. And since the ports lockout of 2002 and the congestion crisis of 2004 has aroused fears in the hearts of shippers and carriers alike, plans for alternatives continue to be developed.

Environmental Revolt

The ports of LA/LB are a gateway to Asian imports for the entire country, but the communities close to them bear an unfair share of the costs of this trade, in the form of pollution, congestion, noise, and eyesores. Pollution is created both by steamships and port trucks, both of which operate on diesel fuel. When the ships are docked, they keep their engines running, so diesel fumes are continually belched into the air. The port truckers often must stand in line at the terminal gates, waiting to pick up a container. They too keep their engines running, adding to the air pollution.

As Deborah Schoch reported in a Los Angeles Times article titled "Study details port pollution threat," a study by the National Resources Defense Council (NRDC) and the Coalition for Clean Air, rated the environmental record of the ten largest ports in the United States (3/22/04, C1). The ports of LA/LB received a C- and C on the rating scale. The port complex is described as the single largest fixed source of air pollution in Southern California, emitting as much diesel exhaust as sixteen thousand tractor-trailers idling twenty-four hours a day would. The POLA alone produces 31.4 tons a day of nitrous oxide and 1.8 tons of particulate matter, primarily from ships and trucks. Another LA Times article by Deborah Schoch, "Ships Are Single Largest Polluter of Air at Port of L.A., Study Finds," describes a more recent 265-page emissions report issued by the POLA, which found that together, the ports generate nearly a quarter of the diesel

[2]Erie (2004, ch. 5) covers a number of threats to the ports of LA/LB, including revenue diversion by the cities, environmental policy challenges, and a secession movement by the L.A. harbor communities of San Pedro and Wilmington. Because he deals with them thoroughly, we feel less need to raise them here.

pollution in the region. It found that oceangoing vessels were the chief source of this pollution (7/8/04, B3).

Congestion is especially problematic on the Long Beach Freeway (Interstate 710), which becomes a veritable sea of port trucks hauling containers at certain hours of the day. This freeway, which is crumbling and in dire need of repair, is operating at maximum capacity, and a single accident brings it to a halt for hours. The problem is only slightly less dramatic on the other freeways in the area, which are also jammed with trucks linked to the ports. There have been some proposals to widen Interstate 710, but they have failed in the face of community opposition led by the home and business owners adjacent to the freeway whose properties would be wiped out.

The railroads, while frequently seen as part of a possible solution to pollution and congestion, can actually contribute to the congestion problem—and are not free from polluting either. When a train crosses a major thoroughfare, traffic can get seriously backed up. The Alameda Corridor project aimed to eliminate this problem in the route from the ports to downtown Los Angeles. But that trip is only a small part of the lengthy rail trips that are involved in moving freight across and out of Southern California. Once trains leave downtown, they must pass through densely populated areas crisscrossed with roads, which leads to community irritation far beyond the immediate ports area. The same holds true for road and freeway congestion.

Communities close to the ports also complain about unsightly eyesores that clutter their surroundings. These include giant cranes sticking high into the air, stacks of empty containers piled up on every piece of vacant land, and trucks or tractors parked overnight in their neighborhoods. All of these complaints extend to the development of warehousing as well. When communities allow warehouses to open, they are encouraging trucks to be driving in and out at all hours of the day and night. Not only are they noisy, but they also contribute to congestion and pollution.

These problems have led to community social movements in some of the cities and communities adjacent to the ports, such as San Pedro and Wilmington, and in some of the cities where warehousing has been or is being developed, including Mira Loma in the Inland Empire and some of the South Bay cities.

China Shipping Suit

For this chapter, the most relevant rebellion has been by community residents over the development of a new giant terminal in the POLA for China Shipping. Community and environmental groups decided to sue the City of Los Angeles over the impact of this terminal on the nearby communities of San Pedro and Wilmington. The major complaints concerned increasing diesel fumes from ships and trucks, increased traffic congestion, sixteen-story-high cranes that block ocean views, and a brownish haze over the coast. Leading the charge was Gail Ruderman Feuer, senior attorney with the NRDC. The suit grew out of a growing recognition that the ports of LA/LB generate more air pollution than any other source in the LA basin but remain largely unregulated. It involved charging the port with not conducting an adequate environment impact report, which enraged residents about the high-handed decision-making of the port authorities.

A settlement favorable to the community groups was reached in March 2003, and the headlong construction of the terminal was brought to a halt. The city had to sign a $60 million agreement with a number of specifications: $10 million for incentives to clean up trucks serving the ports, $20 million for reducing air pollution from port operations, $20 million to mitigate aesthetic impacts on Wilmington and San Pedro, replace four installed cranes with shorter ones, and create a traffic plan for the terminal and other parts of the port. In addition, the port agreed to require nondiesel trucks in the China Shipping terminal yard and to install electric power for docked ships so that they would not have to keep their engines running while in dock. The money would come from port revenues rather than from the city.

This suit was a warning shot for the trade community, which had been operating on the assumption that everyone in the Los Angeles area had benefited from the rapid rise in Asian commerce and rapid growth of the ports. It seemed to them like a win-win situation: more economic activity, more good jobs. How could anyone object to the expansion of these highly profitable ports? Yet here they found that some people were so put out that they were ready to go to court to try to stop port expansion. The China Shipping settlement represented recognition that these social costs needed attention and could no longer be ignored.

Considerable activity has followed. "Greening" of the ports has become an important priority, and a variety of plans have been proposed. Various reforms have been implemented, including "cold-ironing," or the use of dockside electrical power and shutting off the engines of docked ships; burning ultra-low-sulfur diesel fuel; cutting the speed of vessels sailing within twenty miles of the coast; and using ultra-low-sulfur diesel fuel in trucks and trains near the docks. The coordinators of this effort developed the "San Pedro Bay Ports Clean Air Action Plan." The Southern California ports and the surrounding community can take pride in leading the nation's ports in cleaning up.

Alternatives to the Ports of LA/LB

The dominance of the ports of LA/LB raises concerns among major importers, who fear their dependence on this one source of entry. The

West Coast ports lockout of 2002 and the severe congestion in Southern California of 2004 both resulted in the loss of billions of dollars. Even fears of a terrorist attack feed into this equation. So alternatives are continually being proposed, and some of them even get developed.

As a result of the 2004 congestion crisis, more all-water services through the Panama Canal were added, giving a boost to the East Coast ports, which showed significant growth. The Pacific Northwest ports also experienced a boom. To some extent, these alternative ports have continued to show growth. And yet they do not seem to have made a dent in the continued growth of LA/LB, as discussed in the article by Bill Mongelluzzo mentioned above (JoC 4/24/06, 21–22). He points out that some shippers who diverted cargo away from Southern California were returning there, in part because the East Coast ports were reaching capacity, and the natural advantages of LA/LB were still in play. Mongelluzzo quotes the CEO of a terminal operating company: "Cargo can't get away from its heavy reliance on Southern California."

Of course, East Coast ports have plans for expansion, so their limited ability to compete with LA/LB may diminish over time. But their success depends in part on the fate of the Panama Canal. As of this writing, Panama was planning to invest $5.25 billion in widening its canal so that it could handle more traffic and also accommodate the giant post-Panamax container vessels. According to an article in the *Los Angeles Times* by Chris Kraul and Ronald D. White entitled "Panama Is Preparing to Beef up the Canal" the Canal, which already faces delays because of its own congestion, will have to deal with competition from a variety of sources: expansion of U.S. West Coast ports, the Suez Canal as an alternative route, and the development of ports in Mexico (4/26/06, C1).

Mexican ports are being developed in part as a safety valve for any future disruptions at the West Coast ports, especially LA/LB. A number of Mexican ports, including Ensenada and Manzanillo, are candidates for development, but the one that has shown the most immediate promise is the port of Lazaro Cardenas in Michoacán. The Kansas City Southern Railway has set up daily intermodal service from the port through Laredo, Texas, up to Jackson, Mississippi, with a connection to Atlanta.

Meanwhile, the Bush administration is apparently planning to build a NAFTA superhighway through the middle of the country, from the Mexican border at Laredo to the Canadian border north of Duluth, Minnesota. The port of Lazaro Cardenas would be the major point of entry for Asian containers. The advantage of such a plan would be that it would enable global shippers to avoid both the ILWU and the Teamsters (IBT), since Mexican truckers would haul the containers (see Jerome R. Corsi, www. humaneventsonline.com, 6/12/06). According to this source, construction on the superhighway is planned to begin in 2007.

In general, container ports entering the continent on the Mexican West Coast have been showing dramatic growth. According to an article by Eric Watkins entitled "A New Hat in the Ring," in the first nine months of 2005, TEU traffic jumped 12.3 percent (*Marine Digest and Cargo Business News,* 12/05, 10). Still, this was from a very small base—only 1.55 million TEUs were handled in that period. Extrapolation dictates that for the whole of 2005, Mexican ports handled a little over 2 million TEUs. A great deal of investment and growth will be required before LA/LB are threatened.

For the most part, no one in the LA trade community seems especially worried that any of these threats are imminent. True, some business has been lost to East Coast ports, but the Southern California trade community is still anticipating massive growth in imports from Asia and still feels that it faces severe challenges in coping with that flood. In other words, local people do not anticipate a decline at the local ports. On the contrary, their worries are focused on maintaining and expanding the transportation infrastructure so that they can meet the challenges of ever-increasing container freight.

In conclusion, the Southern California ports of LA/LB are together the premier gateway for containerized, mainly manufactured imports to the United States from Asia, especially from China. They are an amazing sight to behold as they disgorge tons and tons of goods on a daily basis, distributing them locally and all over the rest of the country. The ports have become a major logistics center, providing all kinds of services to the international trade community. While some fear exists about the dependence of major corporations and their millions of customers on this one node in the global economy—and efforts are being made to decrease the dependency—in the short run there does not seem to be a good alternative of any magnitude. Meanwhile, the number of containers entering through this particular gateway just keeps growing and growing.

CHAPTER 4

Steamship Lines

Containers are carried across the oceans by steamship lines. These companies are central to the movement of freight in the global economy. Not only do they ply the oceans, but they also play a major role in overseeing the delivery of the containers to their destinations on land. They are an important part of the connective tissue that holds the global economy together. The steamship lines are among the first truly global companies.

As is true for most of the topics covered in this book, there is a tremendous amount to know about the steamship lines. Entire journals are devoted to the topic.[1] And the industry itself is constantly producing materials and analyzing its own performance. Not only is the business complex and multi-layered, but it also keeps changing, so that the facts of today—even apparent trends—can be overturned tomorrow. In this chapter we attempt to combine elements of the vast literature with some interviews that we conducted with several steamship line executives and others who are involved in or otherwise knowledgeable about the steamship companies.

WORLD CONTAINER SHIPPING

In a report by the *American Shipper* on the top 20 container shipping lines, it was reported that as of July 2006, the worldwide capacity for container shipping was 9,887,699 TEUs (9/06, 66–70). The top 20 carriers accounted for 82.8 percent of the total, up from 78.5 percent in July 2005.

---

[1]Cudahy (2006) provides a history of container shipping.

This reflects consolidation in the industry over the previous year, a topic which we shall consider later. The growth in the steamship line business is reflected in the fact that since 2000, the top 20 have increased their capacity from 3.65 million TEUs to 8.2 million in 2006, for growth of 124 percent. From 2005 to 2006 alone, their capacity grew by 20 percent.

Meanwhile, shipyards have orders from these top 20 companies for ships that will add more than 3.25 million TEUs in capacity. Some of the ships on order will be able to carry ten thousand TEUs or more. Indeed, a Korean shipyard has orders for more than thirteen thousand TEU vessels. These ships would be 1,253 feet long (longer than four football fields) and 178 feet wide and are likely to come on line in 2009. Below deck, 6,230 TEUs would be stacked ten high and nineteen wide, while on deck the remaining 7,210 TEUs would be stacked twenty-one across, undoubtedly a sight to behold. Another Korean shipbuilder is developing a twelve thousand–TEU container vessel, which will sell for about $135 million. Meanwhile, Maersk is reported to be developing a ship that can handle fifteen thousand TEUs. There seems to be no stop in the growth of international container shipping or in the size of the ships themselves.

The World's Major Steamship Lines

As of July 2006, the largest container carrier in the world was the A.P. Moller–Maersk group (universally called "Maersk"), with a TEU capacity of 1,725,348 TEUs, a 62 percent increase from the previous year. Maersk accounts for 17.4 percent of total TEU capacity, and 21 percent of the capacity of the top 20 lines. The company owns 171 ships and charters 404 (*American Shipper,* 9/06, 68). Chartering is quite common in this business, as it provides the carriers with some flexibility and avoids tying up too much capital. Maersk is a Danish company. The second-ranked company is Mediterranean Shipping Company S.A. (MSC), with a total capacity of 944,795 TEUs, revealing the domination of Maersk. MSC is based in Switzerland. The rest of the top 20 are as follows: CMA CGM S.A. (France), Evergreen (Taiwan), Hapag-Lloyd (Germany), COSCO (China), China Shipping (China), APL (Singapore), Hanjin (Korea), NYK (Japan), MOL (Japan), OOCL (Hong Kong), "K" Line (Japan), CSAV (Chile), Zim (Israel), Hamburg Sud (Germany), Yang Ming (Taiwan), Hyundai (Korea), Pacific International (Singapore), and Wan Hai (Taiwan). The average capacity of the top 20 is 409,278 TEUs, another demonstration of Maersk's dominance.

A striking feature of this list is the complete absence of the United States—indeed, North America—from the ownership ranks. European countries dominate with 51 percent of top 20 TEU capacity—obviously Maersk plays a hefty role in this. Next come China, Hong Kong, and Taiwan, with

23 percent of capacity, collectively. Japan is next with 11 percent, and Korea and Singapore have 6 percent each, for an Asian total of 46 percent. The tiny remainder is South American (*American Shipper*, 9/06, 70). The loss of U.S. shipping lines will be discussed below.

The steamship business has been ripe for shakeout and consolidation for a number of years, and now it has finally come to pass. In 2005, A.P. Moller–Maersk, which was the largest carrier even then, purchased the third largest line, P&O Nedlloyd, for $2.96 billion, increasing its capacity by 500,000 TEUs (see Cudahy 2006, 203–4). German company Hapag-Lloyd responded by buying CP Ships, adding about 200,000 TEUs, pushing it into fifth place (from sixteenth in 2005). French carrier CMA CGM also acquired a smaller company, boosting its rank from fifth to third. And there were a few smaller deals as well. As a result of these deals, the top 5 container lines now control 43 percent of worldwide and 52 percent of top 20 capacity (*American Shipper*, 9/06, 69–70).

If one looks at imports into the United States, the rankings of the top 20 steamship companies change somewhat. The *Journal of Commerce* provides quarterly reports on the top 50 container lines engaged in the U.S. import trade (see Peter T. Leach, "Shakeout," *JoC*, 6/24/06, 18–20; rankings, 22–26). In the first quarter of 2006, commensurate with its dominance in world container shipping, Maersk tops the list, with 15.1 percent of market share. It is followed by Evergreen, a Taiwanese company, with 8.6 percent, Hanjin (Korea) with 6.6 percent, and APL (Singapore) at 6.4 percent. China Shipping, ranked seventh, increasing its volume of imports 36 percent in comparison with the first quarter of 2005, for the fastest rate of growth of the companies in the top 10.

THE BUSINESS OF THE STEAMSHIP LINES

Liners

The steamship lines are "liners" in the same sense that airlines are. This means that they are common carriers rather than privately serving one particular shipper. They maintain a regular advertised schedule of voyages, which occur at predictable times, and anyone can book passage for their cargo on them. They provide strings of vessels on each route, creating a constant and steady flow of ships between the ports. The idea of liners in the shipping industry goes back to the early days of the British Empire, long predating the emergence of container shipping (Brooks 2000, 2). The major tasks of the steamship lines are to offer regular service and handle the paperwork; to charge a tariff (or rate) that yields a profit; to load the cargo to ensure accessibility and to keep the ship stable; run a fixed service, allowing for delays; and plan tonnage availability (Stopford 1997, 28–29). Bulk shipping focuses on minimizing the unit cost of transportation, whereas liner shipping is more concerned with speed, reliability, and quality of service (Stopford 1997, 25–26). This is especially important for the just-in-time (JIT) production and distribution systems of supply chain management.

Not all ocean shipping is organized as liners. Some ships work for a particular company. Others, like oil tankers, carry only one commodity. Still others, called tramps, make deals to carry particular loads to particular places. The liners, in contrast, provide a general service, and anyone who wants to can use them, so long as space is available.

The steamship lines own the containers in which imports and exports are packed, as is evident if you see containers being hauled on the road; the names of the liners are painted in bold letters on the sides of the containers. This is one way you can identify ocean containers. They bear names like MAERSK, EVERGREEN, APL, or COSCO.

The liners have strings of vessels crossing the Pacific. Take, for example, APL. According to Chuck Savre, vice president of West Coast ports for Eagle Marine Services (an APL affiliate), who kindly let us interview him, APL had five strings into LA from Asia, called PS1, PS2, GCX, MAX, and SAX, each with a different pattern of ports of call. It also had two strings to the East Coast through the Panama Canal: EC1 and EC2. Most strings that just cross the Pacific require four to six ships, depending on the number of port calls. If they provide a weekly service, they need four ships to make the complete circle in twenty-eight days. A trip across the Pacific to the West Coast takes ten days, so going both ways means twenty days on the ocean. That leaves four days in port on each side of the ocean. For big strings with more port stops, they need five or six ships (on the logic of ship scheduling, see Kendall and Buckley 2001, ch. 13).

An advertisement for MSC that often appeared in the *JoC* illustrates three strings. The Orient Express Service circulated among ports in Long Beach, Korea, China, and Japan. It took nine days to sail from Tokyo to Southern California and eleven days to get back to Korea. From the port of Busan, they went to Quingdao, Shanghai, and Ningbo in China, and then back to Busan in Korea, ending up in Tokyo. The Pearl River Service linked China and California. It took ten days to sail from the port of Yantian in Southern China to Long Beach. The ships then went up the coast to Oakland, picked up exports there, and sailed back to China, stopping in Xiamen, Yantian, Hong Kong, and Chiwan. The Pendulum Service had a complicated route that involved sailing from Busan to Manzanillo, Mexico, and then passing through the Panama Canal for deliveries up the East Coast. On the way back it stopped in Long Beach before sailing for Tokyo, several Chinese ports, ending up at Busan.

Intermodal (Landbridge)

As previously stated, landbridge, also known as inland point intermodal, refers to the process of unloading containers on the coast and sending them inland by rail, thereby avoiding the slower Panama Canal, which also is limited in terms of the size of the vessels it can handle. The steamship lines that serve the Pacific can use landbridge to the Eastern part of the country or provide all-water service to East Coast ports. Terminals can provide on-dock rail service, or trucks can haul containers to nearby railheads for shipment to the East, as we shall examine in more detail in the next chapter.

Here is the way APL official Chuck Savre described the liners' calculations regarding landbridge versus all-water routing through the Panama Canal:

> The decision to use landbridge is conditioned, in part, by destination. It makes more sense to use all-water to New York than to Chicago, where you would have to put the container on rail anyway. The main issue is the number of turns you can make with the ship. In the Pacific, it is the number of trips from Asia to North America and back that matter. The more turns you make, the fewer ships you need for a string. All-water strings drive the number of ships up to eight or nine (from four to six in the simple trans-Pacific route) depending on the ports. With all-water, the journey is longer, so you can't cycle back as quickly. So landbridge requires fewer ships than all-water routes, which, needless to say, is a huge economic savings.

Bob Kleist, corporate advisor for Evergreen, estimated that about 45 percent of Evergreen's containers are for the local market, though he could not assess what proportion of these would be transloaded, with their contents shipped East. "As far as we are concerned, the moves are either inland or local. If it's local, we assume it is under the control of the shipper/consignee. We don't follow what happens to local cargo." The rest is landbridge.

We asked Kleist about the proportion of Evergreen's rail moves that are on-dock versus drayed to rail heads. Here is his response:

> To my knowledge, no one has ever put these numbers together. ICTF [Union Pacific's near-dock facility] has six hundred thousand moves a year. At Evergreen's terminal they have eight loading tracks. Evergreen uses four of them, and the next terminal's occupant, NYK, uses the other four. We have about twelve train loads a week, with four hundred containers per train, which amounts to about five thousand a week, for one terminal.

Kleist pointed out that some inland cargo is moved by long-haul trucks as opposed to rail, especially when the container is needed quickly. "We can guarantee that a container will arrive in Chicago within twenty-four hours of its landing in the ports. Sometimes it is quicker. A truck can pick

74

the container up within an hour after it gets off the ship. The truck can be one-third of the way to Chicago by the time we would put it on a train. And at the receiving end the trucker can take it directly to the warehouse."

Endemic Competition

Liner shipping has faced some unique challenges. The steamship lines have very high-cost fixed assets, and there are standard operating costs regardless of whether a vessel is filled or not. This requires them to fill their ships to maximum capacity in order to make a profit. They must offer regular service, but the flows of trade are far from regular. Not only are there seasonal effects, with preparations for the back-to-school and Christmas seasons dominating manufactured imports, but in the Pacific trade there is a major imbalance between eastward and westward flows. Imports from Asia exceed exports to Asia by a huge proportion, and this difference is exacerbated when one takes into account the value of the commodities being shipped.

The shipping industry is also very competitive because companies can enter from any country in the world. Since to be profitable a ship needs to be close to full, some firms undercut standard prices in order to secure customers. The fierce competition that results threatens the stability of an industry that is vital to international commerce. Indeed, this dilemma was a feature of international shipping long before the container age (Brooks 2000, 2–3).

The steamship business shares certain problems with the retailing business. Both are highly competitive industries in which one prominent approach to competing successfully involves taking on everything. For retailing this means expanding into new markets, even if they are already overserved. This logic applies to the steamship lines even more so.

Here is how Chuck Savre described the economics of global shipping: "The growth of shipping has been phenomenal, and it has compelled APL to move into global shipping. APL used to be a trans-Pacific company, but many customers require that we be a global company, so we had to expand. Consequently, there has been an explosion of players. Most of them are foreign carriers."

We raised the question as to whether the likelihood of a shakeout in the industry compels all the big companies to expand. We drew the analogy of retail department stores: Kohl's was entering the saturated Southern California market at the time, even though the last thing the area needs is another chain. Savre replied: "Yes, the rush to be global has had that effect. For example, we entered the trans-Atlantic trade even though it certainly didn't need another carrier. And all the carriers are now entering the trans-Pacific, including Mediterranean Shipping and some others."

In other words, in order to become a premier steamship company, a company almost must provide service everywhere in the world. If a company has significant gaps in its service, shippers may shift their business to another carrier that can service them wherever they want to send or receive cargo. The advantages of dealing with a single liner are often strong for shippers, so they would like global service from their ocean carriers. But this need to cover all markets leads major steamship lines to clog already crowded markets. The result is an intensification of competition in every market. Almost all of the top 20 carriers feel they must cover all the principal trade routes (Brooks 2000, 22–24).

In sum, destructive competition results from a combination of the need to enter all markets and the tendency to undercut the competition by charging lower rates in order to fill the ships.

Liner Conferences

Since international shipping does not occur under the aegis of any single government, it has been the industry itself that has sought a solution to this overcrowded market. Ocean carriers have formed conferences on specific trade routes. These constitute an effective truce in the rate wars. Conferences consist of groups of shipping companies that agree on standard rates for a particular route, such as the trans-Pacific between Asia and North America (Kendall and Buckley 2001, ch. 6; Sletmo and Williams 1981).

Shipping conferences were sanctioned by the United States under the Shipping Act of 1916, which granted them antitrust immunity under the Sherman Antitrust Act. However, they were subject to scrutiny by a regulatory agency, the Federal Maritime Commission (FMC), and had to make their rates public. Non–conference members were not subject to governmental scrutiny (Kendall and Buckley 2001, 95).

Although conferences were sanctioned under U.S. law, they were continually being weakened and so posed no threat of monopoly. At a legal level, the Shipping Act of 1984 introduced the concepts of independent action and service contracts in order to limit the power of conferences (Brooks 2000, 12). But shippers felt that the FMC was allowing the conferences to get away with too much. In 1994, seventeen large shippers and the National Industrial Transportation League (NITL) increased their efforts to remove antitrust immunity for the conferences. One concern that was expressed in opposition to this move was a fear that confidential contracting, as opposed to published conference rates, would increase the power of the big shippers to the detriment of smaller shippers (Brooks 2000, 12–13).

In addition to legal maneuvering, conferences were also eroding because the new steamship lines entering the market found that they could gain market share by undercutting the conference rates. Like so many efforts at collective action, the conferences lost their ability to discipline all of the actors in their universe and insist on their loyalty. As a consequence, the proportion of liner trade operating under conferences gradually declined (Brooks 2000, 3–4).

The final straw in the demise of conferences as a method of private regulation of the industry came with the passage of the Ocean Shipping Reform Act (OSRA) of 1998. Despite the end of conferences as powerful entities that could control rates, they still exist, albeit in muted form. There is a Transpacific Stabilization Agreement (TSA) that recommends rates for shipping across the Pacific. It has no authority to enforce its recommendations, but it does set a kind of standard that carries some moral weight.

In an interview with Bill Mongelluzzo of the *Journal of Commerce*, he described the situation this way: "The Transpacific Stabilization Agreement can discuss rates, but they can only set voluntary guidelines. These are important in that the members represent more than 80 percent of the Pacific trade. They don't set rates but recommend rate increases as voluntary guidelines. But the problem is, they come to an agreement but then someone starts to violate it. This is a truly market-driven environment. In 1998 and 1999, when demand exceeded capacity, the rates went up. But in 2000 and 2001, when there has been excess capacity, rates have declined."

As of this writing, thirteen companies belonged to the TSA, giving an indication of some of the main lines in the trans-Pacific trade. They were, in alphabetical order: APL, CMA CGM, COSCO, Evergreen, Hanjin, Hapag-Lloyd, Hyundai, "K" Line, MOL, NYK, OOCL, P&O Nedlloyd, and Yang Ming. In 2004 Maersk, the largest company, decided to leave the TSA, raising the question of whether even this weaker version of the conference system could survive. Nevertheless, the conference continued to function, raising eastbound rates in 2005. Here are the increases they recommended in February 2005: $285 per FEU container from Asia to West Coast ports; $350 per FEU for inland point intermodal (IPI) and mini-landbridge (MLB) cargo; and $430 per FEU for all-water service to the U.S. East Coast and Gulf ports via the Panama and Suez Canals (www.ftn.fedex.com/usbulletin/021705.htm).

In addition, the TSA recommended a peak season surcharge of $400 per FEU from June 15 to November 30. These figures give one a sense of the relative cost of the various routes. It is interesting that the two canal routes appear to cost about the same, even though they go around the world in opposite directions.

These recommended rate increases are voluntary, and TSA members are still free to engage in confidential negotiations with shippers to set their own rates. The recommendations were based on an analysis of the Asia-U.S. freight market, which they expected to see a cost increase of at least 11 to 12 percent. According to the web article cited above, "Some of the factors behind rising operating costs are port and inland congestion and transportation capacity constraints in the U.S. and Asia, higher trucking and rail expenses, higher labor costs for longshoremen, and delays moving freight through the Panama Canal."

Alliances

Another solution to the problem of filling ships in a steady and predictable manner is the formation of alliances between liner companies (Cariou 2002). Precursors of the alliances were slot charter agreements, in which one liner would lease space on its vessels to another carrier, and vessel-sharing arrangements (Brooks 2000, 26). Full-fledged alliances between liners emerged in the 1990s. Alliances consist of a group of companies agreeing to share capacity, terminal operations, chassis, and other aspects of the business. This form of sharing allows each company to run fewer ships on a particular route while still making sure that its customers are served. It also solves the problem of global coverage for a liner that does not have service available for certain countries. The reader may have noticed the emergence of this practice among the airlines.

The three largest alliances at the end of 2005 were: the Grand Alliance, composed of Hapag-Lloyd, NYK Line, OOCL, and Malaysia International Shipping Company; CYKH, whose members are Cosco, Yang Ming, and Hanjin/Senator; and the New World Alliance, with APL, MOL, and Hyundai. By combining in this way, the Grand Alliance, for example, had access to 337 container ships with a capacity of 982,345 TEUs and had on order another 64 ships with 385,178 TEUs, according an article by Peter T. Leach in the *JoC* entitled "Hanging Together" (9/26/05, 10–12). Maersk was not a member of an alliance because it had almost twice as much capacity as the biggest alliance—in effect it was an alliance unto itself. The alliances helped smaller liners compete with Maersk.

Let us briefly examine the New World Alliance, as described to us by Chuck Savre, to show how the alliances combine. As we have said, APL operated five strings into LA from Asia in early 2003. Its alliance partner, Hyundai, had one string (PSW), and MOL, the other partner, had two (PS3 and PSV). So together, the alliance had eight strings from Asia into LA. This enabled APL not to have to deal with Korean ports, since they were covered by Hyundai.

According to Leach, the alliances have become dominant in the world's busiest trade lanes (cited in "Hanging Together," 10–12). And they were starting to offer new services. They were preparing to add the newest and biggest post-Panamax ships (with seven to eight thousand TEUs) to the East-West trade lanes and to offer new all-water services through the Suez Canal by shifting smaller vessels (in the 5,200-TEU range) to that lane.

Profitability

In an article in the *JoC*, Mark Kadar raises the question: "Are Liner Capital Investments Rational?" (1/03, 33–35). According to Kadar, the most important measure of profitability, from an investor point of view, is return on capital employed (ROCE). He points out that over the previous five years, few if any of the liner companies have been able to meet the lowest threshold for ROCE. The top 20 lines had an average of 4 percent ROCE, compared to an 8 to 9 percent cost of capital for the liner shipping business. This represented a destruction of value for the industry.

Despite this reality, capital continues to pour into the industry, with the extensive building of additional ships of ever-increasing size. Kadar wonders why this investment continues, given the poor return on investment. He explains it by three practices of individual companies, even though they lead to a collective irrationality. The liners feel they cannot pass up a good deal when the cost of ship-building is relatively low. They focus too narrowly on an individual asset, replacing a charter vessel with a new build because it saves money. And they accept the assumption that the market will continue to grow, so they want to be prepared with more capacity in order to avoid losing market share. Each of these assumptions leads the liners to expand capacity, which drives down returns for everyone.

This situation cannot go on forever. Capital sources are likely to dry up. Kadar thinks that companies should stop pursuing the pipe dream of increasing market share and focus instead on customer service and product innovation. They need to be strategic in terms of how they use capital.

The steamship business appears to go through intense swings, with periods of boom and bust. Kadar was writing during a down period, but since then there have been some good years. The volatility is related to the fact that it takes years to build ships, so the steamship lines have to guess about the likely growth of trade. Error in either direction can have severe consequences. In general, a steamship company will operate on the principle of "grow or die," which leads to a tendency to have overcapacity in the industry, which in turn leads to a drop in rates and profitability. The growth in the size of vessels adds to this dilemma. In general, the bigger the ship, the lower the cost per container, but the giant ships are also likely to be harder to fill, unless the growth in trade keeps up with them.

Chassis

In the United States, the steamship lines are also the owners of the chassis (wheels) on which the containers are placed for trucking. This is not the case elsewhere in the world, and it is a big nuisance for the steamship companies to have to make sure that sufficient chassis (as well as containers) are available where they are needed.

Kathleen Gordon, vice president of the West Coast region for Mitsui O.S.K. Lines (MOL), kindly granted us an interview in which she elaborated on this situation:

> There is no reason for the steamship lines to own and maintain chassis. It's a huge expenditure. This is the only country where the steamship lines own the chassis. We want to get out of the chassis business and let the trucking companies take care of them. We even considered it, but we can't right now. We can't do it alone. It will require the industry as a whole to make the change. Chassis are very hard to control. We are in chassis pools with our vessel sharing partners [their alliance partners, APL and Hyundai]—we use each other's chassis. [At this juncture we mentioned speculation that all the lines would share chassis and not bother about ownership.] A company tried to develop a chassis sharing program but it didn't work well and we opted out of it.

The responsibility for the upkeep of chassis has become a political issue.

Relations with Shippers

We asked Gordon whether her company has long-term relations with their shipper customers. This was her response: "We usually do. Sometimes we lose a customer, but that's rare. If we lose them, it's never over service but over rates. The actual contracts can be as long as two years but are usually one year." Their major customers included several electronics companies, apparel retailers, and a couple of giant discounters.

This relative stability of shipper-carrier relations is significant, since it suggests that there is more social structure in this business than first appears to be the case. True, shippers are in a position to threaten to use a lower-priced carrier in bargaining with a steamship line, a threat that may lead to a lowering of rates. But it is not a war of all against all. Rather, longstanding relationships have value and can ensure that during a crunch, more stable customers will receive firmer guarantees of service.

The picture of shipper-carrier relations looks like a set of criss-crossing relations. Each steamship line provides service to multiple shippers, while the bigger shippers use several carriers. The picture of connections could, in principle, be diagrammed. At first glance it might look chaotic, but a closer look would reveal some stable patterns.

Organizations

The steamship lines have other kinds of organizations besides conferences and alliances. One is the World Shipping Council, a Washington, D.C.–based association representing more than forty liner shipping companies engaged in U.S. international trade. The Council's members include the largest container lines as well as other forms of shipping. It also provides intermodal and logistics services to U.S. importers and exporters. According to its website, "The Council's goal is to provide a coordinated voice for the liner shipping industry in its work with policymakers and other industry groups interested in international transportation issues, including: regulatory policy, tax issues, safety, the environment, harbor dredging and upgrading the infrastructure needed to handle America's booming trade" (www.worldshipping.org).

When we began this research, there was also a local organization called the Steamship Association of Southern California (SASC). In June 2003, it merged with its Northern California equivalent, known as the Pacific Merchant Steamship Association (PMSA) and adopted the latter name. The group serves as a lobbying organization, representing the interests of steamship companies, terminal operators, and stevedoring companies at the local and state level. Headquartered in San Francisco, the PMSA maintains an active Southern California branch.

The executive secretary of the SASC from 1985 to 2002 was Jay Winter, whom we interviewed at some length. Here are some of things he said: "Our role is not so much to promote our industry as to protect it. We focus on local government agencies in particular. We watch the ports like a hawk because they can leverage hefty fees. And we watch what local government does because they control the ports."

The SASC filed a lawsuit against the City of Los Angeles, and was joined by the State of California, for using port funds for non-port purposes. Mayor Richard Riordan was the initiator of the raid on port monies and was forced to stop. Before the organizations combined, the PMSA served as a watchdog over Sacramento, responding to state initiatives, but since Southern California is the center of the industry, it made sense for the SASC to have more of a presence in the capitol:

> Steamship lines are a terrible investment [Winter said]. In the last one and a half years they made a little money, that is in 2000 and the first half of 2001. But generally, over the last five years, competition has been very bad. The owners are their own worst enemies because they keep on ordering more capacity. This goes back to the fact that a number of them are subsidized by their governments. In general, asset-based businesses have trouble remaining profitable, and the steamship lines are heavy asset holders. The joke at cocktail parties is: "Only two groups are making money in this business: the ports and the ILWU."

A third organization, one that has a different character from the two lobbying associations, is the Pacific Maritime Association (PMA). This group arose in response to the development of the International Longshore and Warehouse Union (ILWU), the strong dockworkers union on the West Coast.

It is the employer group that engages in collective bargaining with the ILWU and implements the contract with the union. We will have more to say about the PMA when we turn to the issue of labor on the docks.

In Memoriam: Interview with Bob Kleist, Corporate Advisor for Evergreen

We want to close this section with excerpts from an interview we conducted with Bob Kleist. Bob was a respected figure in the steamship business. We met with him in June 2002. He must have been in his eighties at the time, and has since passed away. Because of his length of time in the industry, his extensive knowledge, and his status as an elder statesman, we think it is worthwhile to report some of the things he said. Some of his comments have been reserved for particular topics, and some of the topics he raises will be dealt with further below. Here we present some of his choice opinions as well as some of his observations about Evergreen.

As we already know, it is common practice for the steamship lines to offer door-to-door service, but Bob felt that they should limit themselves to port-to-port service because the landside aspect is not their core competence: "The steamship lines are providing services for which there are legitimate providers that can do it more easily. One liner company started the practice of door-to-door, and the others followed to keep up with the competition."

Evergreen has a ship in dock almost all of the time, he said. "We employ four or five full-time crane operators. They are known as steady men. They come directly to work and don't stop at the dispatch hall, even though they are still connected to it.[2] Each gang is around twelve workers, including the crane operator, a group on the ground and a group on the ship. A good crane operator moves thirty-five containers per hour and gets paid a premium for it. We have five ships per week, and two other steamships dock at our terminal: Wan Hai and Lloyd Triestino, which was purchased by Evergreen."

We had seen Panama listed as the country of registration on a number of Evergreen ships on their website. (This is the "flags of convenience" phenomenon discussed below.) He said that this has declined, and Evergreen is using Taiwanese registration more. According to Bob:

After the Second World War, you had 100 percent U.S.-flag ships. But the shipping companies started to register offshore primarily because of the

---

[2]The ILWU controls access to labor through its use of a dispatch hall. In general, all longshore workers come to the dispatch hall in the morning to be assigned their day's work. However, there are exceptions to this practice. Steady men work regularly for a particular terminal and need not be dispatched by the union on a daily basis. Undoubtedly the steamship lines that employ steady crane operators are paying a premium for their work.

cost of labor. Now there are no American-flag companies left. During the break-bulk period a twenty-thousand ton ship needed a forty-seven person crew. With containerization, a sixty- to seventy-thousand-ton vessel requires fourteen crewmen. If the U.S. shipping companies had tried to stay in business you would probably still have fifty crewmen, because of archaic work rules. And the pay levels would be extremely high. The prevailing wage of the world is about a quarter of the U.S. minimum wage. And, of course, U.S. seafarers were making much more than the minimum wage. It was simply non-competitive to remain here.

Bob also had some comments about the ILWU:

This [the ports of LA/LB] is the most expensive port in the world. The heads of the union are proud of that fact. Their high cost spreads to other areas. We have sixty-five ILWU clericals working in this office. They negotiated a contract a year ago [2001] and are paid thirty-one dollars an hour. And it will go up by one dollar per year until the next three-year contract. China Shipping just signed a contract with the Clerks Local for thirty-five dollars an hour. It is the worst contract I've ever seen. They had to pay fifteen thousand dollars per person as a signing fee. Plus the employees get all kinds of benefits. It's monstrous. Are they conscientious, hard-working people? No, they aren't. [We asked: "How did the union get these extras from China Shipping?"] China Shipping resisted the union for a while, so the union forced them to accept this unfavorable contract. The union had the power to enforce the principle that, if they didn't use union labor, they would get no labor.

Evergreen's parent company is Evergreen Marine Corp. It is traded on the Taiwan stock exchange but is mainly owned by the chairman, Hatsu Y.F. Chang (who has a Japanese name because when he was born, Taiwan was still called Formosa and was under Japanese control). Evergreen's subsidiary, which owns five ships and is jointly owned by a British company, is named Hatsu Marine after him. Bob said that Evergreen is a controlled company but not family-owned, as is the case for some steamship lines.

Bob saw the steamship business as cyclical, with sharp ups and downs. "Part of the problem is that they have a mind-boggling investment." They tend to build ships when business is down because then they are cheaper to build, but that can lead to overcapacity, especially during slow times. "You really can't predict what will happen."

We wanted to know what Bob thought about the big shippers, like Wal-Mart and Target. He said: "They are always trying to drive the rates down. The ocean carriers feel rather powerless to raise the rates. It becomes a real problem because, as soon as slots are close to being filled, new entrants come into the business."

He commented: "The idea that rates are fixed by the steamship lines [violating antitrust principles] is barmy. Ocean freight rates are probably the same as they were forty years ago. What else costs this little? When I first got into the business in the early 1950s we carried cotton bales for ten dollars a bale. They still cost that today!"

We asked about the importance of the Southern California ports to Evergreen. He replied: "Right now Evergreen does about 70 to 80 percent of its West Coast business through LA—higher than the industry average. The company has a terminal in Tacoma, which could handle twice as much as it does now—maybe up to 30 percent of the West Coast traffic."

Why, we asked, is LA such a center?

> It is like the fluctuation in ocean rates. As the area became more sophisticated, the Harbor Departments started making deals, where the steamship lines had to guarantee a minimum amount of business. The more you put through, the less it costs. Evergreen signed a thirty-two-year lease. We expect that the amount we bring in through these ports will grow even higher. However, we can easily meet the minimum and move the rest to Tacoma. The port's required minimum is a lot less than what we bring in. Of course, if we shifted some of our freight to Tacoma, the Harbor Department would not be happy.

At the end of the interview, Bob told us that he had been described as a "legend." He had looked the word up in the dictionary: "a story of dubious truth." He felt that fit him perfectly. We found him to be a charming person.

The Nationality of Ships

The first container ships were operated by U.S. companies, but now, as we have seen, no major U.S. lines remain. Two developments drove the move offshore. First was the use of what is known as "flags of convenience" (FOCs), a phenomenon that predates the container revolution. Second was the shift in ownership outside of the United States. APL was the last U.S.-owned steamship line. It was purchased by Neptune Orient Lines (NOL), a Singaporean company, in January 1998 (for the detailed history of this transaction, see Cudahy 2006, 206–15). Here is how Chuck Savre of APL explained why the industry moved offshore:

> Investors in the United States weren't supportive of transportation. The margins are very small. The stock market didn't support it. Asian investors take a longer-term approach. The U.S. stock market reflects the mood swings of the public. Economics was also involved, labor costs, the cost of operating ships. The flight from the U.S. was, in part, union-driven. There were so many unions in a U.S. crew—six or seven unions were involved. It made the crew size unworkable, given changes in the ships. We now have modern ships.

Technology ran over the U.S. sailors' unions. Because of the low margins in shipping, costs are driven to their lowest level. This means that crew members make a low wage.

Flags of Convenience

To escape U.S. regulation and strong seafaring unions, companies began to register their ships in countries where regulations were weak to nonexistent. The countries involved were among the poorest in the world (Boczek 1962; Gibson and Donovan 2000). Countries that offer flags of convenience, called "open registries" by the United Nations, allow shipping companies of other nationalities to register their ships without paying a tax on income. They face no nationality requirements for their crews, and there are no regulations about where ships must be built or repaired. No government inspection or oversight is offered. In other words, the shipping companies operate in a completely deregulated environment. In exchange they pay a registration fee and an annual fee based on ship tonnage (Gibson and Donovan 2000, 227).

Turning to container shipping in particular, at the beginning of 2003, 33.9 percent of containerships (as measured in dwt) were owned by developed market economies. In contrast, 44.4 percent were owned by open-registry countries (UNCTAD 2003, 29). In 2004, Liberia accounted for 16.12 percent of FOC registrations, followed by Panama at 11.18 percent and Bermuda at 10.18 percent. Then came Cypress, the Bahamas, and Malta (see http://stats.unctad.org). This list gives us a sense of the kinds of countries involved in this practice. Kathleen Gordon of MOL confirmed that in her experience, the majority of their ships are Liberian: "It's just a matter of dollars."

Jay Winter of the SASC laughed at the term *flags of convenience*, saying that people in the steamship business would say they are "flags of necessity." Using them is the only way to compete, he said. "As long as there is a huge block of low-wage labor anywhere in the world, business will move" (12/7/01).

Shift in Ownership

Country of registry says nothing about country of ownership, which is far more important. In the 1970s, 87 percent of the world's tonnage was owned by the United States, Japan, and Western Europe, and 22 percent was operated under FOCs. By 1990, the world's commercial fleet owned by these nations had fallen to 67 percent, and South Korea, Hong Kong, Taiwan, and Singapore had grown as major ship-owning countries (Gibson and Donovan 2000, 230–31). We have seen how thorough the shift away from the United States, in particular, became by the end of the century. There has been a major shift in the ownership of the world's merchant fleet.

The transfer to foreign ownership occurred in part as a result of U.S. unions' opposition to U.S. shipowners' use of FOCs, according to Gibson and Donovan (2000, 232–33). In 1986, the AFL-CIO persuaded Congress to cancel a tax exemption for U.S. owners of FOCs. Consequently, the U.S. owners sold their ships to offshore companies or retained only minority ownership. This blow to U.S. ownership was followed by termination of subsidy programs by President Ronald Reagan. The last two U.S.-flag liner companies were Sealand and APL, both of which were taken over by foreign liners in the 1990s. Sealand was purchased by the Danish company Maersk and became Maersk-Sealand (until Maersk acquired P&O Nedlloyd). And APL, as we have said, was acquired by the Singapore company NOL.

Does Nationality Matter?

Governments differ in their relationship to steamship companies, and that can make a difference in how they operate. We heard, but did not try to verify, complaints that some Asian countries, including China, subsidize their steamship companies. As quasi-public entities they do not need to show a profit for stockholders, which gives them a kind of leeway, including the ability to undercut rates, that is absent for private companies. Some countries have a strong stake in maintaining a presence in global shipping, so will do whatever it takes.

Savre described the importance of nationality as follows: "What is really interesting is the cultural relations of the carriers. The Koreans, the Chinese, the Danish, each do business differently. And each nation has its relationship with its carriers. Each carrier also specializes in its own nationality's ports. Ocean carriers are part of a truly globally competitive industry. The various cultures and societies don't get along that well together anyway. It makes for an interesting dynamic."

We tried to find out whether foreign ownership affects the way in which the steamship companies engage in local politics. Jay Winter, then of the SASC, whose membership consisted predominantly of foreign-owned companies, implied that it did make a difference. The companies were happy to have the SASC speak for them, thereby avoiding drawing attention to their "foreignness." We asked him if the United States still exercised influence over the steamship companies, despite their foreign ownership. He replied: "The owners listen to their senior managers in this country but they make their own decisions. They try to ignore U.S. law. They feel that everyone here should be grateful for all the business they are bringing to this country."

In fact, the companies that serve U.S. ports typically have U.S. branches, which are run by U.S. executives. They are truly transnational corporations in every sense of the word, and when they maintain substantial business in a country, they develop structures that adapt fully to that country's characteristics. Thus, almost all of the steamship lines personnel that we spoke with during this research were Americans. The only exception was Maersk, where the officials were Danish.

RELATIONS WITH THE PORTS

Today the most common relationship between the steamship lines and the ports is that the former are the tenants and the latter are the landlords. Not all ports operate this way. Some are operational ports that are actively involved in running what goes on. The rise of landlord ports can be seen as part of the trend toward port privatization.

The ports provide facilities, that is, terminals, and the steamship lines lease them. These are run by terminal operators, which are typically subsidiaries of the big steamship lines, though there are exceptions. The terminal operators run their terminals as private enterprises. They employ or have their own stevedoring companies, which employ the labor on the docks. Port officials tend to claim that they operate in a hands-off manner and are not involved in any of the ports' operations, but this is not quite the case. Although they do not run the terminals, they get involved in other aspects of port functioning. For example, a port official told us that his employer felt compelled to become a member of the West Coast Waterfront Coalition.

Bob Kleist told us that the ports are not looked on as very significant. "The ports have to realize: A container load doesn't care which port it arrives at. It barely cares which ship it travels in." On the other hand, "here in Los Angeles we have terrific capacity," he said. "The available infrastructure is a marvel. The ports have something to offer."

However, Savre described a more engaged relationship between the shippers and the ports: "The big shippers have clout with the ports. They want their cargo a certain way, and they deal directly with the ports. They make calls on them. If a customer is looking to open a warehouse or DC, the ports help them get the best deal. They introduce them to land and empty DC availability. They try to influence the shippers to bring their goods through their port because that increases their business and revenues. The ports are very competitive. The ports call me. They want to know what they can do to bring business their way."

FREIGHT RATES

The key to most of the international transportation system centers on the rates that shippers pay to the ocean carriers for their services. These rates are expected to cover capital costs, operating costs, port costs, and the costs of land transportation. The steamship lines sit at the top of a hierarchy of relationships that include the railroads and the trucking companies they use. If they fail to get a decent rate from their customers, the shippers (also called "beneficial owners of cargo," or BOCs), then the whole hierarchy is squeezed. This is where the power of the giant retailers is especially relevant.

Here is how Bill Mongelluzzo of the *Journal of Commerce* described the situation during our interview with him:

> The giant retailers are dominating. You can count the most powerful on the fingers of one hand: Wal-Mart, Target, Home Depot, Kmart, Payless Shoe-Source. There are two categories of shippers: retailers and direct importers. They set the freight rates through contract negotiations. The rates are supposed to be secret, but word gets around so that everyone knows what the rates are. Each year they negotiate with the ocean carriers. The contracts are usually finalized by May 1, though sometimes they may run a little late. At that point, the rates are determined for the year. The smaller shippers do worse than the big ones. It all boils down to volume.
>
> The rates that are negotiated determine what happens throughout the entire intermodal system, the total through move, including: ocean carriers, terminal operators, ILWU, trucking, railroads, and 3PLs. They are all affected by the rate negotiated between the shippers and the steamship lines. The big retailers are the benchmark for everyone else. They set the rates that everyone else tries to achieve.

Low Rates, Low Margins

During the period when we did our interviews, the problem of low rates and low margins in the steamship business seemed chronic, although there were fluctuations in the severity of the problem. Most people explained this by simple supply and demand. The steamship business poses some unique supply and demand issues, as we began to discuss in the section on profitability above. According to Savre: "Part of the reason for low rates is overcapacity. The steamship lines build for the future. This goes in surges. They build when the time is right, but when the ship is deployed, the time may not be right. Moreover, ship-building is a long-term investment; the ship is deployed for many years. There is a volume/capacity dynamic that impacts rates."

A big problem with investing in ships is that it takes several years for them to be built. But predicting the demand for container slots in general, let alone for one's particular company, is far from an exact science. The industry is always faced with a possible glut of ships, which drives the rates down. Yet each company must also ensure that it has sufficient capacity for its customers, or else it will face the threat of losing them. The heart of the problem lies in the length of time it takes to build ships and the unpredictability of their market share.

The result is that there are periods of serious overcapacity in the industry, resulting in falling profits and even some periods when the steamship lines lose money. The conference system helped to assuage some of the worst effects of these swings.

We asked Gordon of MOL about how her company calculates rates. They do not look at overall costs but at the average cost per container. They calculate:

· The cost in Asia
· The cost of the voyage
· The cost of discharge
· The cost of throughput
· If it moves inland, the cost of the railroad
· The truck move to the railroad
· If door delivery, the cost (say) of trucking from Chicago to a suburb.

Gordon went on to explain the system in detail:

We have a "Cost Master," and we plug in origin, destination, and whether it is a twenty-foot or forty-foot container. This enables us to work out the net proceed, which is about the same as the profit, except that there can be a few hidden costs that aren't included. This helps us determine the rate we ask of the customers. We use this to figure our profit and loss.

Everything is calculated on a round-trip basis, because of the imbalance of trade. We focus on the net proceed. We look for the least expensive trucker. We figure out whether it is worth shipping back empties or have containers sit around here. On the export side we operate below cost so we have to make it up on the import side. We have established guidelines on when to accept a contract. We call it the Strategic Marketing Initiative. If the rate falls below our guidelines, we won't accept it.

We are under continual pressure to cut costs. It is difficult to cut them on the dock because there is a contract. We try to cut costs on equipment, including containers and chassis. We have been mandated to cut back on empties by 10 percent. If we have fifteen hundred containers for export, we fill the rest of the ship with empties. That helps the Asian side to avoid having to lease boxes.

We use a lot of off-dock facilities for equipment. Maintenance and repair [M&R] is a huge cost item. We try to stop vendors from taking advantage of us in M&R because they try to overcharge. Chassis are a big problem. We try to make sure we have the right amount. We don't want them to pile up.

We asked Bill Mongelluzzo for his opinion about the breakdown of the costs of shipping. Here were his thoughts:

> Let us say the freight rate per container from Asia to the final destination in the U.S. is about two thousand dollars. The inland cost is about four to five hundred dollars. Then there is the debt on the vessel, the labor at the port, the employees of the carrier, the port truck move (which is about a hundred dollars), and the port costs. In terms of the port costs, even though LA/LB are the most expensive ports on the West Coast, and probably in the country, the cost is not enough to discourage the steamship lines from coming here and asking to expand here. The ports aren't profit centers. They charge compensatory rates, that is, they cover their costs and don't take a loss. This is unusual for U.S. ports, many of which, especially in the East, are subsidized in one way or another.
>
> The biggest cost by far is for leasing the terminal. This costs around $125,000 per acre per year. The steamship lines also pay wharfage and dockage fees. The terminals all have slightly different agreements. The bigger ones get better deals. There is also a minimum volume commitment by the carriers to the ports. After that is met, there is a sliding scale for how much the carriers pay in fees.

Even though the port charges sound high, they must be a small part of the total transportation cost. Otherwise LA/LB would not be as big as they are. The steamship lines try to play one port against another, threatening to move if they don't get what they want. But once the deal is negotiated, they sign twenty-year leases. LA/LB is just too attractive for them to contemplate moving elsewhere with any seriousness. Of course, this assessment may have changed since the end of 2001 (when we conducted the interview with Mongelluzzo.

Rates in the Trans-Pacific

UNCTAD provides data on average rates per TEU on a quarterly basis (2003, 66). In the first quarter of 2001, for example, the average Asia-to-U.S. rate per TEU was $1,874, while the average U.S.-to-Asia rate was $877 per TEU. The rates kept dropping to a low of $1,463 for imports and $749 for exports in the second quarter of 2003. Then they rose until the third quarter of 2003, and started falling again. Two patterns are revealed in these statistics: the sharp difference between eastbound and westbound rates and a tendency for the rates to oscillate over time.

The reality is that rates are very sensitive to supply and demand; when there is over-capacity, rates drop, and when it appears that ships will be approaching capacity, rates rise. The drop in rates can cause the liners to lose money, which can ultimately have negative repercussions for many actors.

According to an article in *JoC* by Peter T. Leach entitled "Mental Wars," in the second half of 2006, freight rates fell even as cargo volumes were rising and expenses were up, in part because of the huge increases in the cost of fuel. Consequently, profits were down as much as 50 percent for the ocean liners (8/28/06, 12–15).

Here is the way Kathleen Gordon of MOL described the rate-setting process for her company:

> From Asia one way it costs about eight hundred to a thousand dollars to move a container. On top of that we try to establish a profit line. We say we need X percent. We say we need an extra thousand dollars per move. We can go a bit below that if we can make it up on forty-fives and high cubes [longer and higher containers with greater capacity]. So if it costs a thousand dollars each way, and we add one thousand dollars each to cover profit, the rates should be around four thousand dollars for a good profit. We can get by with three thousand dollars. But right now the Eastbound rates are sometimes as low as twelve or thirteen hundred dollars, and the westbound rates are negative. We try not to go below fourteen or fifteen hundred dollars. Some steamship companies undercut the rates. This is especially common among newcomers, who are trying to enter the market. They sell rates, not service.
>
> Some countries aren't concerned about profits. Rather, they are more interested in getting dollars. This is more likely for the Korean, Taiwanese, and Chinese companies. We [MOL, a Japanese company] have shareholders to answer to. In some cases, no one is watching profitability.
>
> Some companies are aggressive in negotiating the rates down. A liner will get a foot in the door with a customer by reducing rates. We are forced to react in order to retain our business. The customers [shippers] play the lines off against each other. Some of the customers are ruthless. You can tell when they are playing you off against another company and when you can trust them. The dirty dealers are well known in the industry, but if our sales person is green, they won't pick it up.

The Ocean Shipping Reform Act

The conference system was eliminated in 1998 with the passage of OSRA, the most recent legislation deregulating the international transportation system. OSRA allowed for the negotiation of confidential service agreements between shippers and ocean carriers. After its implementation on May 1, 1999, steamship lines could still participate in conferences, but these became advisory and suffered defections.

The basic features of the law include continued limited antitrust immunity for ocean carriers and private service contracts negotiated between shippers and carriers. The limited antitrust immunity allows conferences to continue, though mainly in an advisory capacity. Conferences must allow member lines to enter into service contracts with individual shippers. The service contracts are now secret, eliminating the requirement that tariffs be filed with the Federal Maritime Commission (FMC), so that shippers can strike different deals for themselves.

Some industry observers claim that both shippers and carriers benefited from the passage of OSRA. However, it is noteworthy that the actors who pushed for it came predominantly from the shipper community, especially the National Industrial Transportation League (NITL), the premier shippers' organization in the United States. Kathleen Gordon of MOL said that OSRA "sure doesn't benefit the liners."

Bill Mongelluzzo's position on the question of who benefits most from the law was as follows: "OSRA strengthened the hand of the shippers. That was its purpose. The big retailers who head up the National Industrial Transportation League worked on it. They got together with the major U.S. carriers at the time—Sealand and APL—and worked it out. Before OSRA the carriers could set rates through the FMC. They were visible for all to see. Now they are supposed to be confidential, but they get out."

We believe that the real beneficiaries have been the large shippers over the smaller ones. The bigger shippers, including the giant retailers, are able to use their considerable volume to cut themselves the most favorable deals, getting massive discounts in exchange for commitments of volume. They can use their muscle to bargain down the tariff. OSRA has contributed to the shift in the balance of power from carriers to shippers, and from smaller to bigger shippers. It is one of the factors in the rise in power of the giant retailers.

As Bill Mongelluzzo stated above, contracts are usually signed by May 1, after negotiations between shippers and carriers over the rates. Chuck Savre described the process of rate negotiation this way:

> The key factors involved in rate negotiations are capacity and greed. In general, the more capacity, the lower the rates. And the major shippers are greedy to cut the rates down.
>
> All carriers lost money last year [2002], but they are fearful of losing market share. This year [2003] looks better. The question is whether the carriers will be able to hold out for the full GRI [general rate increase, the rate recommended by the conference]. There may be some erosion as the time for signing gets closer. The proposed GRI is seven hundred dollars per container.

Negotiations typically start around January, although there is variation. The end of April is considered a good time for finalizing the year's rates because it is before the peak season starts in July.

THE POWER OF THE GIANT RETAILERS

Bigger Is Better

The ability of a shipper to gain a favorable freight rate is directly related to size. The more volume a shipper moves, the lower the rates it must pay. The logic behind this is obvious. Since the carriers need to fill their ships, the more a particular shipper can guarantee the use of its slots, the easier life is for the carrier. Big shippers can guarantee filling a large numbers of slots, so they are favored.

It is not difficult to see that this gives the giant retailers, like Wal-Mart, a huge advantage. Indeed, a manufacturer that imports told us that Wal-Mart sets the standard, and then everyone else falls into line behind them. Wal-Mart brings considerable clout to the annual spring rate negotiations table, where it can bargain carriers down. All other shippers use the Wal-Mart rates as a baseline. It would seem that the ability of Wal-Mart to push rates lower than the steamship lines would want has a positive ripple effect for other shippers.

Savre described his company's relationship with Wal-Mart as follows:

> The giant retailers, like Wal-Mart, are able to leverage their volume. They manage to get deals. That is because they are attractive to the carriers. If you cut Wal-Mart in half, the two firms would be the first and second largest importer. They have a lot of clout, though more with some than with others. Wal-Mart tried to get a rate reduction in this round of negotiations [2003], but the carriers are holding the rate. As they say: "You can't haul at cost." Of course, each of the steamship lines has a different cost structure.
>
> The steamship lines feel some anger towards Wal-Mart. Doing business with them is straining. Wal-Mart advertises that it is rolling back prices, and to implement that they have to focus on cost containment. They see transportation as an area where they can cut. The larger shippers negotiate additional free time at the terminal and ask for other conditions that reduce their costs. They sometimes want special gates on weekends and at night. They want to lower other terminal costs. They also want more free time with the container on the street. A reduction in their costs means a rise in ours.

Jay Winter of the Steamship Association said: "The Wal-Marts call the shots. They have all the power." He thinks the giant retailers are a major cause of congestion on the docks. When they run out of warehouse space, they simply store their containers on the docks until they are ready to pick them up. Jay has met with giant retailers Payless Shoes and Target. "They talk about trucking terms. They tell us [the steamship lines] what they expect to do in the way of volume. They want to establish how people will handle their business. They exercise real pressure in their meetings with the carriers. At the Payless Shoes meeting they assembled all of their vendors and told them what to expect during the peak season."

Winter was critical of the use of JIT principles by retailers: "JIT was originally devised for the manufacturing business—to handle their huge inventories. Now the retail business has adopted it, but it isn't the same thing. Manufacturing is spread out over the whole year, but retail typically operates on a peak season of three months. The carrier business used to be spread over the year. The ships were full from January 1 to November 30. Now they sit around waiting until October."

Winter sees the relations between the shippers and ocean carriers as adversarial, despite the reforms of OSRA:

> I heard Ed Emmett of the NIT League [a shippers' organization] give a talk. It was the most honest talk I've ever heard from shippers. Most of the people who deal with the carriers are mid-level managers who report to a higher-level executive. They are told by the executive to cut transportation costs by 10 percent or they will lose their jobs. This puts great pressure on the carriers. I went to a Logistics Annual Convention organized by IMRA [International Mass Retailers Association]. A few ocean carriers were there. One had spoken with a vice president of a retailer which had recently signed a contract with the carrier, but the VP didn't know anything about it. The reality is that transportation is a minor concern to the top executives of these companies.

This means that the shippers, including the giant retailers, are often indifferent to the realities the carriers face—they simply expect lowered costs, or they will switch. This kind of approach leads to the continual emergence of low-cost carriers, which threaten to undercut the industry's standards. As Winter says, "The steamship lines are facing pressure from the shippers. They are caught in a vice: cut your costs by 10 percent, but deliver the goods on time."

Conclusion

We have seen that the steamship lines, powerful though they are, are not the most powerful actors in global transportation. The giant retailers occupy this role. Nevertheless, the steamship companies play a critical role for all the other actors involved in global logistics. They are near the top of a hierarchy of relationships, and they certainly exercise considerable power.

We have also seen that the steamship business is highly competitive, sometimes leading to irrational consequences from a system perspective.

This competition is, in part, foisted upon them by their customers, but it is also a product of the particular economics of this business. The heightened, sometimes ruinous competition reverberates down the system, with negative consequences for those segments of the industry least able to defend themselves.

CHAPTER 5

Landside Transportation

Once it has landed at the ports of LA/LB, where does the cargo go and how does it get there? Who takes charge of these freight movements and how are they coordinated? In other words, how does intermodalism actually work? In this chapter we try to answer these questions. Two major modes of landside transportation are involved, namely, rail and trucking. Important to this story is the process of deregulation and its impact on these modes. The issue of control is another important question—which actors in the complex importing and transportation industry are in charge of freight movement? Apart from the methods and coordination of cargo movement, congestion plagues the industry in Southern California, threatening the future growth and viability of the ports and, ultimately, of international trade itself. What solutions have been tried, and what new ones are being proposed? Is the growth of this complex system sustainable?

MODES OF LANDSIDE TRANSPORTATION

The major modes of landside freight transportation for international imports are rail and trucking. Of course, there is a huge domestic freight transportation industry. We are here concerned only with the international intermodal sector, namely, the movement of the goods that arrive in ocean containers and, within that, the freight movement connected with the Southern California ports. But before examining international intermodalism in detail, let us first look briefly at the two major modes and their development, especially in the West.

Railroads

Power and Decline. Rail was the major mode of freight transportation of the nineteenth and early twentieth centuries. The railroads were seen as powerful monopolies—the dreaded "octopus," to use Frank Norris's name—in the last quarter of the nineteenth century, causing shippers—those who depended on their services—to call for government regulation. The railroads themselves favored regulation because they were worried about potential price wars in the most used corridors. The Interstate Commerce Act of 1887, which regulated the industry, gave the railroads special privileges as well as obligations. Their major obligations were to serve all customers without discrimination and to charge reasonable rates. They were not allowed to abandon service without the approval of the Interstate Commerce Commission (ICC). In exchange the companies were allowed to set minimum rates, practice collusion with competitors, and restrict new entrants, all of which sheltered the railroads from competition (DeBoer and Kaufman 2002, ch. 3; Grimm and Windle 1998, 16).

This cozy arrangement did not last, however. In the 1920s, freight transportation began to move from the railroads to the trucking industry. Trucking provided considerably more flexibility for shippers, and even though it was somewhat more costly, its other advantages overrode the cost factor, especially for high-value, high-rate cargo, such as manufactured goods. Over the following decades, the market share of the railroads continued to decline, from 68.6 percent in 1944, to 56.2 percent in 1950, to 44.1 percent in 1960, to 39.8 percent in 1970, to 37.5 percent in 1980. Meanwhile, the return on investment for the railroads fell, from 3.44 percent in 1947 to 2.13 percent in 1960, to 1.73 percent in 1970, and to 1.20 percent in 1975, levels that were well below par (Talley and Schwarz-Miller 1998, 125).

Deregulation. By the early 1970s, the U.S. railroads were faced with serious financial problems. In 1973, seven major railroads in the northeast declared bankruptcy. To avoid loss of services, Congress enacted the Regional Rail Reorganization Act (1973), creating Conrail. Congress also moved to deregulate the railroads (Talley and Schwarz-Miller 1998, 125–26). The first piece of reform legislation was the Railroad Revitalization and Regulatory Reform Act (the "4-R Act") of 1976. It was followed by the Staggers Act in 1980. Because of all this legislation, the 1970s have been called the decade of deregulation (Larson and Spraggins 2000). The laws sought to increase returns on investment to competitive levels by allowing the market to take over from government regulation. They granted the railroads more flexibility by allowing them more rate-making freedom and the right to shut down unprofitable lines (Grimm and Windle 1998, 18; Talley and Schwarz-Miller 1998, 126).

The most important law for deregulating the railroads was the Staggers Act. It granted the railroads freedom to set rates and made rail freight contracts with individual customers legal and exempt from ICC regulation (Larson and Spraggins 2000). Before Staggers, it was illegal for a railroad and a shipper to make a deal about rates. All rail rates were public, and any changes required ICC approval, which slowed up change considerably. Now parties could sign confidential contracts covering rates and other terms of service. Deals could be cut in which shippers guaranteed volume in exchange for rate reductions and special service. The railroads were able to lower costs as a result, especially by downsizing their employees (DeBoer and Kaufman 2002, 65).

Deregulation improved the rates of return on investment for the railroads. In 1980, the rate was 4.22 percent. It rose significantly to 8.11 percent in 1990 and to 9.37 in 1994 (Talley and Schwartz-Miller 1998, 126). However, by 2000 it had fallen to 6.48 percent, rising to 7.04 percent in 2002 (Association of American Railroads 2003). This performance was still an improvement on the pre-deregulation period and was mainly attributable to savings through mergers and acquisitions, more efficient labor use, and reductions in track mileage. Some of the benefits of deregulation were also passed on to shippers in the form of lower rates (Talley and Schwartz-Miller 1998, 126–27).

The Growth of Intermodalism. Just as the 1970s are described as the decade of deregulation, so the 1980s are termed the decade of intermodalism (Larson and Spraggins 2000). This was a period in which just-in-time (JIT) inventory management was catching on, which led to increased concern over the smooth movement of goods from factory to warehouses and distribution centers. Intermodalism is not restricted to international freight transportation but also was a growing feature of domestic rail-truck moves during the 1980s.

The ability to engage in intermodalism with the steamship lines depended on the passage of the Shipping Act of 1984. This important act permitted the steamship lines to arrange with the railroads to ship containers under a single bill of lading (Shashikumar and Schatz 2000). The technology of double-stacking containers on rail cars, which made such arrangements feasible, had been developed just prior to the change in the law, allowing the steamship lines and railroads to take full advantage of its provisions.

Intermodal is the fastest-growing sector of the railroad business. If it were treated as a separate commodity, it would be the largest of those handled by the railroads, according to a *JoC* article by railroad expert Lawrence H. Kaufman called "Intermodal Insights: Behind the Numbers" (10/25/04, 13). In 1965, the industry moved 1,664,929 trailers and containers. By 1990 this figure had risen to 6,206,782. In 2000 it was 9,176,890, and it continues to grow. Containers generally outnumber trailers, with 6,288,021 containers versus 2,888,630 trailers in 2000 (Association of American Railroads 2003, 26). The term *container* here includes domestic as well as ocean containers, so the rise in their use is not a clear indicator of the rise of international intermodalism.

The increased placement of truck trailers on the railroads is an interesting phenomenon. For decades, the railroads lost business to the trucking companies, especially the most lucrative cargo. Truck transportation was more reliable, and it allowed shippers to lower their inventory costs through JIT delivery. But according to Kaufman, conditions have changed. Highways have become increasingly congested, and diesel fuel costs continue to rise. Meanwhile hours-of-service rules for truckers have led to a drop in driver productivity. The upshot is that it pays for trucking companies to ship their trailers by rail rather than to have them driven as trucks. This is an interesting shift indeed. And since the construction of new highways is so expensive, it is a trend that is likely to grow, at least for the foreseeable future.

Mergers. As a part of deregulation, the ICC became an enthusiastic supporter of railroad mergers during the 1980s. Six major mergers occurred in that decade, four of which involved Western railroads. In 1980 the Burlington Northern took over the St. Louis–San Francisco. In 1982 the Union Pacific (UP) took over the Missouri Pacific and the Western Pacific. In 1988 the Denver and Rio Grande Western gained control of the Southern Pacific and took over its name. In the same year, the UP acquired the Missouri-Kansas-Texas, also called the Katy (Larson and Spraggins 2000). During the 1980s, railroads also acquired trucking companies. In 1984, Burlington Northern acquired three Class I motor carriers, and UP acquired Overnite Express, the largest U.S. non-union trucking company (Larson and Spraggins 2000).

The next decade was even more intense in terms of mergers. Larson and Spraggins describe the 1990s as the decade of "mega-mergers" (2000) During this period, the number of Class I railroads dropped from fourteen to eight. In the West, the Atchison, Topeka and Santa Fe in 1995 consolidated with the Burlington Northern to form the Burlington Northern Santa Fe (BNSF). The ICC was retired in 1995, to be partially replaced by the Surface Transportation Board (STB), and this merger was one of the ICC's last acts. The BNSF emerged as the largest North American railroad. UP tried in vain to block the merger.

Then in 1996 the Southern Pacific merged into the Union Pacific, which enabled the UP to surpass the BNSF as the largest railroad in North America. In the previous year, the UP had also won ICC approval to merge the Chicago and North Western into its system (Larson and Spraggins 2000).

These major mergers left only two Class I railroads in the West. In 1970 there were seventy-one Class I railroads in the United States; by 2000 there were only eight.

Railroad mergers added to the woes of the railroads. In the West, the formation of the BNSF in 1995 was relatively smooth, but UP's mergers were anything but. Most disruptive was their acquisition of the Southern Pacific (SP). UP did not have a good understanding of SP's operations and closed two small but critical Texas terminals. The result was a huge mess that came to be known in the industry as "the great meltdown." Containers piled up along the supply chain, unable to move. It took months to untangle. UP's stock fell from almost $70 in 1997 to below $40 in 1998 (DeBoer and Kaufman 2002, 75).

Competition. Some might contend that having only two railroads on the West Coast limits competition, but this seems not to be the case. Customers constantly pit the UP and the BNSF against each other, which makes each company eager to poach the other's customers whenever possible.

The competition faced by the railroads is not restricted to other railroads but also includes other modes of transportation, notably trucking companies and the airlines. Airlines captured most of the railroads' passengers, while trucking companies captured much of their less-than-carload (LCL) freight. Trucking and the airlines were less hamstrung by government regulations, and they also went through major technological upgrading, while railroad technology changed very little (DeBoer and Kaufman 2002, 55).

Both trucking companies and the airlines have been more service-oriented than the railroads, which put more emphasis on cost-cutting and efficiency. Moreover, the other two modes of freight carriage have been able to consolidate to create nationwide networks, while rail consolidation has required more regulatory review and has faced opposition. After all these years, the railroads are still viewed with suspicion as too powerful (DeBoer and Kaufman 2002, 55).

The railroads feel some bitterness over the fact that trucking is "subsidized" by government at the federal, state, and local levels by public support for highway construction and maintenance. Trucking companies are the beneficiaries of this subsidy. The same is true for the airlines, which benefit from public airports, though the competition between rail and air freight is much less intense than the competition between rail and trucking. Unlike the other two transportation modes, the railroads own their right of way, so they are responsible for building and maintaining the country's rail system. Moreover, they must pay taxes on these assets. This expense makes the railroad industry one of the most capital-intensive in the country. Huge private investment must be made by the railroads to build and maintain the country's rail system (DeBoer and Kaufman 2002, 55).

Trucking companies and railroads continue to vie for long-haul transportation. Generally, the railroads are much cheaper, making them the mode of choice for most of the imports that come through the ports. The higher the value and the smaller the size of the goods, as is the case for electronic products, the more desirable trucking becomes. The advantage of trucking over rail is that it is more flexible, allowing for door-to-door service. In contrast, the railroads can only pick up and deliver at rail terminals, which require local truck hauls at the end points of their routes. Moreover, it takes time to build a train, adding cars until you have enough to make the journey worthwhile, so delivery cannot be as swift as by truck.

Current Problems of the Railroads. DeBoer and Kaufman evaluate the challenges that the railroads have faced since 1990 and continue to face in the twenty-first century (2002, 65–78). Many of the problems of the railroads are self-inflicted; in the course of this research, we often found people in other branches of the international trade community who expressed criticisms of the sector, especially of the Union Pacific. They would roll their eyes in mock dismay when the topic came up.

According to DeBoer and Kaufman, part of the dilemma lies with the business model the railroads developed in response to the historical political hostility and governmental intervention they faced because of opposition to the power of "the octopus." The railroads developed a defensive posture, which was exacerbated by loss of market share to trucking and the airlines, leading risk-taking leaders to leave the industry. Their twin goals became to load their trains to the maximum (they had plenty of capacity) by cutting prices and to cut expenses by abandoning some routes and instituting reductions in the labor force. After deregulation, these patterns became even more entrenched.

Before deregulation, the railroad industry, which was heavily unionized, operated in a "high labor-cost environment." Wage rates were high, the union was able to impose costly work and pay rules, and increases in labor cost were passed on to customers. A central strategy of the railroads to decrease labor costs was to decrease the size of the labor force, which they have pursued relentlessly. Rail employment reached its peak in 1930, with about two million workers. Since then, the numbers have dropped almost every decade so that, by 2000, there were only 250,000 left (DeBoer and Kaufman 2002, 70). Reductions occurred in all segments of railroad operations, including train crew composition, a process that was supported by a conservative political environment. Presidents Reagan and George H. W. Bush set up presidential emergency boards (PEBs) under the Railway Labor Act, enabling the industry to cut crew size (Talley and Schwartz-Miller 1998, 129–30). In the 1990s the railroads eliminated about twenty-five thousand crew jobs, saving about $200 million in annual wages. These reductions improved the profitability of the railroads, but they also contributed to the ports' congestion crisis of the 2004 peak season, as we shall see.

Meanwhile, from the late 1980s to the end of the century, the railroads slashed prices and otherwise increased their efforts to attract traffic as a way to maximize their capacity. Coupled with the reduction in employees, productivity, as measured by revenue per ton-mile per employee, rose dramatically, but revenue per ton-mile fell. During the 1990s, the railroads managed to fill their shrinking capacity and found themselves unable to move all of their customers' commodities.

Trucking

Sectors. The trucking industry is divided into distinctive sectors. The truck load (TL) sector engages in filling the entire trailer with the goods of one company. Transportation involves a single haul, without stops, from origin to destination. Independent TL companies can do for-hire hauls, or firms can own their own corporate fleet of trucks. In contrast, the less than truckload (LTL) sector engages in the consolidation of goods from several companies into a single truck, which makes loading and delivery more complicated, since the truck must make multiple stops. Trucking companies tend to specialize in either TL or LTL, and the businesses are quite different. For one thing, LTL is much more expensive than TL, requiring much more advance planning.

A third sector consists of small package deliveries, by companies such as UPS and FedEx. Although these companies might be seen as part of the LTL sector, they have some unique characteristics, including providing delivery directly to consumers and operating their own airline fleets and logistics companies. They are much bigger than the largest LTL company, and they are transnational corporations.

A fourth type of trucking is known as drayage. It entails the use of chassis (racks on wheels) to haul disconnected containers. Drayage is a key element in intermodal freight transportation. When containers come off ships or trains, they can be hauled (drayed) directly by trucks without having to be unpacked. The same, of course, is the case for loading onto trains or ships. Drayage companies can handle both international and domestic containers. A drayage company can pick up a container at the ports and haul it to a railhead, and a drayage company can pick up the container when it arrives at a rail yard in Chicago and deliver it to the customer. Similarly, a drayage company can haul a domestic container filled with transloaded imports from a distribution center in Ontario to the San Bernardino BNSF rail yard. Our research has focused mainly on harbor drayage, which is a pivotal link in the supply chain that surrounds the ports of LA/LB.

Deregulation. The trucking industry developed much later than the railroads, so it faced regulation much later. The Motor Carrier Act of 1935 brought the trucking companies under the jurisdiction of the ICC. Part of the reason for regulating trucking was to shelter the railroads from growing competition with the trucking industry, which was expanding rapidly. Moreover, motor carriers were in severe competition with each other, and they wanted regulation to stop the destructive competition among them. Shippers also supported greater price stability. The 1935 act controlled competition by restricting new entrants, and it permitted collusion in the setting of rates, which allowed the ICC to play a major role in determining trucking rates (Grimm and Windle 1998, 17).

In a sense, the railroad and trucking industries represent opposite types of industries. Trucking is a naturally competitive industry, with low entry costs and worker skills that are easily acquired. In contrast, the railroads have certain monopoly properties that could easily be exploited to the detriment of their customers. From the perspective of a society, like the United States, that stresses the ideal of competitive markets, regulation was much less necessary in trucking than for the railroads. By limiting entry and engaging in rate regulation, the ICC provided protection for the trucking industry and allowed the flourishing of the Teamsters, which from a certain ideological perspective can be seen as capturing labor rents. In other words, government regulation allowed the industry to charge higher rates than a very competitive market would produce, and when the union pushed for higher wages, the increased costs could be passed on to the customers (Hirsch and Macpherson 1998, 61).

Deregulation of the trucking industry began in the late 1970s with administrative changes enacted by the ICC. The Motor Carrier Act of 1980 codified these changes. Unlike the railroads, which still faced some forms of regulation after the Staggers Act, the trucking industry was completely deregulated in practice, allowing market forces to shape all aspects of the industry, including free entry by new carriers, limitations on collective rate-making, and the freedom to set rates. Trucking companies were now allowed to charge discriminatory prices, including discount pricing for high-volume customers, which, as we have seen in ocean shipping, favors the bigger shippers and supports their consolidation. The Trucking Industry Regulatory Reform Act of 1994, and the Interstate Commerce Commission Termination Act of 1995 brought to an end any remaining pretence of regulation (Belzer 2000, 28–29; Grimm and Windle 1998, 22–23).

A key effect of deregulation was the entrance of "owner-operators," independent contractors in the trucking business. They could be individuals or very small companies with a handful of drivers with whom they subcontract, who each act as independent small businesses. These drivers, who own their own equipment, are paid for a job, and their compensation might be described as piece rate. They are often employees of larger companies in almost every way, except their legal status. Given that they do not receive overtime, benefits, or any of the other advantages of being an employee, they provide a low-cost alternative for trucking companies. Needless to say, they tend to be non-union; indeed, if they try to form or join a union, they may face charges of antitrust violation. The irony that small, independent truck drivers can be charged with breaking antitrust law, while giant steamship companies receive some antitrust immunity, should not be lost on the reader.

Another way to think about the emergence of independent contractors is that it enabled the trucking companies that employ them to become non-asset-based firms. In other words, they were able to avoid having to invest in lots of expensive equipment, which makes it easier for the firm to weather downturns in demand. This point was made clearly to us by John Wall, president of ContainerFreight EIT, a harbor drayage company, and a man with years of experience in the trucking industry (interviewed 7/28/03 and 8/26/03):

> The nation's transportation system—both TL and LTL—has been transformed. If you do an analysis of Wall Street's evaluation of trucking companies, you find that the non-asset-based companies are valued much higher. They are giving a clear message that one needs to move to non-asset-based. This is shown in Yellow's takeover of Roadway in the LTL sector. The problem is that there is tremendous overcapacity in the LTL sector. The non-asset-based companies avoid having to pay fixed cost expenses. If you have assets, during periods of low activity you still have liabilities, like depreciation and interest, even if you aren't using the equipment. So it is better not to hold any.

Here we see one important key to the increase in contingency in our system. By contracting out, a company avoids the problems of unused capacity while improving its position in the financial markets.

Deregulation of the motor carrier business led to increased competition, which created the division of general commodity trucking into the LTL and TL sectors. The LTL sector maintained and extended the existing terminal structure and continued to operate mainly within the Teamsters, whereas TL carriers eliminated terminals, focusing on large shipments of ten thousand pounds or more, which they picked up from shippers and delivered directly to consignees. The TL sector attracted new entrants, including large numbers of independent contractors, thereby avoiding the union and skimming truckload freight from the general freight market—in both the trucking *and* the railroad industries. In sum, out of deregulation was created a non-union trucking sector (Belzer 2000, 15–16).

Meanwhile, in the LTL sector, the number of carriers dropped 78 percent between 1976 and 1993, and revenues fell 40 percent. Concentration developed, with the top four LTL companies increasing their share of the business from 17 percent in 1976 to 43.6 percent in 1993. However, the LTL sector as a whole experienced growing competition from UPS and FedEx (Grimm and Windle 1998, 27–28).

The TL sector has grown since deregulation, as measured by total revenues and ton-miles. The leading TL companies in 1994 were Schneider International, with revenues of $1.32 billion, and J. B. Hunt, with revenues of $1.07 billion. Both firms grew substantially under deregulation. The sector experienced cost reductions and productivity increases (Grimm and Windle 1998, 28). While increased competition may have benefited some companies and customers, there is plenty of evidence to show that it has hurt truck drivers. Or, as Michael Belzer (2000) put it, trucks have become "sweatshops on wheels."

Harbor Drayage. Harbor drayage is a specialized part of the drayage sector of the trucking industry that deals with the hauling (and return) of ocean containers from the docks to either railheads or to warehouses and distribution centers (DCs). In general, harbor drayage companies tend to be smaller businesses, although there has been some consolidation in this sector as well. These companies overwhelmingly tend to hire drivers who are independent contractors. The drivers own their tractor, which they lease to a trucking company. In turn, the trucking company receives jobs from shippers and ocean carriers, and the company sends the drivers out to pick up and deliver the containers.

Wall described the sector this way: "LTL and TL companies don't enter drayage. They pay hourly and fringes, and the power units are on their books. In the ports you can't have expensive equipment on your books because of the rates. This has allowed the drayage companies to create a secondary market. The rates haven't moved in a decade. This is why no trucking companies have entered the ports in the last fifteen to twenty years. It is why we created this market."

The drivers are paid a standard rate for a particular haul, for example, between the docks and the Union Pacific Railroad's intermodal container transfer facility (ICTF) or between the ports and the downtown rail yards of both UP and BNSF. Another standard run is between the ports and the Inland Empire DCs. Drivers performing these jobs are essentially working on piece rate, and the cost of any delays, long lines, or road congestion, is borne by them.

Over three hundred harbor drayage companies operate in conjunction with the ports of LA/LB. They vary in their degree of specialization in this field, with some offering a set of services beyond drayage and others focusing exclusively on this function. Together they employ about ten thousand drivers (Overby 2005). The companies vary tremendously in size and in the variety of services that they provide. Among the bigger trucking companies is California Cartage—the leading company with a number of subsidiaries.

Harbor drayage firms can be hired by shippers, 3PLs, or ocean carriers. Shippers and 3PLs can arrange to have their containers picked up at the ports, or they can leave the process up to the steamship lines, which can take charge of the entire move from door to door. In general, the steamship lines appear to be the largest employers of harbor drayage firms.

Everyone in the transportation industry surrounding the ports recognizes that the port truckers are at the bottom of the food chain. Even their direct employers, who have a decided interest in keeping wages as low as possible, recognize that wages may have fallen too low, leading to a shortage of drivers and exacerbating the problem of a huge backlog at the ports of LA/LB during the peak season of 2004. For example, we first learned of Michael H. Belzer's book *Sweatshops on Wheels* from an executive of one of these companies, Patty Senecal, who clearly felt considerable sympathy for the drivers, even though her firm was caught in a highly competitive world where an individual company could not seriously consider alternatives that might help the drivers. (We deal with the labor issues in this sector in Part III.)

SOUTHERN CALIFORNIA FREIGHT TRANSPORTATION

Trying to track the way freight moves through Southern California is like trying to track all the connections on the Internet. No one seems to have a picture of the whole system, which is mind-boggling in its complexity. We managed to get a glimpse of it by visiting a couple of major rail yards and an associated truck yard. These visits, which involved tours and interviews, opened our eyes to an underbelly of the world of trade that is rarely open to view. It is a dirty, gritty, masculine world of big machines and diesel fuel. It also occupies a lot of space that is generally hidden from the average Angeleno.

Much more research could have been conducted on this topic (as is true for just about every topic covered in this book). We longed to ride a freight train from LA to Barstow and back, to get a feel for the thing. Pictures of standing next to the engineer, pulling the whistle, floated through our heads. The railroad industry has a disparaging term for people like us who idolize trains—they are called *foamers*, for foaming at the mouth. Such a trip probably could have been arranged, but we didn't do it; maybe in another life. So here is an attenuated version of how freight is moved in Southern California.

Railroads. The two Class I railroads in Southern California offer a number of options for freight movement out of the ports. The basic choice is between on-dock and off-dock rail. A number of the terminals at the ports of LA/LB provide on-dock rail facilities to their tenants. However, even if on-dock facilities are available, they are not necessarily used, and we heard of terminals that do not.

The two major railroads generally handle different terminals. Maersk, for example, is served by BNSF, while UP covers the APL and Evergreen terminals. On-dock rail is mainly limited to "dedicated" trains, that is, they are used by one of the major steamship lines, which sends a train to a particular destination, such as Chicago (Meyer, Mohaddes, and Associates 2001, 23–27).

Trains that are loaded on-dock move to the rest of the country via the Alameda Corridor, a set of rail lines that connect the ports to the rail lines running from downtown Los Angeles to points east. Completed in 2002, it was a $2.4 billion project that cuts the time of the move to about an hour and avoids numerous intersections where tracks and roads used to cross, which had caused delays for both modes of transportation. The construction of the Alameda Corridor created an underground passageway, over which road bridges cross. (For a full description of the development of this project, see Erie 2004, 147–62.)

Originally the Alameda Corridor was supposed to provide truck lanes as well to alleviate the congestion on the freeways from the ports, but this part of the project was scrapped. Two rail lines were laid, and a third was planned. Both the UP and the BNSF were using these tracks.

The project was funded with a combination of public and private capital, some of which had to be paid off. As a result, customers were charged a tariff of thirty dollars per FEU until the loans were liquidated. The railroads ended up floating the bonds, according to Chuck Potempa, director of Hobart, BNSF's downtown rail yard. (Potempa wondered why the ports did not float the bonds themselves.) Anyway, the railroads have passed this tariff on to the steamship lines, but the liners feel that they are unable to pass it along to the shippers.

Plans were being developed and, slowly, implemented to extend the Alameda Corridor concept from downtown LA through Los Angeles County and the Inland Empire. The plan, known as Alameda Corridor East, was far less elaborate and costly than the first part of the project. With ACE (as it is called), the main purpose was to fix certain junctures where rail lines and highways cross. The plan was to make certain overpasses and crossings more efficient.

How successful the Alameda Corridor has been is a question for debate. Its key feature is that it provides for the rapid movement of full ocean containers to the eastern part of the country. This practice seems to go through periods of waxing and waning popularity. When emptying the ocean containers in Los Angeles, and transloading them either for local delivery or into domestic containers and trailers for longer hauls is on the rise, shippers have found the Alameda Corridor less useful. As a result, it sometimes has suffered from underused capacity.

Apart from on-dock rail, several off-dock rail facilities are available in Southern California. The ICTF is an important off-dock rail facility run by the Union Pacific railroad. Located in the city of Carson, near the docks, it is also adjacent to the intersection of Interstates 405 and 710. The Terminal Island Freeway (Route 103) ends right in front of the ICTF. Containers are drayed from the ports to the ICTF to be put on rail. The ICTF feeds into the Alameda Corridor. The other major railroad, the BNSF, had plans to build a near-dock facility as well, easing the congestion it faced at its downtown railyard and speeding the movement of containers east.

Downtown Rail Yards: Hobart. Both the BNSF and the UP have intermodal rail yards near downtown Los Angeles. UP has three downtown rail yards: the East LA yard, the LATC near downtown, and a yard in the City of Industry (MTA 2002, 32). The BNSF yard is officially called the BNSF Los Angeles Intermodal Facility but is universally known as Hobart. It is the busiest intermodal rail facility in the country. "For clutter, for noise, for sheer nonstop action deep in the guts of industrial Southern California, few places come close to massive Hobart Yard," wrote David Ferrell in a 2002 *LA Times* article entitled "Hobart Yard" (4/4/02).

Here are some basic statistics. Hobart had 190 acres, with eight loading tracks and fifteen track segments. It operated twenty-four hours, seven days a week, and dealt with twenty-six intermodal trains per day on average. It did 1,040,602 lifts a year (up from under 700,000 in 1995), for a daily average of 2,851, and an average of 5,781 lifts per acre. Its top five customers in terms of lift volume were: Hyundai, UPS, J. B. Hunt, OOCL, and NYK.[1]

We visited Hobart twice (6/5/02 and 6/13/02), receiving an excellent tour that included a look down the Alameda Corridor from above as well as a couple of very informative interviews with Chuck Potempa. (Unfortunately, we could not visit the UP yard.) Hobart receives both international and domestic containers to ship east, but the domestic containers may, in fact, be filled with transloaded imports. We asked Potempa: How much does Hobart handle ocean containers to and from the ports?

The answer isn't completely simple. We deal with various kinds of freight: some is transloaded, some is domestic, and some is headed for Europe as

[1] These statistics were collected in 2001. They have probably changed somewhat since then, but they still give a sense of the size and scope of the railyard.

landbridge. Let's say a hundred boxes come off a ship. Fifty end up locally, broadly speaking. That includes LA, San Diego, Phoenix, Salt Lake City, and the Central Valley. We don't see these boxes. The other fifty go on rail. About five to ten, maybe closer to ten, go to Europe. The rest—forty—go to inland points. The transloaded goods are put into trailers and trucked to places like Salt Lake City. However, some can be trucked across the country to Norfolk, Virginia. This might happen if the goods are high-value, like electronic products. Or they might haul an ocean container all the way by truck. It depends on what the customer wants.

Potempa described Hobart as "the crown jewel of the international trade world," asserting that he did not think anyone would disagree. It handles all types of freight, for all types of companies. Of the boxes they handle, 36 percent are designated "international." This includes movements in both directions, though the ratio is two to one eastbound over westbound, and most of what is sent west is empty. Apparently empty rail cars are sent to other West Coast cities.

Although the Alameda Corridor passes about two miles to the west of Hobart, it does not stop there or at the UP (known as the East LA) yard but swings by. In other words, the yards are an alternative to the Alameda Corridor, particularly for imports that arrive at terminals that do not rely on on-dock rail or, in the case of Hobart, for those that are being shipped on BNSF rather than UP, so they do not use the ICTF. Once trains make use of the Alameda Corridor, they do not stop for unloading until they reach an Eastern destination.

Thus, all the ocean containers that come from the ports to Hobart must be drayed by trucks, and the Alameda Corridor does not change this fact. About a thousand harbor trucks come to Hobart per day (as of June 2002, when the interview was conducted). Potempa calculated: "We do 1,040,000 lifts per year—or did last year. If 36 percent are international, then that's about 350,000 to 400,000 per year, or about a thousand a day. On top of that, some drivers come to pick up containers, and some come to deliver or pick up chassis." He pointed out that, in all, half a million trucks connected with international trade visit Hobart through the ports in a year. And 95 to 98 percent of them move on the 710 freeway.

A typical international move would be by the steamship line Hyundai, according to Potempa. Hyundai did not have on-dock rail at the time of our visit to Hobart. Potempa said that the steamship line would discharge 1,800 containers on Friday and Saturday, and organize a 3 a.m. dray to Hobart of 600 to 1,100 containers. We asked Potempa what proportion of containers were put on rail on-dock and on to the Alameda Corridor rather than being drayed to Hobart. He calculated that in 2001,

BNSF had 422,000 rail lifts on dock (in either direction), and Hobart had 1,040,000, also in either direction, so the ratio is about two to one in favor of drayage.

The trains in Hobart carry both containers, which are always double-stacked, and trailers on flat cars. The latter are LTL trucks, and include such familiar names as Yellow, Roadway, Consolidated Freight, ABF, and UPS. UPS is their biggest-dollar account. We wondered whether the Alameda Corridor would lead to a loss of ports-related business for Hobart as more on-dock rail was built. But Potempa thinks this is unlikely:

> Those terminals that don't have on-dock rail aren't rushing to build it as a result of the Alameda Corridor. They have their ways of doing things. For example, Hyundai drays to Hobart and will probably continue to do so. That's their way of doing business. There are eleven on-dock facilities, and they need to keep building more. Even so, given the growth and expected growth of imports, it will be hard for Hobart to keep up with the flow. What the Alameda Corridor does is, it handles on-dock more efficiently. That means that the trains get out of there and to downtown more quickly. It also benefits the local communities, by getting rid of the 144 grade crossings that used to jam up traffic. That's it.

The Inland Empire Rail Yards. BNSF operates an intermodal rail yard in San Bernardino, while UP has a rail yard in Colton. We have only visited the former, but we heard that UP's Colton yard is not an intermodal facility. The San Bernardino yard operates 24/7 on 154 acres. In 2002 it had 449,786 lifts, for an average of 1,232 per day, and 2,921 per acre. In 1995 it had well below 200,000 lifts per year, so its volume has increased substantially in recent years.

Bob Brendza, director of facility development for the San Bernardino BNSF facility, kindly gave us a tour and granted us an interview. The San Bernardino yard, said Brendza, does not deal with ocean containers and only handles domestic containers and trailers. The railroad does business directly with third parties, that is, trucking companies like Swift, Yellow, Schneider, and J. B. Hunt, and it does not know who the beneficial owner of the cargo, namely the shipper, is. So they cannot tell whether the goods inside are imports or not. All Brendza knows is that a trucking company has arranged to move a domestic container or trailer by rail.

As we have pointed out, however, the domestic containers and trailers may contain transloaded imports. The San Bernardino facility lies to the east of the Ontario warehousing district and probably provides services to those import distribution centers that want to ship imports further east. In fact, the BNSF yard was affected by the lockout at the ports in 2002, though it took thirty days before the impact was felt. "Once it hit, it hit hard." Their peak volumes in 2002 shifted from October to November. This suggests that goods from the ports are normally transloaded before coming to this facility, accounting for the time lag. Another piece of evidence that imports move through this facility is that its growth has mirrored the growth in international trade.

Brendza, an experienced railroad employee, had some comments on the Alameda Corridor. He had read a report that it was being underutilized: "Boxes often go to a place like Cal Cartage [the largest drayage company], where they are re-stuffed and then driven to Hobart. About 60 percent of imports handled by BNSF go to Hobart. On-dock rail loading just isn't that efficient for us. We need another ICTF. There isn't enough capacity on-dock. Some terminals have sufficient space, like Maersk and K-Line, but it uses too much land. It takes too long to load a train to make it that efficient to do on-dock. In fact, 30 percent on dock is probably the most efficient level."

There has been talk about developing an inland port, using rail and replacing trucking as a means of solving the twin social issues of pollution and congestion. Brendza commented on the economics of the situation: "You can get a truck quicker to Ontario than a train, and over such a short haul the train would be more expensive." In addition to problems of rates and speed, there is also an issue of rail capacity. "There is nothing in the marketplace that would support short-haul intermodal," a sentiment that we heard in various forms from a number of railroad employees. "Only government incentives could make it work."

UPS is the BNSF's largest customer, followed by J. B. Hunt. They run a train to Alliance, Texas, near Fort Worth, called the Alliance Train. They have a contract with J. B. Hunt that guarantees arrival in forty-eight hours, which is faster that any truck can move. They call it the J. B. Hunt train. The BNSF has a partnership with J. B. Hunt, which maintains a yard on their San Bernardino property. And Yellow has a property right next to their yard. The contracts with trucking companies are typically short-term, so by having J. B. Hunt as a partner and Yellow nearby—they can convert a short-term relationship into a long-term one. The BNSF also has a relationship with Maersk, which is an anchor tenant at their new logistics park in Chicago.

According to Brendza, "The railroad companies provide wholesale transportation. They sell it cheaply to the trucking companies, providing them with bulk rates. The trucking companies do logistics while the railroads do not, which is why we end up selling transportation wholesale. This facility emphasizes high speed and quality service—and charges for it. They provide the fastest route to Chicago and get paid a premium for it. This is their niche relative to the UP."

When we asked Brendza about the role of the giant mass retailers in transportation, he commented: "They are driving the industry. They drive transportation and logistics. I went to a meeting where Wal-Mart was making a presentation. They were talking in billions of dollars, and pointed to something as a rounding error. Their rounding error was more than our net worth! One of these days, they may decide to buy a railroad. UPS has similar economic clout."

Intersection between the Railroads and Trucking. Following up on the interview with Brendza, we met with Josh Loar of J. B. Hunt, Operations Manager of the facility in the BNSF yard in San Bernardino. This facility only does intermodal work: they load and unload domestic containers and trailers to and from trains. Hunt has an over-the-road (OTR) division. They also maintain a facility in South Gate that also does intermodal work and is more directly linked to the ports. While the San Bernardino facility was affected by the 2002 lockout, the South Gate facility was hit even harder by it, losing 30 to 35 percent of its business.

Loar reported that Hunt is switching more work to intermodal. Intermodal used to be much more difficult, because you had to load and unload trains when you switched between companies. Now the railroads are cooperating more with each other and developing interchanges. They have interchange agreements and special interchange lanes. This allows them to change engines without unloading the train. UP and BNSF do not have such an agreement. Occasionally they will use each other's engines, but at great expense. Interchange agreements allow for no charge. Since the BNSF railroad does much more intermodal work than UP (UP focuses more on the hauling of bulk freight), it has more at stake in the agreement.

A significant amount of Hunt's work from this facility is retailer-based. They do work for Wal-Mart, Target, Kohl's, and J.C. Penney as well as smaller retailers. Wal-Mart is their biggest customer. Loar described how the big retailers handle their imports:

> The big retailers bring the sea containers to downtown LA, where they cross-dock. Then the imports get sent here in domestic containers and trailers. For example, Wal-Mart uses USF in Irwindale. USF is a 3PL that runs the operation for Wal-Mart. There are sixty doors on each side of the building, and trucks are lined up on both sides. They go from there to Wal-Mart's major DCs all over the country. Hudd, in the City of Industry, is another cross-dock facility that works for Wal-Mart. It used to be DSL. There was also a DSL is South Gate that now is Hudd. Wal-Mart also has an import DC in Mira Loma. USF tenders loads to us and we put them on a train. We pick them up and deliver them to Wal-Mart DCs. USF handles both domestic and import freight and was less affected by the ports lockout than was Hudd, which overwhelmingly received ocean containers.

Loar noted that the big retailers want to turn the ocean container around as quickly as possible and send it back to the steamship line. The smaller warehouses in Ontario may receive the ocean container directly. Then they have ten days to unload it and return it to the steamship line.

Loar reported that Hunt commits twelve hundred containers a week to Wal-Mart. The provisions are in Hunt's contract with them. There can be exceptions, in which case it costs them an additional amount:

> Basically we have locked up what we provide and what they will pay. It is all done through our corporate office. We have a yearly contract. Wal-Mart gives us a lane to cover, like San Bernardino to Dallas, from one distribution center to another. These lanes are put up for bid every year. There are some lanes we don't want because there is no freight coming back. We'll only take those if the shipper pays extra. We discuss with them if we plan to use intermodal. It is part of the negotiating process. They know when we use rail because of the cost difference. Generally OTR is 30 percent more expensive, for example, $1 per mile by train and $1.35 to $1.45 per mile by truck. Of course, Wal-Mart gets a volume discount. There are individual differences in rates depending on where the freight is going and how far the destination is from the rail ramp, etc.

The closeness of the relationship with Wal-Mart is revealed in the response to the ports lockout. "During the strike [*sic*] we had daily meetings regarding the ports. It was felt to be a crisis. We met regularly with Wal-Mart. Everyone was wondering when Bush would intervene." These kinds of deals and contracts are probably common in this industry, with shippers and carriers establishing somewhat stable relationships in what looks like a crazy quilt of criss-crossing networks.

WHERE DOES THE CARGO GO?

How much of the freight that arrives at the ports of LA/LB actually remains in the local area? This question is relevant in part because it relates to the continued attraction of the ports. If a good deal of the cargo remains in the region, then LA/LB will likely continue as a major hub regardless of the threatened changes discussed in chapter 3.

The figure that gets mentioned a lot is 50–50, that is, 50 percent of the goods that come through the ports of LA/LB remain in the basin and the other 50 percent move by intermodal transportation to the rest of the country. These figures are based on an estimate of the proportion of ocean containers that are put on rail. If an ocean container is put on a train, it is certainly leaving Southern California for points east. The unstated assumption is that, if the container is not put on rail, the goods in it are going to remain in Southern California (Meyer, Mohaddes, and Associates 2001, 25).

Types of Freight Movement

The story is, of course, far more complicated than this simple picture. The freight that arrives at the ports can be moved in a variety of ways:

1. Put on on-dock railroad and shipped East using the Alameda Corridor
2. Drayed by truck to railheads, either near the docks (ICTF) or at the downtown rail yards
3. Drayed by truck to local warehouses, where it:
    a. Stays in the basin
    b. Is transloaded into domestic containers or trailers for shipment East by rail or truck
4. Drayed by truck to the Inland Empire (Ontario), where it:
    a. Goes back into the basin
    b. Gets shipped to the broader Western United States by rail or truck

Thus, of the containers that are not put on trains either on dock or by being drayed to the local railheads, a certain (unknown) proportion can be transloaded for shipment East. Transloading involves emptying the ocean container and repacking its contents into other kinds of containers, namely domestic containers (also boxes without wheels) or trailers (the back part of trucks, with wheels attached). Either of these can be moved by truck (the container can be put on a chassis, or the trailer can by attached to a tractor) or by train (domestic containers can be double-stacked on railroads like ocean containers, and trailers can be put on railroad flatcars). Domestic containers and trailers are typically larger than the ocean boxes. As we have seen, most ocean containers are forty feet long, with a minority extending to forty-five feet. U.S. trailers can be fifty-three feet long.

Transloading occurs in the LA basin even when the commodities are being sent back East for a number of reasons. First, when the ocean container is shipped East, it takes some time for it to find its way back to the West Coast and to the steamship line that owns it. Because imports vastly outnumber exports, containers tend to accumulate in Eastern locations, creating a costly problem for the liners. They can either be shipped back empty, or an attempt can be made to fill them with something that can be sold on the West Coast or exported, both of which are difficult to accomplish. Moreover, if the containers can be emptied immediately in LA, they can be put back into circulation right away, enhancing their economic value to the steamship company, which can lower its container costs.

A second reason for transloading locally arises from the shippers' interests. Of course, smaller shippers must have their goods transloaded locally because they only use parts of containers and they need to be unpacked so that each owner can claim its part of the contents. But even bigger shippers that mainly use full container loads may want to divide up what is in them by city or even by specific warehouse or store of destination. Sorting it all out beforehand saves having to do it later on and may help to avoid unnecessary transporting of goods to places they do not need to go. Packing the goods into the larger domestic containers and trailers can increase efficiency and decrease costs. The Los Angeles basin is filled with ample cross-docking facilities that can provide precisely this service.

One of the reasons that nobody knows what percentage of goods leave Southern California is that when the railroads receive a domestic container or trailer, even if it is filled entirely with imports, they do not know the origin of the goods. They treat such boxes as domestic moves. In other words, at the BNSF Hobart rail yard downtown, some containers and trailers carry imports and some carry domestic items—but the latter may be filled with imports! The BNSF facility in San Bernardino describes itself as handling entirely domestic traffic, even though its outbound cargo could be coming mainly from the ports, if indirectly.

Percentage Estimates

Some people in the industry are well aware of the problem that we do not really know what percent of imports remain in Southern California. Several of our interviewees told us that the real percentages are unknowable. To find them out would require a detailed survey of every shipper in Southern California or, at a minimum, every warehouse that receives imports. Since no one is willing to fund such a study at the moment, the answer remains a mystery. Still, we did ask several people who were well-placed in the industry to try to give us an estimate.

The person whom we found to be most knowledgeable was John E. Wall. Wall has had many years of experience in all facets of the trucking industry, and he follows its developments carefully.

Here are his estimates. He believes that 65 percent of the containers that arrive in the ports are put immediately on rail for intermodal carriage to an inland destination in the United States. Of this 65 percent, 25 percent is put on the railroads on-dock, and 40 percent is drayed to the railheads.

As for the 35 percent that is drayed locally, Wall estimates that 30 percent goes to South Bay and 70 percent to the Inland Empire. In other words, of the grand total, about 10 percent goes to the basin and about 25 percent goes to the Inland Empire. He also estimates that 40 percent of this 35 percent (about 15 percent of the overall total) will move to the transcontinental market (beyond the Rockies) either by train or truck, and 60 percent (about 20 percent of the grand total) remains in the basin. In sum, according to John's estimates, about 80 percent of the freight moves East, but he admits that no one knows. This is a far cry from the 50–50 figure cited above. We think these figures make sense because the Southern California ports serve as a gateway for most of the country. The local market may be big, but it is not nearly big enough to absorb 50 percent of all the imports that flow through the ports.

Meyer, Mohaddes, and Associates give a somewhat different breakdown (2001, 21). They estimate that 45 to 50 percent of containerized cargo moving through the ports of LA/LB is aimed for the Eastern United States. About 35 to 40 percent is put directly on rail either using on-dock or off-dock loading. The difference of around 10 to 15 percent is accounted for by transloaded cargo. Meyer, Mohaddes, and Associates are of the opinion that transloading is a small part of the total volume, but they see it as rising rapidly, for a number of reasons: some of the large importers, especially the retailers, want to postpone their decisions about merchandise mixes for each distribution center, and they gain two weeks if they transload in Southern California instead of packing by detailed destination in Asia; ocean carriers want faster turn times for their containers because they can make more money by sending empty containers back to Asia as quickly as possible for refilling; some steamship lines are deemphasizing landbridge operations in favor of port-to-port agreements with shippers; some new steamship line entrants to the trans-Pacific trade lack the inland connections and are encouraging transloading rather than taking responsibility for door-to-door deliveries; NVOCCs account for a growing proportion of imports, about 37 percent in 2001, and since they tend to offer less-than-containerload (LCL) service, the containers need to be deconsolidated before their contents can be delivered to their consignees. Acknowledging that no one collects data on transloading, Meyer, Mohaddes, and Associates report an estimate of five hundred thousand TEUs for 1998.

WHO CONTROLS THE MOVES?

Ultimately, the transportation of freight is under the control of the shippers, who are the beneficial cargo owners (BOCs). They hire the transportation providers—3PLs or carriers—to move the freight for them. They pay for the transportation and storage services. In this sense, the work is done for them, and they can always get rid of carriers and 3PLs who do not meet their needs.

In practice, the freight transportation system is hierarchically organized and consists of complex and embedded networks. Who actually takes charge of the move is thus a very different question from who has the ultimate control. Shippers can hand the whole process of transportation over to other actors and simply pay an overall rate for the service. Thus, although they are the ultimate employers of transportation services, they may "contract out" this element of their business and let other actors handle it. So the question remains: who controls the moves?

Steamship Lines in Charge. Steamship lines can sign agreements with shippers such that the steamship company takes complete responsibility for the pickup and delivery of the goods, from a factory in Asia to a final warehouse or store in the United States. These kinds of moves are called door-to-door, or store-door, as opposed to port-to-port moves. The liners make arrangements with the other transportation providers for the freight to be moved. The rate that is paid by the shipper to the steamship line covers all of the landside parts of the move as well as the ocean leg of the journey.

The steamship lines will hire harbor drayage companies and play an important role in controlling the terms under which the port truckers work. Not all port trucking companies are employed by steamship companies, but many are. The steamship lines will also employ the railroads and trucking companies and cover the hiring of drayage companies at the other end of the haul.

Generally speaking, if an ocean container is put on rail, either on-dock or after being drayed to an off-dock rail head, it will be shipped across the country under the control of an ocean carrier (Meyer, Mohaddes, and Associates 2001, 24). In addition to providing this service, the major steamship companies have developed their own logistics subsidiaries that can provide more complete logistics services to shippers. The subsidiaries do not just provide services to shippers that are employing that particular liner, they also act in a semi-autonomous capacity to offer logistics services to any shipper that wants to purchase them.

Trucking Companies in Charge. Port-to-port moves afford the opportunity for other types of carriers to take charge of the landside moves, and here trucking companies have taken charge. J. B. Hunt is a good example. The trucking companies (sometimes simply referred to as "carriers," with the steamship lines referred to as "ocean carriers") do not necessarily drive the goods across the country. Indeed, driving ocean containers by truck across the country is rare. If an ocean container remains unpacked, it is much more likely to be shipped by rail. The trucking companies are more likely to haul containers and trailers that have been transloaded. Even so, it is often cheaper for them to put their now-domestic containers and trailers on rail to ship to the East. In other words, the trucking companies employ the cheaper services of the railroads to take over part of the haul. As we have seen, the trucking companies deliver domestic containers and trailers to the railroads and then pick them up at the other end for delivery to the customer—the shipper.

Railroads Not in Control. According to Chuck Potempa of BNSF's Hobart rail yard, the railroads do not develop legal contracts directly with the shippers. They deal with steamship lines and 3PLs (known as IMCs or intermodal marketing companies in the railroad industry) only, not with manufacturers or retailers. In other words, they are somewhere down the hierarchy of control.

Given that the railroads are vital actors in intermodal transportation, why have they not taken charge of freight movement, like the big trucking companies and the steamship lines? The answer seems to lie less in their structural position in the transportation network than in specific management failures. The railroads had some difficult times in terms of their willingness to engage and invest in innovations. They were late to embrace intermodalism and JIT delivery programs. Consequently, they served as an obstacle in the logistics system. Other actors had to take charge and drag the railroads along (Shashikumar and Schatz 2000).

Third Parties in Charge. A large industry of logistics intermediaries has grown up in recent years. These companies vary in their size and coverage. Some are global firms with the capacity to arrange for the movement of freight anywhere in the world. Others are more modest, providing advice and software to shippers who want to make their logistics systems more efficient. Some 3PLs do not own any assets and engage other asset-based companies to do the actual transporting of cargo. Others own parts of the distribution network. They may own and operate warehouses and distribution centers, for example. Or they may own a fleet of trucks and airplanes, as in the case of UPS and FedEx.

Shippers in Charge. Sometimes the shippers, especially the big shippers, take charge of the transportation themselves. This can take a number of forms. First, the shippers can own their own trucks and take over the cargo directly themselves. Second, they can have favored carriers that they ask the steamship lines to use. For example, they can tell the steamship lines which drayage companies to use. They let the steamship lines arrange the entire move, but they express their preferences along the way; of course, these preferences are likely to be taken seriously when the shipper is a major customer. Third, they can claim the cargo at the docks and hire carriers directly to haul it for them.

Some big shippers are experts at logistics and therefore believe—often correctly—that they can organize and implement their logistics systems better than anyone else. They own transportation equipment or hire transportation providers, maintaining tight control over what the carriers do for them.

Changes in the System

Needless to say, the system of freight transportation is in a constant state of change and development. Nothing stands still in this system. As of this writing (early 2007), two prominent "new" trends have emerged.

First, transloading in the LA area, as opposed to shipping ocean containers directly across the country, seems to be on the rise. The steamship lines are apparently discouraging shippers from having the ocean containers shipped directly East by imposing a surcharge on these moves. The reason is that the steamship lines want to get the empty containers back more quickly, so that they can be sent back to Asia and refilled in a timely manner. This shift has apparently affected the Alameda Corridor, which was not seeing the level of rail traffic that was anticipated.

The second trend is that the giant retailers are increasing the practice of picking their goods up in Asia. In other words, rather than having the steamship lines take care of the entire move, the retailers take possession in Asia and buy space on the vessels from there.

The *Journal of Commerce,* along with other trade journals like the *Pacific Shipper,* the *American Shipper,* and the *Cunningham Report,* is filled with changes of this sort. The winds of fashion and the shifting competitive environment mean that companies are continually adjusting their practices. Such shimmers of change can never be fully captured in a book like this. All we can do is portray snippets of it at particular points in time. What we have tried to understand here is the underlying structures around which the smaller adjustments are constantly playing.

COPING WITH THE GROWTH IN TRADE

Massive Congestion of 2004

The peak season of 2004 demonstrated beyond doubt how susceptible the Southern California ports and their landside distribution systems are to being overwhelmed by the growth in trade. Described by the *Los Angeles Times* as "a huge floating traffic jam" (9/27/04; 11/19/04), ships waited outside of the ports to be allowed entrance to a berth where they could be discharged and reloaded. At its peak, on October 11, 2004, ninety-four vessels were lined up outside of the harbor. Once in the dock, turnaround was taking a week or more, longer than the usual time of perhaps four days. Interestingly, this was a *global* phenomenon, with the Panama Canal and ports in Europe facing the same kinds of congestion and delay.

The "crisis," precipitated by an unexpected 10.4 percent increase in traffic over the same period the previous year, brought together the weaknesses in all of the elements of the system. First, there were not enough trained longshore workers to unload the ships quickly enough. Plans had been developed to extend gate hours to cover the night hours, which would certainly have increased the handling capacity of the ports. But terminal operators decided to postpone this move until March 2005 because there was not enough longshore labor to cover the daytime hours.

Second, the railroads did not have enough equipment or personnel to deal with the crush. The Union Pacific was caught unprepared for the surge in volume, indicating that it planned to hire five thousand employees, mainly in the Southwest, and add seven hundred locomotives and sixty-five hundred freight cars by the end of 2004 and lay $225 million of new track. The BNSF had similar plans, including laying a third line near the Cajon Pass, where the railroad shares tracks with Amtrak and Metrolink.

Third, there appeared to be a shortage of port truckers, as delays proved too costly to the drivers. According to an executive of a port trucking company, 10 percent of his three hundred trucks were idle because he could not find drivers willing to put up with the delays. "We can't compensate the drivers for all of this waiting time, and it's been hard to recoup their own internal costs. . . . This is the worst I have ever seen it." Another stated: "As we continue to shrink in drivers, the import volume is peaking. The driver comes to the gate at 7 a.m., can't get in until 9 a.m. and then can't find the container they are supposed to pick up." An informal survey by the Marine Exchange of Southern California found that hundreds of drivers had quit. (These items were reported in the *Los Angeles Times* by Ronald D. White and Leslie Earnest, "Delays Mount at Local Ports as Shipping Surges," 9/27/04, C1, C5.)

Shippers, especially the giant retailers, were faced with the prospect that the goods they had ordered would not appear on the shelves in time for the Christmas season. Some diverted their cargo to other West Coast ports or to all-water routes. From July through mid-November 2004, over a hundred ships were diverted to Oakland, Manzanillo, and other ports (see Ronald D. White, "L.A. Ports Unclogged but Not in the Clear," *Los Angeles Times*, 11/19/04, C1,C4). But these alternatives could not fully alleviate the congestion, and giant container ships continued to wait outside the harbor for their turn to dock.

By mid-November 2004, the congestion had eased, and sixty ships were in their normal process of being discharged and reloaded. But retailers were assessing the harm they had experienced from delays and added costs, and some were deciding to change their port usage permanently.

The ports of LA/LB were contemplating how to reassure their customers that the problems would be solved.

This state of affairs affected not only the shippers but also the steamship lines, which lost money by having their ships stranded, unable to return quickly to Asia to pick up the next load of freight. They also faced added fuel costs from having to sail faster across the ocean to try to make up for lost time.

Smoother Sailing, for Now?

As a result of this traumatic experience, various changes were instituted. More ILWU and rail personnel were employed, for example. A system for extending gate hours into the night and on Saturdays, known as PierPASS, was implemented, starting July 23, 2005. The basic idea behind the program was to charge forty dollars per TEU and eighty dollars per FEU for containers that were picked up or delivered during regular daytime hours. For these and other reasons, traffic moved smoothly through the ports in peak seasons of 2005 and 2006.

The ports of LA/LB and their surrounding logistics systems were warily watched for any signs of a repeat. Undoubtedly some companies continued to divert cargo to other ports, just in case. And some brought in goods early, afraid that if they waited until peak season, they might get stuck. As a result, peak season was less marked, and traffic flows seemed to be flatter over the course of the year.

Everyone anticipates continued massive growth in trade, especially containerized imports from Asia, and that the ports of LA/LB will have to absorb a goodly portion of it. No one knows for sure whether these projections are accurate, but certainly many believe them. In the short run, at least, they seem to be coming true. Local problems of congestion and pollution are already serious without any additional rise in imports. The ports are located on the edge of a large urban area. Cargo must be moved through the area using the same roads and rail lines that are used for other purposes, including passenger transit. These transit systems are already stressed, so that added trucks and freight trains threaten the system with potential gridlock.

Politicians, public agencies, and industry members hope to gain federal aid for infrastructure projects. They argue, not without merit, that the ports serve the *national* economy and that the Los Angeles region is forced to bear many of the costs at a local level. Since the ports are really serving a national purpose, the federal government has an obligation to help mitigate the local effects by helping to pay for better surface transportation, including expanded roads and railroads.

But cries for increased infrastructure spending meet with resistance in Washington, D.C. First of all, the federal government is engaged in a costly war in Iraq and is building up unprecedented deficits. It can ill afford costly transportation projects, and the amount budgeted to cover major needs all over the country is a small fraction of what is required. This situation is exacerbated by new demands for security, an added expense to an already strained system.

The word out of Washington is clear—costly infrastructure projects will not be funded until the ports and cities use the resources they have to maximum efficiency. This means that the pressure is on to improve operations. The Waterfront Coalition has played a key role in calling for a variety of reforms. In May 2005 they put out a report calling for improvements in the container transportation system, with a host of practical suggestions.

Where will the money for needed investment in upgrading the infrastructure come from? Various proposals keep sprouting up, including proposals for an inland port, and a variety of forms of funding are proposed, from charging shippers for infrastructure improvements to developing large public-private projects similar to the Alameda Corridor. But a fundamental contradiction lies at the heart of this issue, a clash between the public goods of cleaner air and less congested highways and the private interests of shippers, who want quick and cheap transportation and can make the case that their customers want—indeed, demand—the associated lower prices. The problem is that without public funding for the socially desirable outcome, will shippers volunteer to pay more for less to serve the public good? Again, the answer is that it is unlikely. Can local, regional, and state government, as protectors of the public interest, intervene? Possibly, but the industry is united in its fierce opposition to government intervention. Members keep saying, "If we don't solve these problems ourselves, the government will step in and force a solution on us that we won't like," or words to that effect. So they continue to struggle to find a solution.

CHAPTER 6

Warehouses and Distribution Centers

Warehousing is a central supply chain function.[1] Goods must be unpacked, sorted, stored, repacked, and sent out to their correct destinations. Sometimes warehousing involves more than these basic functions. It can entail value-added processes, such as simple assembly, checking for errors and correcting them, and making the goods store-ready. Warehouses and distribution centers (DCs) serve as nodes in the supply chain where the state of inventory is assessed and from which replenishment orders are placed. They are vital to the entire process of moving the goods.

The logistics revolution has changed the character of warehousing. In the old days of "push" production, warehouses served primarily as storage facilities. Goods were made in large batches and stored in warehouses until they were ordered. The modern warehouse and DC, based on "pull" production, aims to minimize the amount of inventory and maximize the flow of goods so that they sit in storage for as little time as possible. The goal is to have goods arrive and depart on a just-in-time (JIT) or as-needed basis. In practice, this goal is rarely achieved in its ideal form, and goods are still stored in large numbers. Nevertheless, today's warehouses and DCs are constantly being reoriented toward perfecting a constant-flow model.

In practice, the warehouse and DC are the central location where "pull" production is made to function. This is where JIT delivery is implemented. The warehouse or DC sits at the nexus between production and distribution, where it serves as a conduit both for information about supply and

[1]Rebecca Giem participated in much of this research, helping to set up interviews and assisting with them. She took the initiative to look into the temp agency industry and helped significantly with the development of contacts in the real estate industry.

demand and makes sure that the balance between them is as accurate and current as possible. Without a good warehousing program, a company has little chance of participating in "lean" retailing.

In Southern California, the most striking warehouse and DC development is the huge complex that has grown up in the western part of the Inland Empire (San Bernardino and Riverside Counties). The giant warehouses that make up this complex lie just to the east of Los Angeles County, within easy driving distance of the ports. The bulk of our research focused on the Inland Empire, but before we turn to that, let us look at the general developments in warehousing in the wake of the logistics revolution.

WAREHOUSING AND DISTRIBUTION CENTER DEVELOPMENTS

Warehouses versus Distribution Centers?

"A distribution center is the antithesis of a warehouse," say Abernathy et al. (1999, 63). They argue that warehouses are primarily storage facilities, whereas DCs are far more active in linking retailers and their suppliers. Because DCs require less storage space, they are smaller than traditional warehouses. They have much higher levels of capital investment, while needing fewer employees, who are more highly skilled in dealing with electronic equipment; capital intensity per worker is much higher in a DC than in a warehouse (63–69).

Rather than focus on the storage of goods, as in the old warehouses, the new DCs engage in two major functions. First, they cross-dock, which means that when a truck arrives at the DC, it is immediately unloaded, the goods are sorted on to conveyor belts depending on their destinations, and trucks are lined up on the other side to receive the packages and get on the road right away rather than sit around in a warehouse. Second, they unpack, sort, and repackage goods to meet the requirements for specified shipments, which is described as a "value-added" function. Abernathy et al. estimate that a major DC of a big retailer cross-docks about 60 to 70 percent of its incoming containers per day, while 30 to 40 percent stay to be processed (1999, 65).

Unfortunately, this sharply drawn contrast is not borne out in practice, at least in Southern California, and we found that here the terms *warehouse* and *DC* are used interchangeably. One can find cross-docking facilities, which come close to the ideal description of the DC. But generally these businesses include both storage and cross-docking functions in different combinations. The mixing of the terms reflects the mixed reality.

Nevertheless, there is truth in the claim that warehousing has changed drastically in recent years such that, whatever we call these entities, they have been transformed as a product of the logistics revolution. As Abernathy et al. point out, the new type of DC or warehouse plays a central role in lean retailing (1999, 65).

Recent Changes in Warehousing

The basic functions performed by warehouses are fourfold: receiving goods from a source, storing goods until they are required, picking goods when they are needed, and shipping goods to the next (or final) user. Despite tremendous innovations, these basic functions have not changed (Tompkins and Smith 1998).

Warehousing has traditionally been thought of as a required cost that adds no value to a company's operations. It has been viewed as a necessary evil. The logistics revolution has challenged this conception, viewing "having the right product in the right place at the right time" as an important value-adding function. Once it is accepted that warehousing is vital to a company's achieving its goals, a more scientific approach to it can be taken. Warehousing has now come to be defined as a central logistics function that deserves full attention (Tompkins and Smith 1998, 5).

Warehouses fall into three types: private, public, and contract. Private warehouses are those that are operated by the company that owns the product. The building itself may be owned or leased, but the warehouse is run by the company. Public warehouses are available for hire on a short- or long-term basis and typically have multiple customers at the same time. They may be specialized to deal with certain kinds of commodities or functions, such as refrigerated warehouses or bonded warehouses, which are licensed by the government to store goods prior to the payment of taxes or customs duties. General merchandise warehouses handle packaged goods. Contract warehousing relies on a long-term contractual relationship with a customer or limited set of customers. These warehouses are run by third-party logistics companies (3PLs), which can offer transportation and other logistics services (Bowersox, Closs, and Cooper 2002, 393–96).

It is not our purpose to delve into the details of the science of warehousing.[2] However, some of the new features associated with the logistics revolution should be noted. As we pointed out in part 1 of this book, product proliferation has caused the number of SKUs to skyrocket. Add to this increased customization to satisfy the demand for variety, and it becomes evident that the modern warehouse has to be much more flexible and agile than a simple storage facility. Another change is the demand for reduction in lead times, shorter product lives, and increased inventory turnover, which

---

[2]Tompkins and Smith (1998) is an almost thousand-page tome that examines the details of warehousing and how it should be managed. Other such textbooks are also available.

are linked to such management philosophies as Quick Response and JIT (Tompkins and Smith 1998, 6–7).

Increasingly, stores need constant shipments. The flagship store of a major department store requires deliveries from eight trucks a night during a typical week, and anywhere from ten to thirty a week during peak season. A single state-of-the-art cross-docking facility for a retailer can handle up to seventy thousand containers and pallets each day of varying size, weight, and fragility. It can load and unload fifty to seventy-five trucks at a time. Back in 1995, a typical Wal-Mart DC served about 150 stores within a 200-mile radius, each of which received about five deliveries per week. In that year, Wal-Mart's own trucks delivered over 688,000 trailer loads from its DCs to its retailer stores (Abernathy et al. 1999, 64–65). These numbers are considerably bigger today.

We interviewed Steve Harrington, president of the Distribution Management Association of Southern California (DMA), an organization of warehouse operators, and he was exceedingly helpful in explaining warehousing to us: "Inventory turns are important in the warehousing business. If you have twelve turns that means you turn the building over once a month. The average used to be four to six, maybe eight. Now if it isn't ten to twelve, you are considered to be doing a poor job. Good operations have twenty-six turns. They turn the entire building over every two weeks." This means that you need half the space, which translates into lower fixed costs, leaving more capital available.

Another change concerns the order-to-cash cycle, which is the time from when a manufacturer ships to a retailer, to the time it gets paid. The goal is to lower the time of this cycle, which greatly affects the warehousing function. Harrington's parent company, a manufacturer of private label pharmaceuticals, for which he runs the Southern California DC, used to have a cycle of fifty-eight days, which it managed to reduce to forty over a period of two years: "The manufacturer has to send in an accurate invoice. Whenever there is any issue, the retailers play a game of challenging you and delaying the payment. Say they have forty days to pay you. If they can sell it in two to three weeks, then they have all that money in the bank earning interest. And if it is $10 million, they are making a lot of money, especially if they are selling on paper-thin margins."[3]

For this reason, Harrington's company is always working to improve its order-to-cash cycle. Using bar-coding technology, DCs are able to handle huge amounts of data, and they, rather than the retail store, become the locus of inventory control. As a result, when a truckload arrives at a store, it is unnecessary for the staff to engage in inventory checking, which used

[3]We came across this issue in a description of "the bank of Wal-Mart," where Wal-Mart makes considerable money off of the discrepancy between the time of sale and the time they pay their suppliers.

to take days and lots of labor. Instead, the ideal is that the goods move rapidly from the truck to the sales floor. This means that the goods should be "floor ready" when they arrive, a requirement that sometimes involves the DC in value-added processing, as we shall see. These features of lean retailing increase both the speed and the accuracy of deliveries (Abernathy et al. 1999, 68–69).

Warehouses are no longer viewed as independent operations but as an important part of the overall logistics strategy of the firm, where the goal is to minimize the cost of product delivery while still providing excellent customer service. Because of this heightened emphasis on the importance of warehousing, third parties (3PLs) have increased their role in this part of the logistics chain. The 3PL may organize the entire logistics system for a company as well as running its warehouses and DCs (Tompkins and Smith 1998, 6–7).

According to a survey of manufacturers regarding their use of 3PLs, warehousing management was chosen most frequently as the most beneficial company function to outsource to a 3PL (Lieb and Hickey 2003a, b). Manufacturers who operate their own warehouses have to deal with all the costs associated with owning real estate as well as the wages and benefits of employees. Moreover, according to a *JoC* article by William Armbruster called "Stacking Up," older warehouses owned by manufacturers are often located in places with poorer transportation connections than those provided by a 3PL (12/1/03, 18–20).

Sometimes 3PLs operate warehouses for multiple clients. However, they may also run dedicated warehouses for a single customer. Under these circumstances, the 3PL is likely to demand a long-term contract. Dedicated (or contract) warehouses are especially common among the giant importers that are the focus of this book.

Value-Added Functions

The 3PL-managed warehouses of today can engage in many more functions than simply receiving, storing, picking, and shipping goods. They can also perform multiple "value-added" functions (Bowersox, Closs, and Cooper 2002). Steve Harrington of the DMA discussed three important recent value-added innovations in warehousing.

Postponement. Steve gave the following example: "Let's say we are making private label aspirin for Wal-Mart and Longs Drugs. It's all the same product, with a Wal-Mart label for Wal-Mart and a Longs label for Longs. There is no need to label the bottles until the orders come in. That way you can balance your stock needs better." This is called a "bright stock" operation. Bright stock is defined as generic stock waiting to be customized. Another example is unpainted car parts that can be painted whatever color the customer wants. Customizing bright stock is one of the value-added functions performed by DCs.

Another example is canned foods, which can be sent to the warehouse in "brights"—cans without labels. When an order for a specific label is received, the warehouse puts the label on the right number of cans and finishes the packaging (Bowersox, Closs, and Cooper 2002, 384). These examples may demonstrate the increased efficiency connected with improved logistics and modernized warehousing, but they also show that many of the apparent "choices" offered to consumers are only label-deep.

Displays. Harrington gave another example from his company, which sells to various retailers. At Vons, one of their customers, they have pre-built displays. The producer puts a group of products together in a cardboard display as a promotion. They would be set up at the end of an aisle. The DC assembles the displays and ships them that way. This way you don't have to send six to eight items separately. Hershey's, for example, will have a display of candies on a disposable pallet. It will be set at hip level near the entrance of the store. Gatorade does something similar, and Costco does a lot of these displays too. The store does not have to handle anything.

Cross-Docking. Harrington described examples of cross-docking in the Inland Empire:

> New Balance has a conveyor belt system, which is put in transit by EDI (electronic data interchange). Every box has a UPC bar on it (bar-coding). When they empty a container, they scan four thousand boxes, using a sidebar scanner. This eliminates all manual paperwork. It sends an electronic message back to the sender of the goods, telling them they have arrived so that the DC can send them the invoice. Now the boxes can move straight to the waiting dock.

Other companies that do this include Target and Toys "R" Us, though most do it to some extent. FedEx and UPS have huge sorting facilities. Every box has a bar code, which is scanned into the computer. At FedEx the building is shaped like a T. At the bar end there are fifty-four doors with fifty-four trucks, each headed for a different zip code. The goods come to the trucks on conveyor belts.

Another company that uses cross-docking extensively is Costco. We spoke with Dale Stephens, Costco's traffic manager. He told us that Costco brings imports into the United States in two major ways. They purchase goods in Asia and then contract with a steamship company for port-to-door delivery. They call this "buying collect." Or they deal with U.S. vendors who have imported the goods themselves, getting the goods from their domestic DCs. This they call "prepaid," because the vendor has already paid for the transportation.

According to Stephens, Costco does not store product in their DCs. It only passes through them, and it is all cross-docked. The goods arrive in containers, are palletized at the DC, and leave the DC on pallets. There are minor exceptions, like some pharmaceuticals, which may move by the case. Stephens continued:

> We call our DCs depots. The goods are shipped out of the depot the night they arrive. They go straight from the depot to the store. We try not to handle the goods, which move from container to pallet to the store to the consumer. Most of this happens on the same day. They start at 2 to 3 a.m. moving the containers to the DCs, and the pallets are out by 8 to 9 p.m. Then they are delivered to the stores by the next morning. All the depots are regional, serving a regional market. We have three on the West Coast: in Tacoma, Oakland, and LA.

Costco does not use 3PLs, according to Stephens: "We think we know what we're doing, so we don't use them. They are just another middleman and incur extra expense."

Some warehouse-managing 3PLs are expanding their services to cover transportation, while some traditional transportation companies, including steamship lines, are acquiring firms that specialize in warehousing in order to expand their logistics services. Given that warehousing appears to be the most beneficially outsourced function, it has become of central importance to logistics companies who want to provide full-package services to their customers, according to the Armbruster article cited above.

Technological Development

New technology, new organization, and new management techniques have been applied to warehousing to make it more efficient. Bar-coding and EDI are examples of new technology. Warehouse facilities can be equipped with conveyor belts so that large parts of the process of selecting and moving goods can be automated. They can also make use of automated "pick and pack" systems, and of wire-guided forklifts. Warehouse buildings have changed as a result. They used to be multi-level structures with low ceilings and a limited number of shipping and receiving doors. Now they are huge single-story spaces with lofty ceilings and shelves that tower above. They require larger and larger parcels of land, which helps to explain the movement out to the Inland Empire in Southern California (Willis et al. 2003, 74–75).

For years, the major technological advance in warehousing involved bar-coding. This enabled goods, cartons, and pallets to be scanned into a computer system for tracking and forwarding. But now, led by Wal-Mart, a new technology, radio-frequency identification (RFID), has been introduced. RFID uses a tag with a ninety-six-bit product code, which contains considerably more information than the bar code. Wal-Mart expected that RFID would allow the retailer to cut inventory by 5 percent, limit out-of-stock merchandise, and lower labor costs in both their stores and their warehouses. It expected warehouse labor costs to drop by 7 percent, because RFID allows for the scanning of tags through cardboard, so that pallets do not have to be broken down when they enter a warehouse. According to a *JoC* article in called "The Race for RFID," by Tony Seideman, it is also possible to identify what has arrived in trucks before unloading them (12/1/03, 16–18).

RFID improves the tracking of goods at all stages of transportation, increasing visibility throughout the supply chain. But introducing it is costly. Seideman reports estimates that large retailers would have to pay $100,000 per retail store and $400,000 per DC. Overall, implementing RFID in a company the size of Wal-Mart would cost $35 to $40 million.

A more sinister side of this new technology is that it enables employers to keep closer track of what their employees are doing. Seideman presents a business perspective on this aspect: "Although some employees may feel spied upon, the new software can actually improve morale by allowing companies to set up bonuses for those who perform exceptionally well." We can certainly quibble with an interpretation that claims that increasing competition between employees is good for morale, but that is not our main concern here.

Some businesses believed that Wal-Mart was moving too quickly on RFID. The new technology requires the replacement of costly investments in bar-coding infrastructure and compels manufacturers, warehouses, ports, and transportation firms to maintain both technologies for a significant period. Moreover, there are lots of glitches in the form of incompatibilities between the systems that currently exist around the world.

Although warehouse management has become much more sophisticated, it is still not well integrated with container and shipment tracking. In other words, warehouse and transportation software have yet to be integrated. Seideman refers to these as "stovepipes of logistics technology," meaning that they stand separately, though efforts are definitely being made to integrate them. According to an industry consultant quoted by Seideman: "Visibility to SKU level across the supply chain is key to increasing efficiencies, improving customer satisfaction, and increasing order velocity."

WAREHOUSING AND DISTRIBUTION CENTERS IN LOS ANGELES COUNTY

Before turning to the Inland Empire DC development, let us briefly consider warehousing in Los Angeles County. Needless to say, there are thousands of warehouses in LA County, and there are a great many even if we limit ourselves to port-related warehouses. These warehouses and DCs often serve the function of first handling imports. They may, for example, transload the contents of ocean containers to domestic containers and trailers, enabling the ocean containers to get back into immediate trans-Pacific carriage. They may also provide for trucking to the next point of destination. Some of them provide cross-docking facilities, while others may engage in some storage or limited value-added activities.

We conducted interviews at a couple of these LA warehouses, although we unfortunately were not able to get into the topic in much depth. Further, the people we interviewed did not want their names or companies revealed. So here, in a general sense, is what we found:

One of the warehouses was run by a logistics subsidiary of a steamship line. We interviewed the representative in 2002. The warehousing firm was a strictly local company that was bought by the steamship line but now works closely with the logistics subsidiary. The warehousing firm ran a number of distribution facilities in Los Angeles. The site where we met the informant was located in South Los Angeles, near the Long Beach Freeway (Interstate 710). The company engaged in transloading here, emptying containers, and loading the goods into truck trailers. This allows for "postponement," providing flexibility for the shipper (BOC) to send the goods to different specific locations at the last minute, as needed. This is the kind of thing that the giant retailers want to be able to do.

The logistics company charged a "cargo management fee" to its customers for information services, EDI, warehousing, and so on: "EDI is huge. We send an advance shipping notice to the customer as soon as the ship leaves the port in Asia. The big companies, like Wal-Mart and Target, demand it. You have to provide them with all the information electronically." This company dealt with Wal-Mart, Target, Federated Department Stores, Nike, Liz Claiborne, and lots of apparel companies. They provided GOH—"garment on hanger," which means they were doing value-added work.

Despite his comment that "EDI is huge" this person also stated: "EDI hasn't taken off like it should. The products that are being made in Asia are all bar coded, so we ought to be ready to go with EDI, but there are a lot of software issues that haven't been resolved. So there is not much EDI or automated distribution." This appears to be a general finding—the ideal of a perfectly automated warehouse operation was rarely met in practice.

Our source gave us a tour of the warehouse, a recent acquisition of the company. The most striking feature was that there were twenty-six miles of conveyor belts that had never been used and were completely rusty. Work was going on between them, while they served as gigantic obstacles. According to our source, "The whole thing was set up so that, when the containers arrived, the goods would be unloaded and immediately scanned, using the bar codes. Then they were either prepared for their destination or stored for easy and quick rehandling. The belts move up to the ceiling, and there is another floor on top for storage. There are two kinds of cross-docking: ACD and MCD, or automated and manual cross-docking."

It is hard to express the impression that this warehouse made on us. This was a state-of-the-art facility, which had obviously required considerable capital investment, and no one was using it. Despite the fanciest technology, it was more efficient to simply hire workers to move the boxes around. The current owner had not yet decided what to do with this facility at the time of the interview.

The basic functions being performed at this location were deconsolidation and transloading. This is a U.S. Customs–bonded container freight station (CFS), which means that the goods do not have to clear customs before they are brought here. The ships arrive at the ports over the weekend, and the containers are brought directly here. Once here they are handled in two ways: they get a PT (permission to transfer) or an IT (immediate transfer). With the former, you clear customs at this site. With IT the goods are cleared by customs at their destination.

The second interview was also conducted in 2002 with the director of logistics services for a company that does harbor drayage, among other things. We met at one of their facilities in Wilmington, a community near the ports. This facility is also customs-bonded, meaning that, for up to thirty days, or about twenty-one days after the ship's departure, a company (BOC) can leave its containers here without clearing customs, and they can clear customs at this facility. The NVOs (non-vessel operating common carriers), also known as OTIs (ocean transportation intermediaries)—in other words, the companies that are handling the freight of a customer— can split out the cargo here and then have it cleared by customs. This is what is meant by cargo (or container) freight station bonding. The facility also provides bonded warehousing; for example, an importer of liquor can leave it indefinitely here and only pay duty on it when they move it out.

This site was also a foreign trade zone, or FTZ. As our guide explained it:

This means that the goods have not yet entered the commerce of the United States. The FTZ enables firms to manipulate cargo. For example, if the duty rate on auto parts is 10 percent, and on completed autos is 6 percent, the importer can assemble cars in an FTZ, and only pay duty on the completed auto. Another example involved jackets imported by Wal-Mart. Wal-Mart did not want to take possession of them, so they were sold to a Chilean company. The warehousing firm took out the Wal-Mart labels and sewed in the Chilean ones. They were exported and no one had to pay duty for their coming into the United States.

The company that granted us this interview and tour was engaged in warehousing, deconsolidation, and trucking. Our respondent clarified that transloading and deconsolidation are not the same thing. Transloading refers to the transferring of the cargo from one mode of transportation to another, for example from an ocean container to a rail car, while deconsolidation means the unloading of a container and dividing its contents up either for different towns or different destinations.

In general, LA County is running out of land for large warehouses, especially near the ports. Land is just too expensive in LA, and it can be impossible to put together large enough packages of land. As a result, LA warehouses and DCs tend to be older and smaller than those in the Inland Empire.

WAREHOUSING IN THE INLAND EMPIRE

The West End of the Inland Empire, centered on the city of Ontario, has become a major warehousing and DC area for Southern California in recent years. The Inland Empire consists of two large counties, San Bernardino and Riverside, that stretch across California to the Nevada border. So the West End lies to the immediate east of Los Angeles County. The DCs that have been developed there are thus perched on the edge of LA County, ready to have goods trucked to them from the ports, which are about fifty miles away.

Anyone driving east or west along Route 60 (the Pomona Freeway) can see DCs as they approach Route 15. They are the huge windowless structures that stretch both north and south of the freeway. To get the full flavor, one should drive up or down Route 15 and exit anywhere. As far as the eye can see in every direction are these giant warehousing structures. The atmosphere is like a moonscape, with no visible human beings on the streets. The lack of windows contributes to the alien character of the landscape. Near the edges of this development are dairy farms and vineyards, which have clearly been pushed off the land by the more lucrative DCs. It is strange indeed to see cows grazing right next to these outsized temples of world trade.

Logistics in the Inland Empire

The Inland Empire is promoting itself as a logistics center. The Inland Empire Economic Partnership (IEEP), a promotional organization, describes the region's logistics industry as follows: "The Inland Empire region, comprised of Riverside and San Bernardino counties, has leveraged Southern California's transportation infrastructure as well as the region's growing base of skilled workers and affordable real estate to become the center of the logistics industry expansion." The IEEP's website lists some of the Fortune 500 companies that have established warehouses there: Wal-Mart Stores, Home Depot, Target, Costco Wholesale, Sears, Walgreens, United Parcel Service, Lowe's, FedEx, Anheuser-Busch, Staples, Kohl's, Toys "R" Us, Black and Decker, Fisher Scientific International, Big Lots, and Ross Stores (see www.ieep.com). This impressive list, heavy in big box retailers, is only a small sampling of the number of DCs in the region.

John E. Husing is a leading economist of the Inland Empire who puts out the *Inland Empire Quarterly Economic Report*. In the July 2005 edition, he pointed out that wholesale and distribution (logistics) grew from 79,320 jobs in the Inland Empire in 2000 to 96,440 in 2005, a gain of 17,120 jobs. The average pay for these jobs was $40,290 in 2004. Husing also reported that one estimate of the number of truck trips bringing containers from the ports to inland facilities and driving back was 1.28 million in 2004. The IEEP also reports that "nearly all of Southern California's major trucking companies including JB Hunt Transport Inc, Swift Transportation, Yellow Freight Systems, Roadway Express, UPS and Federal Express have . . . established cross-dock hubs in the area."

In a report for the second quarter of 2005, Grubb and Ellis, a real estate firm, reported that the vacancy rate had been dropping, leading to more construction, especially along the I-215 corridor (north and south of I-60). New building was going up on the western part of the former March Airforce Base, and Ross Stores had moved into a new DC in the Moreno Valley. "With China's exports forecasted to increase 1,600 percent within 15 years and the numbers of containers passing though Los Angeles' ports to hit 32 million by 2025, job creation in the logistics sector is inevitable." These kinds of real estate reports, which are put out by all of the major real estate firms in the area, show ebbs and flows in the growth and spread of warehousing in the area.

Reasons for Location in the Inland Empire

Location decisions for distribution centers depend on the availability of relatively low-cost land as well as skilled and relatively low-cost labor; easy access to transportation in terms of delivery, so that nearness to the ports is a consideration in this instance; good means of transportation (roads, railroads, airports) from the DCs to the destinations for delivery; and closeness to population centers where large proportions of the goods are to be delivered. These requirements add up to a pretty good portrait of the Inland Empire.

The West End of the Inland Empire has proved to be an ideal location for the development of warehouses for several reasons. First, DCs often need a "large footprint" (up to sixty acres, Husing told us in a phone interview), which can be difficult to assemble in a densely populated urban area. In the Inland Empire, unused land, or "dirt," as the real estate industry refers to it, was available and at a relatively low cost. Consequently, warehouse rents were lower per square foot than they were in the neighboring counties of Los Angeles and Orange. Because the Inland Empire DCs are generally newer than those in Los Angeles County and because more land is available, they can satisfy DC operators' most up-to-date needs. The DCs in the Inland Empire are generally larger and more modern than the warehouses in the South Bay of LA County. In terms of size, many exceed seven hundred thousand square feet, and some are much bigger, more than a million square feet. They have been constructed for the needs of the modern warehouse operator, including higher ceilings and various high-tech features.

Second, a low-wage local labor force is available. In general, the Inland Empire's employment opportunities are far more limited than those of LA County. Some of the Inland Empire's towns and cities serve as bedroom communities for their western neighbors because housing prices are significantly lower there, but these employees suffer from an impossible commute on heavily congested freeways. The morning rush hour driving west on the Pomona and San Bernardino Freeways into Los Angeles starts before 6 a.m. and remains a nightmare for several hours. The desirability of avoiding such commutes means that local workers are willing to accept lower-wage jobs (combined with the savings from not having to commute). They are a kind of captive workforce. Given that there are not many competing jobs for a work force that is mainly limited to a high school education, the warehouse sector can get away with paying lower wages than it could elsewhere.

In his *Quarterly Economic Report* of July 2005, Husing reported that wages for logistics workers in Southern California averaged $45,314 in 2003, compared to $37,161 for the Inland Empire. He also noted that 50.3 percent of adults in the Inland Empire had a high school education or less, compared to 46.8 percent for the Southern California region as a whole, so he considers the pay for these jobs relatively advantageous. As he put it: "The logistics group provides unskilled workers with entry-level pay well above the minimum wage at $8.07 to $10.45 an hour depending on the sector." They can work their way up to $12.96 and $14.91 an hour and up from there. Still, the relatively lower pay for Inland Empire workers remains an attraction to DC operators.

A third attraction is Ontario International Airport. The IEEP reports that it handles nearly five hundred thousand tons of cargo annually, and it is expected to be one of the top ten cargo airports in the United States by 2015. The airport is developing the Pacific Gateway Cargo Center. It will have a million square feet of warehouse, office, and operations space, 400 truck docks, and up to sixteen aircraft parking spaces. The IEEP anticipates that it will be the largest cargo-related facility in the Los Angeles airport system. Moreover, UPS operates a major hub near the airport, which is another attraction for local warehouses.

Additionally, good roads stretch to the east and north, enabling the DCs to serve as regional distribution centers covering the West and Southwest of the United States. As Steve Harrington of the DMA (which, significantly, maintains its headquarters in the Inland Empire) pointed out, 85 percent of the people in the Western United States live within two days of the Inland Empire. Salt Lake City is one day away, as is San Francisco. A DC here can provide next-day delivery to a Wal-Mart in Red Bluff, at the northern edge of California. "We are one day out of Los Angeles," he said, "but don't have to deal with LA's congestion, though it is getting worse here." He was speaking, of course, not of the horrific congestion between LA and the Inland Empire, but from the Inland Empire to areas to the East and North.

Perhaps most important in the rise of the Inland Empire as a DC center is the nearness of the ports. The Ontario area serves as a delivery point for containers, which are hauled there by port truckers. The containers are then unloaded in the Inland Empire, and the goods are sent from there to their ultimate destinations. No one knows exactly what proportion of the warehousing that is done in the Inland Empire is port-related, but everyone estimates that it is substantial.

The link to the ports raises a major problem of congestion on the roads that connect the Inland Empire to the ports, over and above the problem of pollution from the diesel engines of trucks moving to and from the DCs. Even though the ports are relatively near and accessible, traffic can be very slow, causing delays in delivery. As a result, some have proposed developing a stronger rail link from the ports to the Inland Empire. However, this appears to be unfeasible on a couple of grounds: It takes longer and is more costly to load a train with containers than is the case for putting the containers on chassis and moving them by truck. The railroads themselves are reluctant to develop such a project because it would be economically inefficient for them. They contend that a trip of five hundred miles is the minimum they require for the movement of cargo by rail.

136

WHAT IS THERE?

What kinds of companies have put up DCs and warehouses in the West End of the Inland Empire? In an article in the *Ontario Daily Bulletin,* reporter Adam Eventov developed a list of the twenty-three biggest DCs in the area, along with their location and square footage. Nine of them were over a million square feet in size, and the smallest on the list had seven hundred thousand square feet. These are indeed *big* boxes.

The largest was Wal-Mart's in Mira Loma, an unincorporated area of Riverside County. Wal-Mart's DC is actually a campus of four buildings comprising 2.7 million square feet of warehousing space. Next came Kmart in Ontario, with 1.7 million square feet. It was followed by GATX and Pic 'N' Save in Rancho Cucamonga, with 1.4 and 1.35 million square feet, respectively. Target in Fontana was next with 1.2 million square feet. Among the remainder of this list were Price Costco, Pier 1 Imports, Staples, Nestlé, Home Depot, Sears, Mattel, Sanyo, Toyota, and Skechers. Clearly retailers occupy a solid place among the biggest DCs in the area. The four communities mentioned, Ontario, Rancho Cucamonga, Fontana, and Mira Loma, account for most of the DC locations, though Mira Loma and Chino also make an appearance on the list.

We attempted to compile more up-to-date and thorough lists of DCs from city, real estate, and newspaper data. We contacted the cities of Ontario, Rancho Cucamonga, Chino, and Fontana to see if they had lists. They did, but they were in various states of confusion, sometimes not separating out DCs from other types of commercial and industrial property. We could not obtain a list from Mira Loma because it lacks a city government.

The list is lengthy and contains many well-known corporations. Automobile companies, such as Honda, BMW, Volkswagen, and Toyota, and tire companies like Bridgestone/Firestone and Goodyear maintain large DCs in the area. (We visited a huge Toyota warehouse in Ontario and were generously given a tour. We also visited one for Toyo Tires and were granted a wonderful interview by their vice president of logistics, Jay Carroll, a very knowledgeable logistics expert.) Home improvement companies, such as Home Depot, Lowe's, and Ikea, are present on the list. All of the major retailers seem to be present, including not only Wal-Mart, Target, and Kmart, but also such companies as Toys "R" Us, Kohl's, Walgreens, and so forth. Manufacturers, food companies, and pharmaceutical businesses all have DCs in the area. Third parties (3PLs), including UPS, were prominent occupants of the area's DCs, sometimes running public warehouses for multiple clients and sometimes running dedicated warehouses for a particular client. In fact, just about every kind of company imaginable maintains a warehouse in this region. The IEEP and John Husing, among others, have described the Inland Empire DCs as catering to the Fortune 1000—the largest corporations in the United States. We might refine this to say that they cater primarily to those of the Fortune 1000 that engage in importing in a significant way.

We visited the DCs of three of the biggest retailers: Target, Wal-Mart, and Costco. Here is what we found out.

Target's Import Warehouse

We interviewed Kayle Schreiber, import transportation manager at Target's Ontario import center. This facility is located in a complex of warehouses and DCs on Haven Avenue in Ontario. They are all giant, windowless boxes. The building had a long line of trucks down one side. We had to show our driver's licenses to a security camera before being allowed to enter.

The facility was an import warehouse. Target has sixteen regional DCs around the country, the closest of which was in Fontana. Each one is 1.3 to 1.8 million square feet. This facility is different from the company's standard DCs. It is a pure warehouse, used for holding imports. Much of the import product they handle is slow-moving. If it went directly to a regular DC, it might sit there for a while, taking up room that is needed for faster-moving goods like paper diapers. The high-selling items tend to be made domestically. Storing imports in the DCs would result in stockouts in the stores for the faster-moving items.

As a result, Target decided to create import warehouses, according to Schreiber. This one, Target's first, was built in August 2001. Wal-Mart and Kmart were already using them, so Target knew it was a workable idea. At the time of the interview (2003), Target had two more import warehouses, in Washington state and Virginia.

This facility was 725,000 square feet, and next to it was another Target warehouse of 500,000 square feet. The company was planning to build a bigger facility, of about 3 million square feet, in Rialto. They rented this facility. Target uses a third-party consolidator, NYK Logistics, in Carson. When containers arrive, Target's marketing department checks the goods. If there is no immediate need, they send the container to an import warehouse. If some of the goods are needed, they are sent to the deconsolidator for transloading. The trailers are then sent to the DCs, which is turn send them to the stores. Some of the transloaded cargo is also sent to this facility. Said Schreiber:

> We get about 50 percent of full containers sent directly from the ports, and 50 percent of trailers that have been deconsolidated by NYK. Annually that amounts to six thousand containers and about three thousand trailers. The flow is somewhat volatile. We deal with about seven steamship terminals,

each with ships arriving on different schedules. Besides, ships can face bad weather and be delayed.

The company sends goods to the DCs from this facility. About 75 percent of the moves are by rail. It tends to send to the closer DCs, in such locations as Arizona or California. In other words, this warehouse services the Western United States primarily.

Ninety percent of Target's imports were out of Asia at the time of the interview, with the vast majority coming from Hong Kong. (This may be changing with the rise of China's other ports.) Fifty percent of its Asian imports moved through the ports of LA/LB. However, the company was trying to develop more all-water service to the East Coast. (Note that this interview occurred not too long after what Schreiber described as "a painful port lockout." He said that even though Target now had a six-year contract with the facility, there was still some sensitivity.) On the West Coast, Target's imports were divided 50–50 between LA and Seattle. Out of Asia, the East Coast accounted for about 20 percent, so there was a 20–40–40 distribution for the three points of entry from Asia.

Each import warehouse services its closest DCs. The company strives for the shortest distance. Schreiber said that they send more to Phoenix than New York. Target uses very little landbridge, because other methods are cheaper. That they are slower doesn't matter, because the imports are the less time-sensitive items. It is okay if it takes the goods twelve days to get to New York.

At the time of this interview, Target imported about 18 percent of the goods it sold, but was planning to move the percentage up to 25. And it was likely to continue to grow thereafter. However, if you went into one of its stores, you would find that 62 to 63 percent of the goods were made outside of the United States and were imported. The difference is accounted for by the fact that the maker of the goods is the importer, and Target is only "importing" them indirectly. For example, Target can buy the goods domestically from a vendor, like Sony. Sony would import the goods to their own DCs and then send them to Target. This can mean sending them from LA to Chicago and then back out to LA, which adds unnecessary cost and time.

The 18 percent figure refers to direct imports by Target. But now the company was developing an initiative to convert from indirect to direct importing and to bring the goods in directly themselves. According to Schreiber:

> The main reason is that we are the third-largest containerized importer in the country, which enables us to get favorable shipping rates. If we bring the goods in directly, then we can get a better deal on the shipping rates than the

vendor, who passes on those added costs to us. . . . One advantage we have with the steamship lines is that we do a better job of forecasting. We tell them at the beginning of the year how much we are bringing in and from where. This allows them to plan. Wal-Mart doesn't do that, partly because they are so big they don't feel they need to. They just make a demand to the steamship line. As a result, we didn't miss a single container last year, even when the capacity got tight [due to the lockout], while Wal-Mart missed a lot of containers—like thousands.

With indirect imports, there are two DC moves, as described in the Sony example. Target's goal is to cut down domestic transportation, which is a way to cut costs. However, the main reason for the move to direct importing is the reduction in the rates paid to the steamship lines, which are very expensive, Schreiber said.

So what Target planned to do is to take possession of the goods at the factory in Asia. Then the retailer decides how they get to their destinations. It uses seven or eight steamship lines, including Maersk and APL. It likes to spread out the work so that it is not too dependent on one company.

Target runs all of its logistics operations in-house and does not work with 3PLs. The company feels that it can take care of shipping more cheaply and efficiently than others. It has logistics teams at its headquarters in Minneapolis, one of which deals with vendor-to-port operations, one with port-to-port, and one with port-to-deconsolidator or -warehouse. The only outsiders Target uses are Customs Brokers, who clear its containers on entry and handle the paperwork. Almost all of its cargo is cleared before it lands.

Target does not put goods directly on the railroads. Rather, it books with its carriers (trucking companies), and they decide whether to use the railroads. Its carriers are companies like Hub Distribution, Hunt, Schneider, Swift, and so on. However, the company does know when the trains leave. It finds out the cut time of a particular train—that is, when it will no longer accept loads—and tells the carriers when the trailers can be picked up so that they can get to the railroads on time. However, this is not an exact science. Schreiber says that the DC only sends a trailer off when it is 100 percent full. "It costs a couple of thousand dollars to send a trailer to New York, so it doesn't pay to send it 80 percent full. . . . The carriers have a certain number of days to get the trailer to its destination. It's up to them to determine how they use the railroads. The railroads are expensive. We maintain contact with them—they keep us informed of their capacity. For example, it is a headache to get in and out of Chicago because of congestion, and they let us know if it is tight. We only use the BNSF from here, not the UP."

Target was affected by the port lockout. It brought freight in early and used different ports of entry, but it could not anticipate precisely when the lockout would occur, so it was still caught by it. The contract ended in June, and the company expected work to stop in July, but work did not stop until September. "Of the 150 ships stranded in the harbor, you can be sure that we had containers on almost all of them." The problem is that the lead time on imports from Asia is so long that you can't anticipate, according to Schreiber.

Schreiber expressed support for operating the port terminals 24/7. They plan to double their imports in five or six years, and so will others like Wal-Mart. "We are looking at gridlock. The ports can't continue to operate five days a week. The costs [of night gates] will have to come down." (As of this writing, night and weekend gates had been established at the ports.)

Wal-Mart's Import Warehouse

Wal-Mart has an import warehouse in Mira Loma. Unlike Target, it was run by the 3PL, Exel, at the time of our visit, and the person we interviewed, Tony Girodo, Manager of Retail Americas, was an Exel employee. At this site was a campus of Wal-Mart warehouses. Like others in this part of the Inland Empire, they appear from the outside to be giant window-less boxes with trucks lined up outside. We saw Wal-Mart and Schneider trucks. On the door of the main building was a sign reading, "No cameras or recording devices allowed past this point," and a security guard required an ID to sign us in. Since there was a wait, we went outside to take some photos, which produced a flurry of security guard interest. We were politely asked why we were taking photos and were informed that we would need permission to do so, but they did not confiscate our film.

Girodo told us that this facility is an import DC, that is, its sole purpose is to receive inbound containers, all of which come directly from the ports. He estimated that they receive about sixty containers a day. The goods are deconsolidated, housed, and shipped from here. Wal-Mart also has a transloading facility in Southgate, which used to be DSL before it was bought by Hudd. Hudd is also responsible for draying to this Mira Loma facility, where they receive only ocean containers, and ship goods out in fifty-three-foot trailers.

From here, goods get shipped to regional DCs. They send goods both by TL and rail, using rail when the journey is over five hundred miles long. The service area of this facility extends for about a thousand miles, including Texas and the Pacific Northwest. They basically cover the West. All shipments go to regional DCs, which then send them to the stores. There is a division of labor, with import warehouses serving as the first receivers of goods from the ports. Girodo believes that all of the big retailers operate this way. Some of the smaller companies might send ocean containers directly to their stores. By sending all the imports to a centralized location, they can ship by TL instead of LTL, saving a lot on costs.

Exel handles a number of accounts in the Inland Empire, in retail, automotive, and chemicals. They operate eight or nine retail DCs. Exel is an English company; its world headquarters are in England and its U.S. headquarters are in Ohio. It provides comprehensive logistics services, including planning, transportation, and warehousing. Exel tries to develop a "campus" network (which is the way it refers to its DC clusters), where there is labor-sharing across campuses. They do extensive training, bringing together workers from all the local campuses. Then when they are slow somewhere, they can ship workers around. This form of cost-saving is one of Exel's strengths, says Girodo.

This facility is dedicated solely to Wal-Mart. Exel does not provide Wal-Mart with comprehensive logistics, because Wal-Mart does its own. The company can negotiate lucrative deals because of its volume. This campus was new—about four years old at the time of the interview (2003). It used to be near the port. Exel provides only the warehousing for Wal-Mart and does not contract their transportation. But Exel certainly can handle transportation. They provide home delivery for Sears, and they have an extensive relationship with the railroads through a company of their own called Mark 7, which buys space on the railroads, ensuring that Exel loads get carried. Exel also owns its own trucks, both TL and LTL.

Like Target's import warehouse, this one stores goods and does not operate on a JIT basis. Rather, JIT is used by the regional DCs, and this facility serves as a source for them. That is because importing requires time delays. This warehouse, therefore, is not geared to everyday replenishments. Rather, it handles large volumes. (This suggests that flexible production with constant replenishment does not function so much in global production; rather, these import warehouses bring in the goods in bulk and *then* the constant replenishment kicks in.)

However, they do use POS information to order imports. It is mainly oriented toward replenishing staple stock. Overseas production and distribution take around three months: "Maybe you can get it down to forty-five days, but that would be tight. That's because you have to allow two weeks on the water. And then it can take from a day to a week to get the goods through customs, which is a big variable." What they deal with here is mainly items that are constantly on the shelf: high-volume, rapid-turnover replenishment items. Girodo distinguishes this kind of inventory from promotional items, which work differently. With this kind of inventory, the rule of thumb is that you have 70 percent in stock and hold back 30 percent. Then you ship directly to specific stores based on sales. For staple stock, in contrast, there is no such rule. It all depends on the supplier.

This facility uses a temp agency called StaffMark. They try to staff for the lowest level of the year and then add temps during the busier seasons. When we visited, it was late July, and Girodo thought that they were a little over 50–50, with somewhat more full-time workers. They were gearing up for the busiest season, which starts around August or September.

The ports lockout of 2002 affected this facility, but Girodo felt it wasn't too bad. Had it lasted longer than ten days, the impact would have been major. Also, the timing of the lockout meant that a substantial percentage of the goods for the season were already here. Had it happened earlier, the damage would have been worse. Still, Wal-Mart containers were left sitting on ships and were stuck on the docks in the subsequent jam, meaning that the retailer had to pay demurrage, a cost that was then passed on to the consumer. Wal-Mart did ship to other ports, but it costs a lot to relocate the containers back here for shipment back to Asia. Girodo believes that the billion-dollars-a-day estimate of the cost of the lockout is reasonable.

We asked if the lockout led to a longer-term shift away from the West Coast ports. Wal-Mart has opened up several new import warehouses in the East and is making use of more all-water services to East Coast ports. Interestingly, however, Girodo sees no diminution at this facility, suggesting that the tremendous growth in Wal-Mart imports is what is being shifted to the East, rather than their base-level imports.

We also interviewed another source, who wished to remain anonymous. This person had served as manager of the Wal-Mart DC as an employee of Exel, and who currently (2003) ran a 3PL in the area. Working for Exel, this person was in charge of eight million square feet of warehousing, from the territory west of Texas to the Canadian border. One of this person's major accounts was a major toy-maker. We were especially interested in the account of this person's Wal-Mart experiences:

Wal-Mart used to publicize "Made in the USA," but they quietly phased it out. Since then they have increased their imports tenfold. Look at this pen: It costs one dollar to make in the United States and three cents in China. There has been no serious inflation in the last decade because of Wal-Mart. They are the most impactful company in the world—much more impactful than Microsoft.

Wal-Mart is hard to do business with. I left Exel for my health. I'm a pretty healthy person. I have always been athletic. I had a "cardiac episode" while working for them, which the doctors said was induced by stress. My spouse insisted that I leave. I faced a relentless onslaught. I ran all of their imports. I was in charge of three million square feet of Wal-Mart warehousing. I faced continuous pressure. Nothing is good enough for them. They keep shifting priorities, everything is an emergency, and you face constant unpredictability. You are never allowed to be comfortable. The better you are, the crappier they are. They treat you like shit. They are like the preacher who is determined to keep you humble.

I had to deal with eight of their managers, who took turns giving me grief. They were the West Coast team. The main person was ex-military, out of West Point. There are lots of West Pointers in Wal-Mart's management. They operate with a strict chain of command. They talk about having an open door policy, but it's all a bunch of rhetoric. Their attitude is: "We're Wal-Mart, so you had better do what we say." They talk about partnership with their vendors, but it's a bunch of hooey. They expect their vendors to come to them, hat in hand, and say "yes sir."

There are endless stories. They just fired Exel in Mira Loma. Now they are using Commodity Logistics out of Ohio. They fired Exel over a conflict of philosophy. Wal-Mart wants to run the business. Their position is that you do what they say and express no opinions. The problem is that you need to do business with them. Exel was a little arrogant. They could have worked with Wal-Mart, but they said to them that Unilever and Procter and Gamble were bigger customers and that Wal-Mart was their number-three business. The Wal-Mart people didn't like that.

If you get in the club, you can make money. Not from Wal-Mart, which holds you to a 7 to 8 percent margin, but from ancillary business. You get dubbed a "preferred provider." They tell other vendors to do business with you.

Wal-Mart sets the transportation rates. They do it for all aspects of transportation—for sea, over-the-road, et cetera. If you are short of capacity, they will go to another service provider and double the rates they are paying you in order to ensure that they will get priority.

Our interviewee also worked for Target for nine years, before moving to Wal-Mart/Exel. This person found Target very different. They have more of an environment of cooperation. For example, Johnson Wax was one of their vendors, selling to Target through a third party. Target went to them and worked with them to set up a sophisticated cross-docking system. It made their relationship more efficient and was a great deal for both of them.

We talked about the role of 3PLs in the DC industry. Our informant estimated that about 50 percent of the DCs in the Western Inland Empire were run by 3PLs and thought that their role would grow, though our source also felt some bitterness about the process: "The retailers pit the 3PLs against each other. They accept bids, using an RFP [request for proposal] process. The 3PLs then do transportation studies in order to win the bid. This ends up as free consulting and research for the retailers. The 3PLs need to start charging for their proposals. The research is expensive. We spend $10,000 to $15,000 on research for a project. The problem is that someone needs to start charging, and no one is in a position to go first." Margins are thin in the 3PL business, according to our informant, but the business is growing. However, no one is making a lot of money.

Costco Depot, Mira Loma

We were given a tour of a Costco DC in Mira Loma, by Dave Neumann, assistant depot manager, in the late summer of 2004. The structure was built in 1997 and is 700,000 square feet, though the company was planning to construct an additional 350,000 square feet. The building is shaped like a T, with the top of the T containing 400,000 square feet and the stem 300,000. Cross-docking is done in the stem.

Fifteen percent of what arrived here came directly from the ports in ocean containers. They received about thirty containers a day from Long Beach, using Hanjin and Evergreen. The rest came from their vendors, and Neumann had no idea whether they included imported goods from the ports or not. They received over 400 trucks a day, and had about 225 outbounds per day, so they handled 600 to 700 truckloads of freight in a day.

This depot, which was their largest DC, delivered to seventy-five locations, fifty-five of which were local (Southern California). They covered the territory from Santa Barbara and Bakersfield in the north to Mexico in the South, and East to Palm Springs. They sent goods from here to five Mexican locations and to Japan. There was another depot in Laredo, Texas, which shipped to deeper locations in Mexico.

Various functions were being performed in the bar of the T. One section dealt with e-commerce, which involved a set of long tables for sorting and packing. This facility handled 25 to 30 percent of all the company's on-line sales. Neumann showed us labels that had lots of information. They had two sets of barcodes on all pallets, one of which was read by an RF gun; these identified the location of the pallet. They were testing RFID but were not using it yet. In another section they were inspecting garments and sewing in labels before shipping them to Japan and Mexico. They checked the fiber content and translated the labels into the appropriate language. They added stickers to items for the international market so that they could track them.

Costco used its own fleet of trucks and also contracted some of the trucking out. The company had 75 tractors, 100 wet trailers and 253 dry trailers. It used its own trucks within a radius of one hundred miles as the crow flies, about an eight- to nine-hour run. All of the company trucks were leased, with a maintenance agreement. The drivers were company employees, not owner-operators.

This depot did not do "live unloads." This means that the trucker drops off the trailer and picks up another one, typically an empty one or one loaded with pallets, rather than wait to be reloaded. They call this a "drop and hook." The next delivery arrived in an hour, and the driver would pick up the unloaded trailer, so the DC had an hour to unload it. This facility faced about four hundred inbound trucks a day, which rose to six hundred for the Christmas season.

In one section workers were building pallets. This DC received pallet-loads of goods, which are large. The workers undo the full pallets and build pallets with smaller numbers of combined items for each store. These pallets go right to the sales floor, and goods are sold from the pallets. Each pallet was being built for a different location. When a full palletload is sent, it is cross-docked, so this is the "less than palletload" section of the T.

Pallets also get built by using a "layered" technique, wherein each layer comes from a different original pallet. They try to build a nice cube. A pallet is 40 by 48 inches and can be built up to seven feet or so. Every location to which they ship returns their pallets here. We saw stacks and stacks of them. They have conveyor belts and an employee inspecting them for repairs. Costco is unusual for its use of pallets. They are a store fixture. People buy off the pallets. Other stores stock shelves, but Costco cuts out this step. This facility had an average of twenty-five thousand pallets returned each day, with more (about thirty thousand) on Monday through Wednesday and fewer by Friday, when they tried to catch up.

Neumann pointed out that they operate a season ahead. They were finishing up with fall goods (at the end of August) and preparing for Christmas. They dealt with patio furniture in February. After Christmas they wanted the stores to look full, so they filled them with furniture.

Three hundred and fifty people worked at this DC at the time of our tour. They appeared to be a diverse group, including lots of women. People were whipping around on forklifts, honking as they went. They come from the local area, says Neumann, although some had moved here.

Cross-docking occurred in the stem of the T. We expected to see conveyor belts, but there were none. Neumann said they were very expensive, not worth it. He imagined how a conveyor belt might work. It would have to form an oval railroad up high and drop goods off at the appropriate doors. If the truck was not ready, the box would have to make the full circle again. This might work with small packages, but not with heavy pallets weighing two thousand pounds apiece. He thinks that conveyor belts wouldn't work in terms of ROI (return on investment).

The DC had something like sixty-five doors on each side of this part of the building, with trucks on both sides. The goods were moved out in less than a day. Workers were busy unloading goods and putting them on pallets, when necessary. The ocean containers typically do not have pallets—they are "cubed out," and their contents need to be palletized.

Walking around a giant DC and seeing its processes firsthand certainly brought our topic to life. It is amazing to see these thousands and thousands of goods moving rapidly through the system and on to their specific destinations. The logistics systems that are required to make this all happen efficiently are impressive indeed.

Role of the Real Estate Industry

The real estate industry has played a major role in the development of DCs in the Inland Empire (and also provided key informants for this research). Real estate companies have developed warehouses and DCs "on spec," meaning that they have worked with developers to build them in the hope that a company will either lease or purchase them. They also have played a role in helping companies to build their own DCs and have worked with them to locate suitable existing facilities.

The real estate industry also keeps track of what is happening in the industry. Some of the real estate companies have aerial maps of the Western Inland Empire and can point out where all the major DCs are located. They know which facilities are empty and which are filled. They know what construction is going on. In other words, they are gold mines of information about what is happening in this sector, even as they influence what happens in it.

While corporations may own their own DCs, most of them are leased, which means that there is a layer of building owner/developers who actually own the warehouse buildings. The leases tend to be long-term, leading to a certain stability in the tenant population. Corporations cannot simply get up and leave the region without paying a major penalty. Thus there is a level of stability in the Inland Empire DC population, with change coming mainly from growth. Of course we should recognize that there are layers of tenants. A 3PL may lease a DC and run it for a changing set of occupants. And a public warehouse may face continually changing customers. Thus a particular manufacturer or retailer, the "real" user of the warehouse or DC, may have more flexibility than the owner or direct leaser of the building.

One of the real estate people we interviewed was Kent Hindes of Cushman and Wakefield in Ontario. Here is how he opened the interview, linking the Inland Empire DC development to the ports:

> The port drives this market, from goods that move by rail to those that move by tractor-trailer. You can't do manufacturing here any more because of the lower cost of labor elsewhere. This is true for furniture, apparel, and lots of other products. First they moved to Mexico, where it costs six to seven dollars. Now they are moving to Asia where they pay forty-two cents. You can buy a lot of transportation when you are paying that little for labor.

Here is the way he described the DC real estate situation in the West End of the Inland Empire:

> There is 196 million square feet available in the West End. Of that, 110 to 120 million is in big box warehouses, defined as those that are 100,000 square feet or bigger. When I came here in 1985, 100,000 square feet was a big transaction. Now I just did a 750,000 square feet building for Wal-Mart, and I have a 600,000 square feet building for spec under construction. The DCs have gotten bigger and bigger because of the changing patterns of distribution, the reliance on JIT.

There were big aerial maps on the walls of his office, and Hindes could point to any building and tell us what it was. He pointed to the Wal-Mart complex in Mira Loma, which consisted of two groups of three buildings each, all close together. He believed they were all part of the retailer's import warehouse system. These building were of the following sizes: 900,000 sq. ft., 750,000 sq. ft., two of 600,000 sq. ft., and two of 400,000 sq. ft., for a total of 3.65 million sq. ft. Target has a 1.3 million–sq. ft. DC in Fontana, and two in Ontario at 900,000 and 750,000 sq. ft. And it had a 1.7 million–sq. ft. DC in Shafter, near the Nevada border, which adds up to 4.65 million sq. ft. in the region.

At the time of the interview (2003), all that was left in the West End was fill-in. "There is hardly any dirt left," which was evident on the maps. "There is dirt in Mira Loma, but it is environmentally challenged [protected by the Endangered Species Act], and there is community opposition over air pollution." It should be pointed out that the residents of San Bernardino County are bearing much of the brunt of the logistics revolution. San Bernardino recently ranked worst in the nation in terms of particulate matter in the air, a circumstance surely related to all of the diesel trucks in the area.

One could see on the map residential areas that were directly adjacent to warehouse development. "If someone came into this market and asked you to assemble one million square feet for development, there would be only two possible locations left. The price of dirt has gone up, but rents have stabilized. But there isn't much to buy."

Where are the DCs moving, we asked? East towards the cities of San Bernardino and Riverside, Hindes answered. They are building just south of March Air Force Base. Walgreens has 1.3 million sq. ft. there, and Lowe's has 1.1 million sq. ft. "The industry isn't moving to Victorville [in the Mojave Desert] because it's too far from the ports, and you have to climb over the Cajon Pass. It doesn't make sense to take a container from the port all the way to Victorville." DCs were also moving to the North, up Route 5, to the Tejon Ranch. IKEA has a DC up there, but Hindes didn't know whether any more development was occurring in that area.

"Everything is driven by the delta between occupancy cost and transportation," said Hindes. "This is ground zero." In other words, the Ontario ideal minimizes both land and transportation costs. All more distant locations have to find a balance between them. Generally, the further out, the cheaper the land but the more expensive the dray. He estimated that the dray rate to Chino was $135–175, to Ontario was $150–180, to San Bernardino was $165–200; to the high desert was around $225. Moreover, there was much more backhaul traffic from the West End than, say, from the high desert.

According to Hindes, the preponderance of freight in the Ontario area DCs comes from the ports and moves outward. He believed that about 60 percent of the freight that was processed here remained in the Western region of the country and that the remainder was shipped by rail from San Bernardino or by truck to the Eastern United States.

The vast majority of companies did not own the buildings where their DCs and warehouses were located. Wal-Mart did not own the buildings, Target owned one of them, and Kmart and Toyota owned their buildings. However, the majority of companies did not own. "Most would prefer to invest in product rather than bricks and mortar." They rented from developers. He believed that 60 to 70 percent of the DCs in this area were built on spec, not knowing who the resident would be.

The internal architecture of DCs has been changing, according to Hindes. They have grown higher—they now (in 2003) cleared 32 feet. The column spacing has grown wider and was now 50 to 52 feet. There were fewer impediments in building racking systems. All the equipment involved was more sophisticated, and it was now possible to stack goods higher. Even though buildings were developed on spec, they were built with the sophisticated warehouse concept in mind.

Hindes said the typical leases are five to fifteen years, with options to extend them. He said the DC occupants are tied not to the area but to the developer. However, if they do not pay the rent to the developer, they will certainly get sued. In that sense they are tied to the area. The 3PLs play an important role, according to Hindes. The Wal-Mart campus was run entirely by Exel (at the time of the interview). Sanyo's DC was run by UPS Logistics. "This is the 3PL capital of the world." He reckoned that 50 to 60 percent of the DCs here were run by 3PLs. The predominant ones were Exel, APL Logistics, and National Distribution Center, out of New Jersey.

"UPS Logistics was one of the big ones but it is falling on its ass," Hindes said. "They don't know what they are doing. UPS has a venture capital fund and has been buying other companies. But the integration has been difficult." He drew a sharp distinction between UPS Parcel Service, a client of his, and UPS Logistics—the former was a well-run company.

149

Real estate is very competitive out here, said Hindes. There are a hand-ful of companies that are active, including CB Richard Ellis, Grubb and Ellis, Colliers Seeley, and Cushman and Wakefield. Their business is devel-opment, property management, and financing: "Wall Street investors are buying up the Ontario DCs because they see them as a solid and profitable investment." Cushman and Wakefield developed and leased a building, which was purchased by Alliance Insurance. "The investors are loading up on real estate."

One of the real estate people we talked with had a project with Wal-Mart. This person had close dealings with the retailer and found it difficult to use restrained language when describing the experience:

> Wal-Mart isn't a retailer. They are a bank. You should see how they negotiate a contract. For example, Procter and Gamble was making Crest toothpaste for them. The order comes, and it leaves the factory in two days. Maybe it is two days in transit, and has a twelve-hour shelf life. So maybe it takes five days to cycle through. Wal-Mart has a net 90 deal with P&G. So they float on the money for two months.

"I've never dealt with tougher sons of bitches," said this source. Logistics is Wal-Mart's core competency. The current leadership comes entirely from the logistics sector. They are also products of the military. Many graduated from West Point or the Air Force Academy. "They mess with all the people they deal with. They messed with us. They are pricks. They keep driving." Our informant wanted to say to them, and maybe did at times, "Why don't you guys go to hell!" "They screw with everybody." Here is the story of the real estate dealings between Wal-Mart and our informant:

> We had the biggest box out here and they wanted it, but they negotiated and pressured until the last minute. It never ended. The final lease is this thick [indicating 2–3 inches with his fingers]. When we came down to the final lease, called the signature lease, they talked about creating a separate entity as the lessee—not Wal-Mart Stores Inc., but Wal-Mart Stores West. There was no guarantee, and I wanted them to sign one, but they resisted. I said: "Stop fucking with me. I don't need this. Go take your business elsewhere." They said: "What are you talking about? We're Wal-Mart. You have to deal with us. We're too big." Until the last day they were still trying to dick with me.

Wal-Mart is horrible with its vendors, our informant reported, who assumed that it was the same with their transportation providers. With regard to Exel, Wal-Mart's 3PL, this person indicated that "everyone jerks with their 3PLs." Wal-Mart will go to all the 3PLs and offer each an undercutting deal. The 3PLs are continually pitted against each other—and they have miniscule margins to begin with.

A great deal more information could be obtained from the real estate companies. Each puts out a quarterly report that tells about the real estate activity in the Inland Empire. They mention new warehouse and DC openings or changes in occupancy. One could probably develop a thorough, up-to-the-minute mapping of all Inland Empire DCs from them, and they have their fingers on the pulse of the latest trends and developments.

We also attended a meeting of the National Association of Industrial and Office Properties, a forum for the commercial real estate industry, in July 2002. NAIOP has an Inland Empire chapter. A group consisting of an economist (the ubiquitous John Husing), real estate experts, 3PLs, and DC occupants made a presentation. These events are held regularly and provide a valued opportunity to schmooze as well as to find out the latest news.

The Role of Cities and Counties

The DCs are mainly concentrated in the cities of Ontario, Rancho Cucamonga, Fontana, and Chino and in the unincorporated area of Riverside County called Mira Loma. They are not limited to these areas, and as they have filled up, DC construction has moved east and north. DCs are now located in the cities of San Bernardino and Riverside, which are further east, as well as in many other locations. Still, there is a pronounced concentration of DCs in these five areas, and we have focused our research on them. Part of the reason for this concentration lies in trucking rates. The further east one moves, the more expensive it is to haul containers there.

Have the Inland Empire cities in question encouraged the development of the DCs? Have the counties of Riverside and San Bernardino played a part? In other words, is this development in part a product of public sector encouragement? We looked into the subject and discovered that while there has been some encouragement, the growth has mainly been a product of private sector interests.

The West End cities, like all California cities, suffer from an inadequate revenue base. They depend heavily on sales taxes and as a consequence have an interest in encouraging retailers to locate stores there. In general, the DCs are not an important source of city taxes, unless they have a direct sales aspect, so they are not an especially desirable type of facility from a tax point of view.

On the other hand, they do provide jobs. True, their ratio of space to jobs is quite low, especially as warehouses become increasingly mechanized. Manufacturing facilities are much more attractive on this account because they employ people more densely. Still, some employment opportunities are better than none, and the cities would rather provide a valued location for some form of economic activity. Giant DCs may not be the ideal choice, but they appear to be the best that is available, especially given a large relatively unskilled labor pool. Efforts are under way to develop high-tech industries in the Inland Empire, such as bioengineering, that would take advantage of the concentration of universities in the region.

Cities did not appear to have done much to try to induce warehouses to choose them as a location site, nor did they seem to have much leverage to do so. One thing that they could offer was tax abatement for a certain number of years. They could also offer information about the availability of free trade zones and other types of zones that could afford companies various financial breaks. In addition, the counties offered training, as did some local high schools and colleges; public agencies could inform prospective DC users of these possibilities.

Steve Harrington of the DMA told us that some courting by cities does occur. For example, the Home Shopping Network DC was pursued by Ontario, Mira Loma, and Fontana. Fontana ended up giving them free land. In exchange, they became Fontana's biggest taxpayer as well as providing jobs. But, he reported, this was a controversial issue because the city gave them $25 million worth of land, for which the taxpayers had to foot the bill. There were grumblings about it.

Kent Hindes, of Cushman and Wakefield, said that the cities had an interest in DC development. "But they are a bunch of eunuchs. They can't do anything to incentivize. Lowe's approached us to develop a DC for them. They brought a caravan from Sacramento. They were looking for breaks. In most places, the state or city pays for the land. That doesn't happen here. First, we can't afford to. Second, we don't need to." Eventually, however, Lowe's did get a cut-rate deal. They set up a DC south of March Air Force Base.

According to Hindes, cities can waive fees if there is a retail component. Then they can share the 1 percent sales tax with the corporation. This is about all they can do. The cities around the Inland Empire vary in their eagerness to promote the DCs. Ironically, the major benefit that public entities in the Inland Empire could offer corporations for situating their DCs there was *lack* of interference. The Inland Empire is noteworthy for its unregulated economic growth. Development has occurred in a wildly haphazard, unplanned manner. Land has been gobbled up in a frenzy of development. True, some community forces have mobilized to fight against it due to the inevitable social costs associated with such growth, as we shall see. But the development forces have basically steamrolled over the opposition.

There is a lot to be said about the effects of this tumultuous and uncontrolled growth on the social and political climate of the Inland Empire. For one thing, underlying social structures have not developed at the same rate, leaving a population with a dearth of informal social services of all kinds. What we are witnessing here is the effects of unchecked private enterprise almost completely free of government interference, and the end result is far from pretty.

Organizations

The warehouse industry is represented by a number of organizations, including the Council of Logistics Management (CLM), the International Logistics and Warehouse Association (ILWA), and the Warehouse Education Research Council (WERC). These are national organizations that tend to cater to the independent 3PL branch of the industry. They mainly aim to help 3PLs become more proficient in offering logistics services and expanding their value-added activities. These and related organizations hold conferences, put out educational materials, and publish trade journals. In other words, there has been considerable sharing of ideas in the hopes of developing the industry as a whole.

At the local level, the Distribution Management Association of Southern California (DMA), run by president Steve Harrington, is an organization that brings together a group of local warehouse operators to share ways to improve their industry. Here is how the organization described itself in its 2003 Membership Resource Guide, which we obtained from Harrington: "The Distribution Management Association (DMA) is a nonprofit trade organization for logistics and supply chain leaders devoted to the advancement of distribution, warehousing and transportation. . . . An association of robust vision, the DMA is determined to become the Inland Empire's premier supply chain trade association—a true community resource wielding legislative influence, promoting two-way educational programs, and serving as a single point of contact for the logistics industry."

In 2003, the DMA had 101 listed members. These consisted of shippers, like Home Depot and Ralphs Grocery Company; governmental agencies, such as the city of Ontario; 3PLs like APL Logistics; educational institutions such as Cerritos College; real estate agents like Cushman and Wakefield; transportation firms like UPS; and labor-providing temp agencies like Team One Employment Specialists, LLC. The organization brings these diverse interests together and provides educational and resource information.

Community Reactions

As we have already suggested, it was not all smooth sailing for the warehousing industry of the Inland Empire. Opposition had arisen over the speed and recklessness of development. And it had arisen over the two major negative by-products of warehousing, namely congestion and pollution. The constant arrival and departure of diesel trucks added to the nightmare of the daily commute from the Inland Empire to Los Angeles and back. And health problems in young children, especially lung diseases of various sorts, alarmed the public. Some Inland Empire communities had some of the dirtiest, most polluted air in the nation.

A frontal assault on these problems has been difficult, though community organizations have formed to try to launch them. One of the most useful tools has been the Endangered Species Act. An endangered species was found in Mira Loma, bringing warehouse development there to a quick halt. Mira Loma residents were especially upset about the degradation of their way of life. Many families had moved there in the hopes of pursuing a semi-rural lifestyle, with horses and so forth, on a few acres of land. Now they found themselves surrounded by looming warehouse buildings, congested roads and highways, and foul air. They were angry. Using the Endangered Species Act, local residents were able to put construction of warehouses temporarily on hold there.

The public sector of San Bernardino and Riverside recognized that a social problem was brewing. The San Bernardino Association of Governments (affectionately known as SanBag) was fully aware that the regional impact of the DC development was not all positive. Indeed, they recognized that there is a major discrepancy between national benefit and local cost. The intermodal distribution of Asian imports benefits a national market. While the Inland Empire gets some economic benefit from its strategic location in this system, it also bears an unusual, almost certainly unfair amount of the costs. For this reason, SanBag feels it has the right to make a claim on the federal government to help deal with some of these externalities. In particular, they hoped to get aid in improving and expanding both rail and road/truck transportation systems. A railroad project was already under way. Called the Alameda Corridor East (ACE) project and described briefly in the previous chapter, this endeavor was intended to improve rail crossings so that they would cease to block traffic and would allow for uninterrupted movement of freight trains through the region.

For a while the idea has been floating around of developing an inland port. A facility would be developed in the Inland Empire, perhaps at a former Air Force base, such as March AFB in Riverside County. Containers would be discharged directly to a short-haul rail line, which would bring them out to the inland port for all the handling that normally goes on at or near the dock. Such a scheme would alleviate both the congestion and pollution generated by constant truck traffic. However, plans like this face the enormous obstacle of cost, even if one leaves aside the willingness and ability of the railroads to operate such a line profitably.

The Future of Inland Empire Warehousing

The West End is pretty much filled in now; there is hardly any "dirt" left for fresh construction. New firms will, of course, keep coming into the area as old ones leave. But the "gold rush" of the warehousing industry in the area is almost over. Consequently, assuming that imports from Asia continue to grow at their present pace and that the ports of LA/LB continue to be major reception points, new locations for warehousing will have to be found.

Already there are signs of setting up DCs further out, in the eastern parts of the Inland Empire and up toward Victorville in the Mojave Desert. Some major DCs have also been established up the San Diego Freeway (the 405) as far north as Bakersfield. This expansion may be inevitable, but it is also more expensive from a port trucking point of view. Nevertheless, the future is likely to hold an expansion of warehousing in these directions.

In our interview with B. J. Patterson, who is vice president of a 3PL, the Inland Empire will continue to grow. The industry will move out to the Moreno Valley and Perris. Lowe's opened a DC out there, for example. Here is what he said about the high desert:

> There is a lot of land out there. The mayor of Barstow is ready to see the industry grow and says it is ten years away. But the cost of drayage is out of this world. Crossing the Cajon Pass is a slow haul. And the capacity of railroad track isn't good. Here [in Ontario] we can turn containers in three days, and drayage costs 250 to 275 dollars [in 2003]. In the high desert drayage costs 350 to 400 dollars. There is traffic up there, and none of the communities support it. And there is a time factor. The only possibility would be if there was landbridge to there, but there isn't enough rail capacity. For example, if Wal-Mart opened a facility there they would want to bring in a hundred containers, and it couldn't be handled. People talk about track upgrading, but it doesn't happen. The BNSF doesn't have the money. The developers don't have the money. It will only be considered when they run out of land.

Kent Hindes provided his opinion:

> The industry will keep moving east. First it moved from the South Bay to the City of Industry. Then it hopscotched over Pomona and came to the West End. It continues to follow the roads and railroads, down the 10. Now there is a new 1.2 million–square-foot Mattel's, and a 600,000–square-foot Kohl's south of March AFB. It's moving down the 215 and up the 15. They are looking at Shafter, Tejon Ranch, Bakersfield. Michael's, Best Buy and some others are in Bakersfield. To the northeast, the Cajon Pass is a barrier—the grades are steep and it's costly to truck.

This brings us to the end of the line in terms of the logistics systems of Southern California. From the warehouses and DCs, the goods are moved to retail outlets, where they will be sold, POS data will be collected, and the whole process will start again. We now change our own course in part 3 by turning to the issue of labor conditions throughout the Southern California logistics system.

PART THREE

LABOR

CHAPTER 7

Maritime Workers

The logistics revolution, without a doubt, has made business enterprises more efficient. Inventory has been cut, transportation costs have declined, and the prices of manufactured consumer goods have been slashed. The delivery of goods to retail stores has been streamlined so that even though the number of specific products (SKUs) has climbed enormously, the right goods find their way to the right stores at the right time far more frequently. Both stockouts of high-demand products and excess inventory that can only be sold by fierce promotions have diminished. No question: the logistics revolution is good for business!

But is it good for labor? Have any of the admitted benefits of these changes actually helped the workers who implement them? Are there losers as well as winners from the logistics revolution? If there are, what has been lost, and by whom? In this section of the book we do not undertake to examine all the types of workers who may (or may not) be suffering as a result of the logistics revolution, including, importantly, production and sales workers and white collar corporate employees. We have a narrower focus here, on the logistics workers themselves: the transportation and warehouse workers who actually move the goods and who bring "supply chain management" to life through their labor.

Here is what we will be looking for. Recall from chapter 1 our theoretical predictions regarding the logistics revolution's impact on labor:

Increased contingency. A consequence of flexible production and capital's tendency to seek out cheaper and more readily exploitable labor forces is likely to be a rise in temporary workers throughout the logistics and productive sectors, outsourcing, independent contractors, and employment by contingent contractors. Contingency-based workforces are more difficult to organize and more susceptible to exploitive labor practices.

Weakened unions. Attacks on organized labor are likely to have accompanied the shift in the way goods are produced and transported in the current wave of globalization. These attacks will be linked to increased contingency and, more broadly, to neoliberal economic and social policies.

Racialization. Much of the burden of the deteriorating working conditions associated with the logistics revolution is likely to have fallen on the shoulders of workers with fewer rights and less political power, both domestically and offshore. We expect that companies will seek out racialized workforces to whom they can pay the least amount, often under extreme working conditions.

Lowered labor standards. Declining wages and deteriorating working conditions will probably be associated with all of the above consequences of the logistics revolution and are likely to be a defining characteristic for most segments of logistics workers. Lowered labor standards, we predict, are a global phenomenon affecting workers in both the Global North and the South.

We start with the two major groups of maritime workers: the seafarers who work on the ships and the dock workers who load and unload them. We are interested not only in the conditions under which these workers are employed but also in their efforts to improve them.

Labor on the Ships

Brief Seafarer History

U.S. seafarers have a history of labor militancy. The definitive history of U.S. seafaring unions is by Bruce Nelson (1988). In chapter 1 of his book, Nelson describes the history of maltreatment of seamen, including the practice of flogging and other forms of tyrannical abuse. He also discusses the development of union traditions among these workers, including their involvement with the International Workers of the World (IWW), and the creation of such unions as the National Maritime Union (NMU), the Coast Seamen's Union (CSU), the Sailors Union of the Pacific (SUP), and the International Seamen's Union (ISU). Their militancy was not constant, and their organizing saw significant highs and lows.

The ISU was founded in 1899, bringing together a number of preexisting unions; it lasted until 1937. Union president Andrew Furuseth, along with most of the union leadership, strongly supported craft unionism and was part of the leadership of the AFL (Nelson 1988, 39). Various strikes were waged by the seafarers during the first third of the twentieth century, including a major one in 1921 and the great maritime strike of 1934 that joined seafarers with longshore workers, culminating in the historic general strike in San Francisco.

The employers were extremely repressive during this period and were often successful in crushing the militant seafarers. The ship owners were part of a larger coalition, called the Industrial Association of San Francisco, which was composed of major corporations like the Southern Pacific Railroad and Standard Oil. This organization and its members were fiercely anti-union and campaigned for the open shop (Nelson 1988, 72–73).

For a period, seafarers and longshore workers on the West Coast were able to develop strong solidarity, as evidenced in the 1934 strike; their efforts were institutionalized in the Maritime Federation of the Pacific. But the two unions were in competition over dock work, and in 1928, after a battle on the San Francisco docks, the Sailors' Union of the Pacific (SUP) voted to withdraw from the CIO-based Maritime Federation and reaffiliate with the AFL (Nelson 1992, 22).

There is certainly more to know about the history of the seafarers' unions, including their ultimate demise, but it is not centrally relevant to our main story. However, we look briefly at the racism issue in this sector, because it has important reverberations today.

Racism in Seafaring Unions

In the early twentieth century there was a division of labor on board the ships, which corresponded both to status ranking and ethnicity. In the United States, the highest-ranked seafarers, the officers, were immigrants from Britain and Northern Europe. Scandinavian immigrants occupied the second tier of deck sailors. The "black gang" that ran the engine room was heavily Irish, while stewards ranked at the bottom and were multinational. On the West Coast, ship owners recruited Chinese and Filipino workers, first as stewards and then for higher-ranked levels of work. "This led the ISU leadership to engage in increasingly strident calls for 'Asiatic exclusion'" (Nelson 1988, 32).

Furuseth himself was committed to white supremacy, as were a number of the seamen's unions. For example, the Marine Cooks and Stewards Association of the Pacific Coast, which was founded in 1901, declared that one of its primary goals was to "relieve ourselves of the degrading necessity of competing with an alien and inferior race." They formed the union mainly for the purpose of replacing Chinese and Japanese seafarers with "American citizens" (Nelson 1988, 48).

Furuseth saw the employment of Asian workers on ships as "a peril to Christian civilization" (cited in Nelson 1988, 48). However, the anti-Asian sentiment was not confined to craft unionists like Furuseth. Even the socialist leader of the SUP was a known racist. The leaders of these seamen's unions helped to form the Japanese and Korean Exclusion League in 1905 and continued to advocate Asian exclusion until at least 1929.[1]

The militance of the white seafarers and the extremely repressive tendencies of the employers undoubtedly played a role in the racism of these workers. Employers saw an opportunity to weaken their unions by displacing white workers with Asian immigrants. Rather than join with the new workers, however, the white seamen defended themselves in racial terms, weakening their position still further.

Seafarers and the Logistics Revolution

What has the logistics revolution meant for seafarers? One major effect has been severe job loss for U.S. seafarers due to the movement of their work offshore. Not only has foreign ownership of the steamship lines led to U.S. job loss, but the increasing use of flags of convenience (FOCs) has also contributed to the employment, as seafarers, of some of the most unprotected workers in the world. Containerization is another major source of change. It has altered the rhythms of shipping as well as the kind of work that must be done at sea. These two changes have been associated with the decline of U.S. seafarers (and their unions) and a shift to low-wage, racialized, and contingent workers.

Containerization itself may have improved conditions on board to some extent. The container lines need to be highly efficient and professional. They must run on time. They cannot afford to lose cargo. There is little room for error. Thus there may be ways in which these ships are better run and more comfortable for seafarers than some other types of shipping. But there are costs associated with this efficiency, as we shall see.

Flags of Convenience. We briefly examined the phenomenon of flags of convenience in chapter 4, primarily from an industry point of view. Here we consider how this practice is affecting labor, in particular the seafarers who work on FOC ships. The International Transport Workers Federation (ITF) has an FOC campaign, which has been active for 50 years (see www.itfglobal.org/flags-convenience/index.cfm). Since they have studied this phenomenon in depth, we rely heavily on their reporting, in particular their description of the campaign in their 2004 annual report, titled *Campaign against Flags of Convenience and Substandard Shipping*, and the *ITF Seafarers' Bulletin* 20, both available on their website.

According to the annual report, "FOCs provide a means of avoiding labour regulation in the country of ownership, and become a vehicle for

[1]For a thorough study of the anti-Chinese movement among white workers and unions on the West Coast, see Saxton (1971).

paying low wages and forcing long hours of work and unsafe working conditions. Since FOC ships have no real nationality, they are beyond the reach of any single national seafarers' trade union." Lane makes a similar point: "A very substantial part of the rationale of the resort to Flags of Convenience was the avoidance of wage and other employment costs associated with Japanese and European labour markets and the unrestricted ability to recruit crews from low wage countries" (1997, 101). For this reason, the ITF took on the role of a kind of international trade union to organize and negotiate on behalf of FOC crews. Their efforts are a rare example of successful international trade union organizing.

The ITF defines an FOC as a situation where the beneficial ownership and control of a ship lies in another country from the flag that the vessel is flying. The purpose of the ITF campaign is twofold: to push for the elimination of this system and to organize to protect seafarers who work on FOC ships from exploitation by the ship owners. They seek to establish minimum standards, and they have produced an ITF standard collective bargaining agreement that sets wages and working conditions for all crew members on FOC vessels, regardless of nationality. Shipping companies can become signatories of this agreement, and about one quarter of all FOC ships are so covered, providing protection to over ninety thousand seafarers. About a hundred ITF inspectors in ports around the world enforce the agreement. Dockworkers' unions (including the ILWU) have helped to provide the enforcement personnel.

As of January 1, 2005, the top fifty flags—countries that engaged in world shipping—included 13 FOCs (*ITF Seafarers' Bulletin* 2006, 28). The top three, in terms of gross tonnage, were Panama, Liberia, and the Bahamas, all three FOC countries. The other FOCs among the top 50 are the Marshall Islands, Malta, Cyprus, Antigua and Barbuda, St. Vincent, Bermuda, Cayman Islands, Vanuatu, Belize, and the Netherlands Antilles. The true nationality of the top ship-owning countries at the time was, in order of rank, Greece, Japan, Germany, China, Russia, the United States, Norway, and so on down the line, based on the number of ships owned.[2] In other words, many of the ship owners in these countries were registering ships in the small, poor countries that provide FOCs.

According to the ITF, FOCs have a negative effect on the conditions of seafarers. FOC registers do not enforce minimum social standards, which is what makes them attractive to the ship owners. The home countries of the crews, which are different yet again from the countries of ship registration, have difficulty protecting them because the rules that apply on board

[2]The United States appears on this list because it is not limited to container vessels. While container shipping has moved almost completely offshore, this is not the case for some other types of shipping.

are those of the country of registration, not that of the crew. The abuses connected with the FOC system include the following:

> *Unsafe and substandard vessels.* The ships tend to be older on average and badly maintained. They are more prone to accidents.
>
> *Poor safety standards.* There are over 2,000 deaths a year among seafarers. It is difficult for seafarers who suffer serious accidents on FOC ships to win compensation.
>
> *Nonpayment.* Crew members are sometimes owed large sums of money, because payment is withheld, delayed, or otherwise denied. In 2004 a total of $25.1 million in unpaid wages was collected by the ITF for seafarers on FOC vessels, which indicates the extent of the problem.
>
> *Abandonment.* Seafarers are sometimes left behind in strange countries, with no way of getting home.
>
> *No Shore Leave.* It is not uncommon for workers to be stranded on the ship indefinitely while in port, especially in the post-9/11 era. (see 2004 *ITF Annual Report* and "What Do FOC's Mean to Seafarers?" www.itfglobal.org)

Writing about Philippine seafarers, Amante (2004) describes how globalized the labor market for seafarers is. Ship operators can employ workers from any country in the world, picking them up at specified ports. "Greek owners can register their ship and fly the flag of Liberia (and thereby follow the employment and labor laws of that country). The ship could then be chartered by a Chinese company in Hong Kong, and recruit Philippine seafarers and officers from India or Malaysia for a six-month contract aboard."

The container steamship lines commonly use FOCs and employ workers from the poorest countries in the world, including China, India, the Philippines, and Vietnam.

Manning the Ships. Manning or crewing agencies are hired to recruit seamen, establishing agencies in the targeted countries. Since the late 1970s, state and industry regulatory bodies have been severely undermined in their oversight over crewing. State agencies, along with trade unions, used to supervise the employment of maritime contracts. This system has since been replaced by private, uncontrolled, labor contracting firms (see *ITF Seafarers Bulletin* 12). The effects of the deregulation of transport crew hiring practices are significant. Today, the employment of seafarers is mainly contractually based temporary work. In other words, seafarers are employed on a contingent basis. Crewing agencies are located throughout the world, especially in poor countries in the Global South. The majority of shipping companies use such crewing agencies as their primary basis for recruitment. Most seafarers are classified as overseas contract workers

(OCW). The status of OCWs places seafarers in a precarious position in terms of their power to organize, making collective bargaining agreements harder to obtain, implement, and enforce.

In our interview with Bob Kleist (chapter 4), he made it clear that seafarers used to be Americans, but now they are all from offshore. Evergreen, for example, uses Taiwanese, Pilipino, Indonesian, and Malaysian seafarers to work on its ships. The choice of Malaysians is linked to the fact that Evergreen has other businesses there. He said that there is a link between the nationality of registration (FOCs) and crewing, though it appears to us that this is far from a stable relationship.

According to Kleist:

> Most maritime countries have a Maritime Academy, where seafarers receive training. Almost every shipping nation has this kind of training or an agreement with a nation nearby that provides it. The ships are now sophisticated and only require small crews, including specialists and generalists. I don't know the operations end of the company [Evergreen] well, but I assume that the officers include the captain, a chief mate, a second mate, an engineer and a second engineer—five officers total. The rest are crewmen, maybe nine or ten of them. Generally they have some background and experience. Forty-five years ago San Pedro was considered the roughest waterfront in the world. Sailors hung out in bars waiting for captains. Captains would take drunken sailors aboard before they knew it. They no longer staff ships that way.

Here is how Kathleen Gordon of MOL, a Japanese-owned company, described the process of employing seafarers: "We have a subsidiary that operates training centers in the Philippines and India. All our crews come from there. Our officers are all Japanese. We used to have Japanese crews, but they got too expensive. We do our own training because the Japanese are very particular. There are usually nineteen people in the crew including the officers. The cost has been reduced by the use of foreign labor."

The manning agencies are located in the Third World. Most shipping companies work through them. They use management companies, which may be the same as the manning agency or may be another layer. The management company may employ the manning agency. For example, the manning of APL vessels is done by a third-party provider, American Ship Management. They do everything regarding the crews.

Conditions on Container Ships

As we have suggested, containerization has had a mixed impact on seafarers. On the one hand, the ships are safer and cleaner. Other kinds of ships, including tankers and cruise lines, have notoriously worse conditions. Despite the relative advantages for sailors on containerships, conditions are still pretty bad and, on some dimensions, have deteriorated. Seafarers must stay on the ships for longer tours of duty, work long hours, and suffer from restricted shore leave, as mentioned above. Rats and poor food are common problems, and occasionally seafarers die in accidents. Horror stories of conditions on board the ships are spread around, and seafarers are known to abandon ship as their only way out.

Under its flags of convenience campaign, the ITF maintains representatives in every major port, typically by employing a local longshore worker. In 2002, we interviewed the ITF representative for the ports of LA/LB, ILWU member Rudy Vanderhider. This is what he told us:

> There are eighty thousand ships in the world registered with Lloyds of London. They each have a Lloyds Number, which is the same as an ILO [International Labor Organization] number. Twenty-six thousand of them are FOCs. The ITF thinks that 98 percent of labor abuses occur on FOC vessels, so the ITF targets them. It is the ITF's stated goal that it wants all ships to register under their national flag, but it will never happen.
>
> On the whole, containerization has benefited seafarers. True, U.S. seafarers have lost jobs, but Third World workers have gained them. Before containerization, you had break bulk, which took a long time at sea. They were like trampers and weren't accountable. In contrast, containerized shipping is efficient and standardized. The companies don't want any trouble. They run on a time charter. They use a ship for six or seven years. The seafarers contract to the same ship, sailing the same route to the same ports.
>
> The ITF contract says that you have to pay $890 per month for an AB [able-bodied average seaman]. The ILO also has a standard, which is much lower. All the major steamship lines have signed the ITF contract, including NYK, APL, MOL, and others.

The ITF has a safe manning requirement, according to Vanderhider. It specifies the number of seafarers that should serve in each position on a ship. For example, the larger container vessels should have 18 to 22 workers.

Crewing companies are found in every labor-supplying country. Some of these companies are good, and some are not. Some falsify documents. Some get the sailors to pay a certain amount up front in order to get the job. Some ships maintain double books. They pay their crew members $300 even though they claim to pay the ITF rate. So sweatshops are found on the high seas as well as on land. As Vanderhider stated: "There are some shyster ship owners."

The practice of forcing seafarers to pay kickbacks in order to get the job happens often, according to Vanderhider. He describes this as "virtual indentured servitude." The worker has to pay a "placement fee." This can be worth the first three or four months of his wages, but he is hoping that he will get a career out of it. "It is a gamble. The manning agency gets the fee, and the worker waits for a callout. He doesn't know where he will be sent and has no say in the matter. He can be sent to Dubai and put on a scuzzy ship for six to eight months, not eat properly, and at the end there is no renewal. He is back where he started."

Seafarers work under a contract. The best case is a six-month contract, according to Vanderhider, after which the worker gets off the ship for three months and then go back. The worst are contracts in the FOC country of Karabati, in the South Pacific, which has fourteen-month contracts. He continued: "Shore leave is a huge issue. The time charter ships [liners] go back and forth, following a predictable circuit. Sometimes the seafarers can't get ashore either in the United States or in Asia. In LA/LB you generally can get ashore, especially if you have seaman's documents. Some don't and only have passports, which the INS is more reluctant to approve, for fear that people will jump ship. If you have seaman's documents it shows you have a commitment to the job and are making decent money."

The owner of the ship has to notify the INS four to five days before the ship docks to clear shore leave for the crew, and they often do not do it. The situation has deteriorated since 9/11. Now the authorities are worried about porous borders. There was a flurry of Chinese stowaways in containers that caused alarm. Container ships are only in port for two days. Sometimes seafarers call the ITF about shore leave, and Vanderhider has to tell them that it isn't covered in the ITF contract. Officials are most concerned about Chinese and Burmese crews escaping, given conditions in their countries.

According to Vanderhider: "Cosco and China Shipping [China-owned steamship lines] both have ITF contracts, but they are bogus. They don't pay the rate or honor the contract. I went after Cosco on the issue of lashing. They were having seafarers lash containers at sea, which is a major safety problem since it is a dangerous activity even in dock. I finally managed to hammer something out with them, after threatening to go to the press with their story."

Vanderhider is on retainer with the ITF and is on call 24/7. He can get buried in calls from seafarers who are having problems. The issues include food, wages, roach infestations, lack of basic equipment like gloves and jackets, health care, and abandonment. Medical care is a big issue, since usually none is provided on board.

The ITF has to have a union affiliate in a country in order to help its seafarers. But many ITF-affiliated unions are weak or indifferent. The situation is the worst for Chinese and Burmese seafarers, who are often too intimidated to talk with an ITF official. If Vanderhider tries, they just walk away. An ITF inspector might be able to get the workers paid, but there is no guarantee that they will be able to keep the money. The ship will likely take it back from them as soon as the ITF representative leaves.

According to Vanderhider, "Some steamship lines don't want any trouble and operate cleanly. But there are certainly scumbags in the LA/LB harbor. You can clean them up, but they are always backsliding." Vanderhider generally does random inspections of FOC vessels. If called he goes on a national flag vessel, but he isn't sure that this is legal. He gives out ITF publications to seafarers and also collects information, sending it out to other ITF inspectors so that they are prepared for an incoming vessel. The ITF inspectors work as an international network.

The ILO and the International Maritime Organization (IMO), creations of the UN that set standards for seafarers, rely upon the ITF. Neither of them has an enforcement capability. Vanderhider told us that the ITF shows up at ILO and IMO meetings and tells them what needs to be resolved. "The ITF is the brains and heart, as well as the policeman."

Interview with Koko Khiang

Vanderhider put us in touch with Koko Khiang, a Burmese seafarer who led an attempt to organize a union among Burmese seafarers, even though such activity was illegal in his country. He is an amazing person.

Khiang worked as a crewman for a Taiwanese steamship company that was not engaged in the trans-Pacific trade but instead sailed among Taiwan, Korea, and Hong Kong. His own experience may be limited, but he is certainly familiar with the conditions faced by many seafarers. Here are some of the things he said:

> Seafarers sign a one-year contract. The Burmese seafarers are paid $320 a month. They are supposed to have breaks, but many work for three years straight because they need the money. I worked for two and a half years without a break.
>
> You get the job through an agent or broker, and you have to pay him $1000 to get the job. This means that you are afraid to speak up or argue. You have to take care of your investment. If you have a problem with the master officer, you can get fired. They deduct $50 a month from your pay for three months for a security fund, to cover your air ticket home if you are fired, and for a replacement fund to find someone to take your place. The brokers are mainly from Singapore and Bangkok. They guarantee the ship managers that you are not connected with the ITF. Right now [2002] the price to become a Burmese seafarer is $2500. It is similar for the seafarers from Vietnam and Indonesia. That is what they have to pay the brokers.

Many seafarers are from the Philippines. Filipino seafarers are generally better off and have unions that are affiliated with the ITF. They only have to pay one month's salary to the Philippines Overseas Employment Association, rather than the large amounts paid to brokers in some other countries. In contrast, seafarers from China are the worst off. They get paid $100 to $150 a month and have no union. "Life on board a ship is very boring," said Khiang. "You don't have much time to sleep. You are supposed to work eight hours a day, but end up working sixteen—without overtime pay. You get no days off at all, but you feel you have no choice."

Khiang described the treatment he received as abusive. The Taiwanese officers would yell at them, and they discriminated against the Burmese. There is a kind of hierarchy of treatment among seafarers. Filipinos are at the top, Indonesians, Vietnamese, and Burmese are in the middle, and Chinese are at the bottom: "There are more and more Chinese seafarers, and they could easily take over all the jobs." He thinks the Chinese are coming to dominate the market in part because they don't speak English, so have another disadvantage that weakens their position. Indonesia has a seafarer's union, but the leaders are part of the military, or were until 2000. Consequently, the ITF would not let them affiliate. This may have changed with increased democracy in the country.

The union that Khiang led was the Seafarers' Union of Burma. In 1948 Burma gained freedom from the British, and for a while unions were permitted. In 1962 there was a military coup, and unions were banned. Since Khiang was born (in the mid-1960s) until at least 2002, when we conducted the interview, there were no unions in Burma. Unions were illegal, so the Burmese seafarers started their union in Bangkok in 1991. The union faced opposition and oppression from both the ship owners and the Burmese government. If they worked with the ITF, their money was taken away and their Seafarers' Book, a form of credential, was revoked. Khiang gave an example: "In 1993 a Burmese crew got assistance from the ITF in Australia. The ITF helped them get back pay that they were owed. They were being cheated out of their wages. The seafarers were going home from Sydney through Singapore and Bangkok to Burma. The Burmese authorities came to the Singapore Airport, picked them up, arrested them, and forced them to return to Burma."

Khiang testified at the International Tribunal on Workers Rights in Canada in 1997. After that he wasn't safe, even in Thailand, since it shares a border with Burma. He sought and received political asylum in the United States in 2000. He gave us a copy of a report on labor practices in Burma from September 1998 that was put out by the U.S. Department of Labor's Bureau of International Labor Affairs. It has a description of how Burmese seafarers are harassed and punished if they try to contact a union and explains that their contract prohibits them from contacting the ITF.

In sum, while there are some differences in the vulnerability and experiences of seafarers from different countries as well as in the types of ships they work on, there can be no doubt that job conditions and pay have declined substantially as the work has moved offshore. Given the "captive" character of work on a ship, the need for protective institutions appears very evident.

Racialized Labor among Seafarers

The majority of seafarers worldwide are men of color from the Global South.[3] Of the remaining seafarers who are white, most are from poor Eastern European nations such as Romania or Ukraine. Racialized labor forces allow employers to exploit workers at higher rates under worse conditions, usually for less pay. The seafaring industry is a good example of the implications of racialized labor. Today's seafarers make a fraction of what white U.S. seafarers used to make prior to the industry's erosion. The racialized process of crewing, selecting poor workers from the Global South, contributes to a lowering of labor standards on the ships.

As we have seen, a major purpose of the FOCs is to avoid the labor standards established by industrialized countries and their unions. Now the shipping companies employ workers from the poorest countries in the world, including China, India, the Philippines, and Vietnam. Manning or crewing agencies are hired to recruit seamen, establishing agencies in the targeted countries.

In racialized labor regimes, racialized exploitation and harassment often are present. It is not uncommon for seafarers to experience unfair treatment due to their race or nationality. According to a 1996 ITF-assisted survey of over six thousand seafarers in 93 countries, a quarter of all seafarers reported that "they had been unfairly treated because of their race or nationality. . . . 10 percent reported incidents of physical abuse and 14 percent had been told not to contact a trade union" (reported in the ITF Seafarer's Bulletin 12). Filipino and Indonesian seafarers reported the highest rates of physical abuse on the high seas. This is especially significant in that Filipinos make up the world's largest population of seafarers—approximately 28 percent of the world's 1.2 million seafarers (Santiago 2005). Racially motivated abuse was highest on FOC ships, where 29 percent of crewmembers reported being racially targeted.

---

[3]The term Global South is used to refer to the former colonial world, or what used to be called the "Third World." It is less a geographic designation than a description of power relations. The Global South is dominated by the Global North—the developed countries of Western Europe, North America, and Japan.

According to the ITF survey, about half of all merchant seafarers earned less than $1,200 a month, with 15 percent making less than $500 a month. The survey found that 55 percent of seafarers supported between two and five people, while a quarter supported five or more people. Many of the lowest-paid nationals were Filipino, Eastern European, African, Chinese, and Indonesian. Japanese seafarers were paid the most, although 37 percent of (non-Japanese) seafarers on Japanese-flag ships earned less than $500 a month. Many seafarers (42 percent) worked on ships where their native language was not spoken, making it difficult to understand colleagues and to report safety or health violations. It also creates difficulties for labor organizing.

Undercutting of wages has also been on the rise in the seafaring industry. With the collapse of the Soviet Union, many dispossessed Eastern Europeans were utilized as cheaper labor to bring down real wages in the industry. Since then, this process has most recently taken place as a result of the increased presence of Chinese seafarers. Many Filipino seafarers were preparing for the influx of Chinese seafarers, and resentment and competition among these groups is increasing. Chinese workers were becoming the most attractive labor force to employers due to their high levels of training and low wages (Carillo 2002). Annual crewing costs reflected this shift; the pay rates for Chinese seafarers were 10 to 20 percent lower than for Filipino seafarers.

Evaluation

In the case of seafarers, many of the direst predictions regarding the effects of the logistics revolution appear to have come true. The work is contingent, the unions have been weakened or eliminated, the work has been shifted offshore and racialized, and working conditions have deteriorated. True, containerization has had some benefits, but the overall picture is one of a decline for this group of workers.

However, there is also some good news. Described in *Global Links* (November 2006), a newsletter of a coalition of international longshore and mining trade unions, the ILO adopted the Consolidated Maritime Convention, popularly known as the Seafarers' Bill of Rights, in February 2006. Taking five years of negotiations to accomplish, the new Bill of Rights sets minimum requirements for seafarers, including hours of work and rest, accommodation, recreational facilities, food, health care, and so on. Unusually, the convention has some enforcement provisions. It has been endorsed by the International Shipping Federation, which represents ship owners associations in thirty-four countries, covering most of the world's ocean shipping, and by the ITF. Such an agreement between management and labor suggests how low standards had sunk.

Labor on the Docks

Brief History of the West Coast Longshore Workers

Longshore workers and seafarers have some things in common. In the early decades of the twentieth century, many longshoremen on the West Coast had been seamen before choosing to settle down as dock workers. They were less transient and isolated from society than the seamen, but they shared the experience of raw exploitation. The irregular nature of the work led them to live near the waterfront, alongside seafarers. Both groups of workers developed a cosmopolitan perspective because of their exposure to peoples from all over the world (Nelson 1988, 2–3).

Before containerization in the 1960s, during the "break-bulk" era, cargo was loaded on and off ships in wooden pallets, nets, or cases. Each box or package had to be carefully stowed, and the hull of the ship had to be packed in such a way as to maintain the ship's balance. This was a slow and arduous process, forcing ships to remain in dock for many days. Similarly, the discharge of a vessel required the detailed work of pulling out packages in small numbers. The symbol of the longshoreman was the hook used to move the stowed objects in and out of the hold.

When a ship came into harbor, the main method of getting labor to discharge and reload it was the shape-up. Anyone who has seen the movie *On the Waterfront* will remember this process. Men would come to the gate and be chosen on the spot to do the work. As demonstrated in the film, this arrangement could allow for favoritism and corruption. Dock workers had no guarantee of hours, job choice, or pay rates. Foremen on the waterfront represented the interests of the employers and exercised complete power over the workers by determining who worked and for what wages. Acts of favoritism and discrimination were common. It was not unusual for workers to resort to bribes to pay their employers or managers in order to receive work. A longshore worker could wait around for three or more days hoping to get a job, and if work was granted, he might have had to work straight through for twenty-four to thirty-six hours.

The 1934 Strike and the Formation of the ILWU

The ILWU website provides a history of the union (www.ilwu.org). Briefly, longshore unions began to form on the West Coast in the nineteenth century. By 1902 they were affiliated with the AFL's International Longshoremen's Association (ILA), but the ties of the locals to the international were weak. In 1910 the Pacific District of the ILA was formed as an affiliate of the ILA, with considerable autonomy for the district and for the local chapters within it.

Strike action was taken local by local, allowing the employers to pit workers against each other. They imported strike breakers or diverted cargo from a struck port to defeat strikes in 1916, 1919, and 1921. The union was rebuilt in 1933 following the principles of the militant IWW, which was active around the waterfront. Indeed, the new union would adopt the famous IWW slogan: "An injury to one is an injury to all."

In 1933, the West Coast longshoremen renewed their charter from the ILA, but this time they established their organization as a single, coast-wise unit. The chief demands they wanted to extract from the employ-ers (the ship owners) were a union-controlled hiring hall that would end all forms of favoritism and equalize work opportunities and a coastwise contract with all longshore workers on the Pacific Coast working for the same basic wages and under the same conditions. As one can imag-ine, the ship owners resisted these demands, and a strike was called for May 1934.

The 1934 strike proved to be a pivotal moment in the history of the West Coast. The employers mobilized private industry, state and local gov-ernments, and the police to smash it, while the seafarers and longshoremen joined together in opposition. Importantly, the national ILA did not sup-port the strike. New leaders emerged among the strikers, including Harry Bridges, who was later elected president of the ILA's Pacific Coast District and then president of the ILWU when it formed.

Nelson points to four crucial features of the strike. First, the strikers were able to maintain discipline and militancy even though their oppo-nents brought out every weapon against them, including private security guards, vigilantes, and the National Guard. Second, old craft antagonisms disappeared as workers from a variety of jobs joined together in a gen-eral strike. Third, rank-and-file union members took power into their own hands, often defying the AFL and its leaders. And fourth, given the hysteri-cal anticommunist propaganda of their opponents, workers came to view "Red-baiting" as a tactic of the employer and resisted the attacks on the leftist participants in their ranks (1988, 128).

During the strike, violence erupted as employers tried to force the docks open using goon squads, tear gas, and the National Guard. Battles occurred in San Francisco, Portland, Seattle, and San Pedro. Hundreds of strikers and bystanders were arrested and injured. On July 5, 1934, "Bloody Thurs-day," two workers were shot and killed. This led the San Francisco labor movement to join the maritime strikers in the general strike. Although the general strike lasted only four days, it demonstrated to the employers and government that the waterfront workers had widespread support among Bay Area unions. The strikers also received support from workers in other countries. The strike ended when the federal government intervened, and the union agreed to arbitration of all of the issues. It won, in principle, its major demands, leading to, among other things, the formation of the first multi-employer collective bargaining unit covering the entire industry.

The Pacific Coast District of the ILA strongly supported industrial over craft unionism, and it was urged to join the newly formed Committee for Industrial Organization (CIO). Meanwhile, the national ILA was solidly situated within the AFL. They tried to impose a dues assessment to fight the CIO, an obvious affront to their West Coast members. As a result, the Pacific Coast District held a referendum and voted to disaffiliate from the ILA. The ILWU was born in 1937 and soon voted to join the CIO.

The ILWU's leadership stands in stark contrast to the conservative leadership of the ILA on the East Coast. Kimmeldorf (1988) has conducted an extensive comparison of the two unions, trying to understand why one longshore union, the ILA, became mob-infested and corrupt, while the other, the ILWU, became radical and remained very principled. The different political trajectories of the two organizations also affected their strength as unions. The ILA's ties to organized crime proved to be a factor in weakening the East Coast union, whereas the radicalism and commitment to union democracy of the ILWU leadership led it to be a force to be reckoned with.

Joseph Ryan, president of the ILA International, was a fanatical anti-communist, and was obsessed with Soviet infiltration, while Harry Bridges, the ILWU leader, was a leftist who had participated in the IWW (Kimeldorf 1988, 14). The differences between the two unions remain to this day. For example, in 2005, the U.S. government filed a racketeering lawsuit against the ILA for alleged ties to the mob.

Since its inception, the ILWU has been known as a left-wing union. From its founding the ILWU adopted an anti-fascist stance, opposed the Marshall Plan, favored trade with China, and spoke out against both the Korean and Vietnam Wars (Fairley 1979). The ILWU's radical tendencies eventually got it expelled from the CIO in 1950, during the peak of anti-communist witch hunts. Structurally, the ILWU has striven to maintain a commitment to democratic decision-making and transparency, including regular chapter elections with term limits. While some have criticized the union for having an elitist decision-making process despite its apparent democratic structure, other labor scholars have touted the ILWU for its democracy (for an account of the democratic structure of the ILWU, see Kimeldorf 1988).

Whether the ILWU is a paragon of democracy or not, it is clear that the structure of the union attempts to maintain a commitment to democratic representation of its rank and file. The union has direct elections of officers and referenda on contracts and other major issues. The ILWU's democratic principles were not only a defense against the anticommunist crusades of the time; they also strengthened rank-and-file participation (Wellman 1995).

Racism in the ILWU

During the early years of the ILWU, race was a major source of division. African Americans were brought in as strikebreakers by the employers in the strikes of 1916, 1919, and 1921. According to the ILWU website, this changed with the 1934 strike: "For the first time, most minority workers refused to scab, thanks to the longshoremen's developing policy against racial discrimination" (www.ilwu.org).

The ILWU has certainly prided itself on its progressive attitude regarding racial discrimination. Third among the union's ten guiding principles, formally adopted in 1953, is the following:

> Workers are indivisible. There can be no discrimination because of race, color, creed, national origin, religious or political belief. Any division among the workers can help no one but the employers. Discrimination of worker against worker is suicide. Discrimination is a weapon of the boss. Its entire history is proof that it has served no other purpose than to pit worker against worker to their own destruction. (www.ilwu.org)

These fine words are certainly to be applauded, but, as might be expected, the ILWU has not always lived up to them. Of course, it is better to have them enshrined in one's guiding principles than not. But to implement them in a society riddled with racial division is not so easy, and it would have been miraculous indeed if the ILWU had not had some shortcomings in this regard. For example, in its early exuberance, the ILWU tried to organize dockworkers in New Orleans in 1937, but faced an overwhelming—and, to ILWU organizers, surprising—electoral defeat from the majority African-American workforce there. Union organizers did not understand the bitter racial competition that characterized longshore work in the city, and they were unprepared for African-American suspicion of their intentions (Nelson 1992, 20).

True, there were some successes. Even though longshore unions had historically excluded African Americans before the formation of the strike of 1934, Bridges and the Communists had tried to overturn this record, and the San Francisco longshore local had three African-American members on its executive board in 1937. But up and down the coast, the legacy of racism had a tendency to persist (Nelson 1992, 23).

During World War II, with the expansion of waterfront activity, at least one out of five new workers in the warehouse division was African- or Mexican-American, and the percentage was higher in the longshore division. Slowdowns and work stoppages arose as whites resisted the entry and promotion of these workers. The ILWU leadership underestimated the strength of racist beliefs among the rank and file. Bridges spoke out against it, but the leadership made only limited efforts to rid the union of it in practice. Quam-Wickham (1992) reviewed interviews with a number of longshoremen of color about the conditions in the 1940s and came across many grievances. She found that the hiring hall, as an institution, could be used by white workers to keep workers of color from certain jobs. These practices were not challenged by the ILWU leadership, in part in the name of local autonomy.

Promotions were another arena of unchallenged racist practice in the 1940s. ILWU longshoremen were not promoted solely on the basis of seniority. In San Pedro, members of the promotion committee of the longshore Local 13 used their position to deny African Americans promotion to the position of gang boss, for example. They would throw African-Americans applications away, or the committee members would harass them with hostile questions. In 1945, a wartime labor shortage led a Local 13 job dispatcher to send a African-American man out as a gang boss. The white workers refused to work for him and walked off the job. The employer fired him because the gang would not work, and the dispatcher was reprimanded by his superior for sending a African-American man out as a boss. As a result, a coastwise policy was adopted by both employers and the union that no man could be a boss unless he had worked five years in the industry—a thin veil to keep out the more recently arrived African-American longshore workers (Quam-Wickham 1992, 64–66).

Apart from possible discrimination in the hiring hall, other mechanisms also made it hard to get into the union. Registered longshore workers' kin were granted preference for membership in the union once the worker died or retired. Before the early 1970s, ILWU members could sponsor people to enter the union. As one can imagine, these practices tended to create ethnic (white) homogeneity among members. In the face of a series of affirmative action lawsuits, changes were introduced to open up membership to women and people of color. (For further analysis of the history of racism and racial division among longshore workers, both in the ILWU and around the country, see Nelson 1998, 2001; Winslow 1998.)

Longshore Workers and the Logistics Revolution

The story of the longshore workers might be considered to be the polar opposite of that of the seafarers. The longshore workers of Southern California have been able to hold on to their powerful union, the ILWU. They have not suffered the decimation and degradation faced by seafarers. But the logistics revolution has certainly had an impact on them, and it threatens to have more of an impact as time goes by. The key shift was the advent of containerization, which completely altered the nature of their work and led to a historic agreement. But since then, efforts to introduce new technology and to weaken the union have continued, culminating recently in the lockout of 2002. The story of the ILWU is by no means over, as new conflicts are brewing to limit the union's power.

Containerization had a major impact on the way longshore work was done. Before the introduction of containers, longshore workers would go down into the hold of a ship and load and unload packages sent down by pallet. Containers completely changed the work. They are loaded by an overhead crane whose operator is highly skilled. The containers on deck are then lashed into place to secure them. The process is reversed for the discharge of ships.

Talley (2002) examined the effects of containerization and deregulation of the shipping industry (by the Shipping Act of 1984) on the wages of dock workers versus railroad and trucking workers. We shall examine the latter two in the next chapter; here we focus on his findings regarding longshore workers. Under the break-bulk system, 20 dockworkers could load 20 tons of cargo per hour. With containers, perhaps 10 men could load 400 to 500 tons per hour. Needless to say, this change meant that the demand for longshore labor fell sharply, by as much as 60 percent in some countries. In the Port of New York/New Jersey, for example, employment dropped from 30,000 longshore workers in 1970 to 7,400 in 1986 (Talley 2002, 2–4).

This situation led to a surplus of dockworkers. However, the passage of the Shipping Act of 1984 led to a decrease in this labor surplus and an increase in the bargaining power of dockworkers. The act (it will be recalled) allowed door-to-door rates, hence intermodal freight transportation. These changes stimulated the growth in containerized trade, leading in turn to growth in the demand for dockworkers.

Containerization is also associated with growth in capital investment in the ports. The ports had to make huge investments in infrastructure in order to handle the giant container ships. Moreover, the ports were in competition with each other to attract the ships, since intermodalism means that the steamship lines (and shippers) are freer to choose which ports they use, because they can ship the containers via different routes to their final destinations. The result was an increase in port capital-labor ratios. The ports—and their customers—could ill afford work stoppages. Given that labor costs are a relatively small percentage of total costs, this situation gives power to the dockworkers to bid up their wages and gain favorable work conditions. The steamship lines would rather give in to dockworker demands and pay the extra, rather than face a strike or some other glitch in the movement of cargo. In sum, the shift to containerization increased the bargaining power of dockworkers, leading to improved wages (Talley 2002, 5–6).

This bargaining power allows some longshore workers, especially the valuable crane operators, to cut special deals and get extras. The union has also been able to use its leverage to advantage. Work rules are favorable to the workers, and under-the-table deals are cut by the steamship lines in order to get a particular worker or ensure his or her loyalty. In other words, the pressure to get the hugely expensive ships in and out of port allows for lots of side deals to the benefit of workers. We heard many complaints about it. Companies blame each other for undercutting the contract. People would say, "We don't mind paying them well, if only they did a fair day's work" (for a detailed description of such deals, see Finlay 1988).

The Mechanization and Modernization Agreement

When containers were first introduced, the ILWU leadership had to decide how to respond. To their credit, instead of resisting technological advancement, Harry Bridges and the ILWU leadership became convinced that technological change was inevitable—if the union were to remain strong, it must embrace it and shape it as much as possible for the benefit of labor. This led to the signing of the historic Mechanization and Modernization (M&M) Agreement.

On October 18, 1960, the ILWU and the Pacific Maritime Association, the main organization representing the interests of waterfront employers (steamship and stevedoring companies) on the West Coast, negotiated the M&M Agreement in an effort to deal with the union's concern over the threat of job loss from labor-reducing technology. The M&M Agreement resulted in both advantages and costs to the ILWU. It allowed the employers to introduce cutting-edge technologies (mechanization) on the waterfront in exchange for a jointly trusted fund, guaranteeing lifetime employment for fully registered longshore workers, thirty-five-hour work weeks, early retirement options for dock workers who had been working for over twenty-five years, and extended benefits (Finlay 1988; Wellman 1995).

The M&M Agreement placed an emphasis on speed and efficiency, transforming the waterfront. New methods of handling cargo were introduced along with containerization, giving employers an immediate payoff in terms of decreased labor costs and increased productivity (Finlay 1988). The use of containers streamlined the movement of goods and allowed for more volume to be moved in a shorter period of time. These improvements, along with newly designed ships, eventually led to drastic increases in tonnage entering the Pacific ports. Between 1968 and 2001, productivity soared. In this period, annual tonnage handled by the West Coast ports grew 465 percent on the docks, while productivity grew 6.6 percent a year. This increase in productivity occurred simultaneously with a shrinking workforce.

Containerization has brought many changes to the waterfront. Work has become less physically demanding, less reliant on brute strength, and more dependent on precision and speed (Finlay 1988). At the same time, the rapid movement of thirty-ton containers through the air means that the docks remain a dangerous work environment, resulting in a number of deaths and serious injuries each year. Since the M&M Agreement, technological change has remained a hot-button issue for longshore workers and their employees.

The ILWU Today

Despite the fact that the ILWU has only forty-two thousand members, the union is still a force to be reckoned with. It is a strong presence on the West Coast ports from California to Oregon, Washington, Alaska, and Hawaii. Its members are truly "the lords of the docks." Whenever we have attended port-related events, "labor" has always been included, and labor is defined by the ILWU. The other ports and logistics-related workers and unions, such as the port truckers, the IBT, or the railroad workers or unions, are not even considered. This appears to us to be a relatively rare status for a U.S. trade union.

An important aspect of the ILWU's power lies in its retention and control over the union's hiring hall, which has remained virtually unchanged in its seventy years of existence. The hiring (or dispatch) hall gives the ILWU full control over the day-to-day distribution of work loads and duties for the longshore workers. Today's dispatch process works on a per-shift basis. Employers phone in their work orders specifying how many workers will be needed and the type of work that will be carried out (PMA 2005). In order to ensure that work allocation is administered on a fair basis, the ILWU utilizes a system of job sharing called "low-man-out" dispatching. Low-man-out gives the worker with the fewest accumulated hours the first opportunity to work. Longshore workers have the right to decide which jobs they want to take, with the option not to work on a daily basis. Instead of employers selecting their workers, the reverse happens in the dispatch hall—workers select their employers. This gives the union and workers tremendous power (Finlay 1988).

The dispatch system is set up to act as a leveling mechanism in which work is allocated on an impartial basis, at least for registered longshore workers (Schneider and Siegel 1956, 16). Ability and performance are not taken into consideration in work allocation. This means that ILWU members do not work directly for any particular employer, although there are exceptions, with certain union members having a "steady" status with certain employers. The hall also functions as a regulatory body, ensuring safety standards and working conditions. During the last contract negotiations between the PMA and ILWU, it was agreed that the PMA would pay 85 percent of all operating costs of the hiring hall on a yearly basis, at just under $18 million (PMA 2005).

Pacific Maritime Association

The PMA, founded in 1949, is the principal organization that represents the interests of the maritime employers, including ocean carriers and terminal operators, on the West Coast. The PMA negotiates all of the collective bargaining agreements with the ILWU. It also funds the hiring hall operations, as noted above, along with managing other administrative duties, such as pension plans, vacation time, and personnel records (Hartman 1969). Throughout its existence, the PMA has been in charge of paying dock workers. The carriers and stevedoring companies pay the PMA, which then cuts checks to the workers. This frees the workers from being too closely tied to any particular employer. Needless to say, this creates a very different power dynamic between employer and employee (Wellman 1995).

We met with Chuck Wallace, vice president of the PMA for Southern California, the highest position in the region in 2002, shortly before the West Coast lockout. We asked what the PMA does. He said that all of its functions flow from collective bargaining. It has a legal department, which is a bit less tied to collective bargaining, but the rest of the functions are connected with it. They include such things as training, payroll, federal health and safety regulations, accident and preventions, and labor relations. He said that huge sums are involved in the contract, as can be seen from the PMA's annual reports.

We asked, somewhat hesitantly, about how much the PMA itself costs (something not mentioned in the annual report). He said that about $16 million goes to training, and that mainly ends up going to the workers. It spends about $20 million on the dispatch halls, which also goes to the workers. Staff and rent cost about $30 million a year. It has a staff of 125, down from the 1960s.

Here is the way Wallace described the interests of steamship lines, the main components of the PMA:

> The ocean carriers are in business to move freight. Their goal is to move it as quickly as possible. They now have a complete system [meaning door-to-door], which is what the customer wants. We have eliminated the warehouse. We provide a reliable source of goods. The consignees, like Wal-Mart, can count on their Christmas goods being there on time at a reasonable cost. They avoid having an extra stage of holding goods in warehouses. They can buy their products later. The ships are now moving warehouses. A container pulled by a truck is a warehouse on wheels.

We asked about how united the steamship lines are. Wallace said that they are competitors, of course, but there is more unity than there was before. We then asked about the problem of paying longshoremen extra under the table, and he agreed that this is common. It involves undercutting the contract. He sees it happening regularly; it is widespread. And the union has great negotiators who are able to get as much as possible. He thinks the biggest issue is whether the employer gets something extra for the money. "You have a problem when you don't put the deal on paper. People forget. There is no clear deal, and you end up negotiating every day. This is not good management."

We raised the question of shipper (importer and exporter) pressures on the PMA. Wallace said that they don't usually interact with the PMA. The PMA only hears from them—and then incessantly—when the contract is coming up. Then they want to know the chances of getting their goods. However, the shippers want to cut down on transportation costs. He pointed to one shipper: "Wal-Mart puts pressure on everyone—on all their customers and we are all their customers—even the Asian producers. They are the ultimate. They call the shots. We get it from the SS Lines. They are pressured from the top."

Here is Wallace's candid assessment of the purpose of the PMA: "Our role is keeping the union in check. We make sure that it doesn't get too huge. We prevent it from becoming so powerful that it is impossible to operate efficiently. Our orientation is that we look to work with labor. We want to get better quality people. We want them to be more efficient. As I said, we spend $17 million on training."

We talked about ILWU power. Wallace said that they are a funnel through which all trade must flow. He thinks that longshore workers are powerful all over the world. They are in a position to manipulate the flow of goods. And here they have no competition. In Europe, other ports compete—they can shift from Bremerhaven to Rotterdam, but in LA there is no alternative.

We wondered if the union could be broken if the shippers, carriers, PMA, or the U.S. government really wanted to. Wallace said he thought it could be broken, that there is enough money to do it. But he does not want that to happen, because "my job would go down the tubes." This was the most remarkable statement in this interview. The PMA is dependent on the union's continued good health for its existence and continuation. Although they are on opposite sides of the bargaining table, they are bound to each other. This reality makes the PMA pro-union, in a strange way.

The PMA's chief concern is a belief that productivity has been declining in recent years. For years it went up steadily, but now it is going down. The PMA wants to improve training and hire better people. They want to set higher standards for the initial hire by developing a two-year junior college program covering basic English, the history of the industry, and certain skills like truck driving and basic welding. There could also be a class on union history. The PMA also wants to provide more sophisticated training for those people who are already employed and to have the workers within their skill sets. Sometimes a skilled worker is needed for a job and a casual employee is assigned. The PMA also wants the workers to come to work on time. And they want more steady workers.

We asked how the PMA feels about the dispatch hall. Wallace said that the PMA doesn't care about it, and neither do the employers. If the employees work hard, they have no complaints. We found this surprising, imagining that the employers would want to gain direct control over their workforce and that the union's control over dispatching is a key source of its power. He agreed that the dispatch hall gives the union power, but he thinks it is an important part of their tradition. The big strikes of 1934 to 1936 were all about keeping dispatch halls. He sees it as an accepted part of the union's image.

Wallace said that the PMA is at loggerheads with the union over all of the issues already mentioned, plus technology—especially with the marine clerks over introducing labor-saving technology that would eliminate many jobs (an issue that became critical in the 2002 contract negotiations). He said: "The biggest ideological difference with the union is over freedom of choice on the job. They want too much freedom, like the right not to show up for work on the day of the Super Bowl, or to send someone who isn't adequately skilled for the job."

Wages and Working Conditions

The current coastwise agreement between the PMA and the ILWU expires on July 1, 2008. This agreement covers all of the work-related issues and regulations on the docks. On the waterfront, work assignments are dispatched depending on the employee's status. Workers are divided into Class A longshore workers, Class B longshore workers, Identified casual workers, and Temporary unidentified casual workers. The vast majority of all Class A workers are members of the ILWU. These are the workers with the most privileges. Class B workers are also eligible for union membership on a limited basis—for example, they get limited voting rights and can advance to A status after five years. Casual longshore workers are not members of the union and must report out of a separate hiring hall. Casual workers can only receive work once Class A and B workers have been offered the job and have turned it down. They are only hired for one work shift (or task) at a time. Being designated a casual worker does not guarantee that one will be needed on any given day, although specific work tasks often take multiple shifts to complete. These workers are also not eligible for benefits.

Registered union members fall into three categories: Longshore workers, Clerks, and Walking bosses/Foremen. Longshore workers handle all of the duties associated with the unloading and loading of cargo on ships. Class A longshore registrants make an average of just over $93,000 a year. Marine clerks are responsible for many administrative responsibilities, including those associated with receiving, maintaining information on the inventory of containers, and keeping detailed records of water-front activity. Clerks process all of the cargo at the docks and report damages. They make an average salary of just under $126,000. Walking bosses supervise dock activity and oversee longshore work. They are in charge of all of the unloading and loading of the cargo. Walking bosses also report to a stevedoring company superintendent. Walking bosses/Foremen make the most of any of the three categories, at approximately $177,000 a year on average (PMA 2005). That they are members of the ILWU is important, as these positions used to be controlled by the employers.

During the 2002 negotiations, rhetoric was directed at the ILWU that implied that blue-collar workers were not entitled to the high wages and benefits that longshore workers received. They were described as the best-paid blue collar workers in the United States, as if their pay was out of line. Perhaps this view is enhanced by the presence of large numbers of workers of color on the docks, which brings out a hidden belief that such workers should not be paid high wages. According to director of organizing for the ILWU, Peter Olney, this sentiment is unwarranted: "Given the enormous productivity gains on the waterfront over the last 40 years and the danger of longshoring, second only to mine work in the rate of death and injury, and the degree of physical difficulty, these excellent wages would seem justified" (2003, 33).

The severe congestion and delays at the ports in 2004 prompted drastic action in terms of longshore employment, since one of the reasons for the delays was a shortage of longshore workers. The PMA and ILWU announced the hiring of several thousand new workers. The applicant pool for this hiring was immense. Approximately three hundred thousand names were sent in the form of a postcard for a chance to be a casual worker on the waterfront. Even though casuals are not guaranteed steady employment, this class still starts at $20.66 per hour. The applicants were mostly selected by lottery. Not only did the year 2004 bring in five thousand new workers to the Southern California ports to deal with the record volume of imports, but nearly two thousand existing casuals were also promoted into the ranks of union membership (PMA 2005). The process of expanding the ranks of steady longshore workers has continued.[4]

EDNA'S DAY ON THE DOCKS WITH CRAIG BAGDASAR

Craig Bagdasar is a walking boss from Local 94, the foremen's local. He was very helpful to me in this research, introducing me to union people, and we have become friends. I asked him about the possibility of spending a day with him while he was working, simply following him around to see how things work. He very kindly agreed to set this up, and we met at the Maersk terminal at Pier 400 on April 23, 2003. He usually works the "hoot shift" (3 to 8 a.m.), so this may have been a bit of a hardship for him. We arranged to meet at 6:50 a.m. in the parking lot near the terminal building. Pier 400 is on Terminal Island, and I had to cross the magnificent Vincent Thomas Bridge to get there. The terminal is on landfill, stretching out into the bay. It is run by APM terminals, which is a subsidiary of Maersk.

Unlike the APL terminal, which I had visited previously, no security guards were visible. In order to get in I just had to show a driver's license. At 6:50 a.m., the parking lot had bunches of men going to work, carrying lunch buckets and backpacks. Craig came out and we drove in a yard truck over to a building called Marine Vessel Operations, where three ships were lined up. He didn't have a clear job assigned yet and had to arrange to get one. He had brought me a hardhat and two safety jackets, so while he was inside negotiating I tried them on. Craig was assigned to be a hatch boss; he usually serves as a ship boss—the person that oversees the entire discharge and reloading of the vessel. He chose a job that would protect my safety. As we drove to work, he pointed out the *Axel Maersk,* which was on its maiden voyage. He described it as beautiful, which indeed it is—huge and blue. He said it is as big as they come.

Crane

We started by going up in a crane—a giant blue one, new, with the latest technology. These cranes were expensive (nearly $12 million), made by a German company in Abu Dhabi. The terminals are now buying cheaper cranes made in China. We took a cramped elevator up one of the legs of

---

[4]Edna has participated a little in this process, serving as a guest speaker in some of the classes taught by Craig Bagdasar, which have recruited new supervisors into Local 94 from the ranks of the other locals.

the crane. We exited on to a narrow wire-net platform 150 feet up. It is built to sway in the wind, and I felt the potential for seasickness. I took some photos. Then we walked across and entered the cabin. This little exercise is definitely not for the claustrophobic or the acrophobic.

The crane operator was named Bobby. Craig asked him what he thought of this crane, and he showed us how the seat wobbled. He felt the best ones were at the TraPac Terminal. We were close to the ship to which Craig was assigned—the *Innovator*. He was going to work with Bobby. He had an intercom and was continually receiving messages over it. We could see workers below us, busy unlashing the containers and unlocking the corner cones, which is done by hand. The first four levels of containers are unlocked from the deck, and higher ones are unlocked from above. The unlocking starts at 7:00 a.m., in preparation for the workers to start at 8:00 a.m. When the unlashing and unlocking is done, these workers are free to go home, even though they are paid for the day.

Bobby had been working for forty-four years. He was a steady worker for Maersk, and had worked for thirty-two years for Sealand. (Indeed, we ran into lots of old Sealand employees here, since Sealand had been taken over by Maersk.) He thought this was a good job. He could move thirty-five to forty containers an hour, but it depended on the UTR drivers, and whether they had a good foreman.(UTRs are small vehicles that are used to move containers around the terminal yard. When a container comes off a ship, it is typically hauled off by a UTR, which then parks it somewhere to be picked up later by a port trucker.) Bobby said: "You have to pay attention, so you don't hurt anyone. And they watch your productivity. But it's warm and comfortable up here, and you can listen to the radio. You can also work on flex time. It takes about two and a half to three days to do a ship." He talked with awe about one ship that had sixty-five hundred containers on it.

The Sealand *Innovator*

The *Innovator* is an older ship, from the 1960s. Craig called it a "rust bucket." We met two dock bosses, Darrel and Pete, both steadies, and the ship boss, Ron—also a steady. They were holding a crew meeting on the dock and giving the workers a safety talk. The workers were of mixed race. They had been sent from the dispatch hall. There were four per crane. This ship had three cranes working it, leading to a lashing crew of twelve. Jobs were assigned by a random procedure, like using coins or drawing tickets. This is the way they were assigned to the forward, mid, or aft crane. The procedure was used, of course, because it was fair. I think this speaks to past racial discrimination. Craig said that older African Americans say that there is still "benign" racism on the docks.

185

Craig's job involved making sure that everything was okay as containers were moved off. When a problem arose—like a cone wasn't properly unlocked—he jumped to fix it. We hung out on the ship along the side and kept an eye on the process of discharge. Craig said that the job involves more effort when they are loading because the hatch boss has to make sure that everything is in the right place, given its port of destination.

Tom, the lashing boss, told us he had worked here since he was 17—he was 54 in 2003. Thirty years ago, he said, there was no safety. Workers were exposed to asbestos, spit up blood. There has been a change now—a loss of pride. Workers just want to get what they can and get out. It gets worse every year: "When I finish, I stick around and help with the next ship. Others just go home." They are paid for the whole day, and it can take a whole day, if most of the workers are less experienced casuals. Experienced workers can do it in a couple of hours. People learn the tricks of how not to strain their muscles. Knowledge makes all the difference. Tom always works on a ship, never on the dock. "You are always dealing with personalities when you deal with the UTR drivers." He said he doesn't care about race or gender, but he doesn't like lazy workers. The culture is macho.

At 8:30 a.m., the unlashing was finished, and they started the discharge. UTRs with bomb carts—long flatbed trailers—lined up under the cranes to pick up the cans. These are all ILWU people. Drayage drivers only come to pick up and deliver in the yard, not next to the ships. Reloading was going on simultaneously with discharging. Most of it was headed for the Far East. Some was for Hawaii and Australia.

The big vessels were from Asia. A lot of them were carrying Wal-Mart, which received priority at this terminal. Wal-Mart's cans were put on wheels quicker, and they sat on the dock longer. When Maersk faced a big backlog, it tried to tell Wal-Mart to get its boxes out.

The Job

Craig showed me a set of sheets he was given listing each container. It showed their destination, including whether local or elsewhere in the country. Destinations like Chicago, Memphis, Dallas, Newark, were common. It also showed the weight of each container, which can be very variable.

The UTRs, pulling the bomb carts, are moving containers that will be grounded. If they are to be wheeled, the UTRs would be hauling chassis. Grounding them makes the unloading process quicker, because the crane operator doesn't need to aim as well. Not putting them on wheels means that they need to be handled twice, but it seems that Maersk is concerned with the speed with which the ship can leave the harbor more than the cost of double handling. Stowing is more demanding than discharging because the worker needs to make sure that everything is in its proper place. Equipment includes lashes and unlocking poles, both of which are long poles.

There are ten cranes working this terminal so far. APL and Hanjin both have twelve; Craig thought that Stevedoring Services of America (SSA) in LB may have sixteen, though they don't use them all. When Maersk moved here from the POLB, its expenses went up. Craig thought it used to cost $179 per container for throughput. Here it costs $230. This is for a variety of reasons: the cost of new equipment, the cost of the lease, the necessity for more labor, and the inevitable bugs in a new operation.

Clerks

We drove over to Marine Vessel Operations. We entered a large room overlooking the ships, all lined up. A few clerks were working here, apparently overseeing the assignment of yard equipment, like top haulers and transtainers. My protection vest had *SSA* written on it, and Local 63 member Gennaro Rippo objected and demanded that I take it off. (SSA is soundly loathed by the ILWU as the most anti-union of the terminal operators.) He was also upset with Craig that he had not cleared my visit with the local chapter president. So Craig called.

I chatted with a woman named Tommie, a chief supervisor. She was counting containers being discharged and loaded, directing the flow of cargo. She assigned floor runners, the worker bees. She assigned top handlers to certain workers regarding certain cargo. One sheet said "TP6." This is the largest ship Maersk has, carrying 3800 cans. They put most of them on rail. The cans were preassigned a location from superintendents in the yard, who passed on the information to vessel superintendents, who passed it on to the clerks, who assigned the machines.

Supervisor's Analysis

A supervisor from the Clerk's Local talked with me. He had an analysis of what was going on, but he wanted it to be off the record because some of it was speculative, so I am leaving his name out. Here is what he said:

> Maersk is the biggest employer in Denmark. They own supermarkets and other kinds of businesses. They build their own ships. They bought Sealand, which became CSX, in order to be able to carry U.S. military materials. They use various registries [FOCs].
>
> Yellow Freight and Roadway, two anti-union trucking companies, handle trucking for Maersk. The steamship line has former Yellow and Roadway employees working for them. Their biggest ship can now handle 8020 TEUs. They almost named it the *Wal-Mart*. At this terminal they get ships that are loaded exclusively for Wal-Mart. I believe that a steamship company named

Great Western Shipping has links to Wal-Mart. GWS sails only between Hong Kong and LA, back and forth. Great Western used to be big for textile shippers. It's propped up by a Hong Kong firm. They don't handle reefers—only dry boxes. They do charters, including charters for Wal-Mart.

Wal-Mart is a good customer of Maersk, but they also use other steamship lines, like Evergreen. They play them off against each other. Evergreen waves demurrage charges for Wal-Mart for thirty days, to undercut Maersk. All of the steamship lines jump through hoops to get Wal-Mart.

The terminals are running out of space because of the storage practices of companies like Wal-Mart. People blame the ILWU for this, claiming that it is their lack of productivity that is the source of the problem. But it isn't true. We have a high tech storage yard, with $11 to $12 million cranes, and other expensive equipment, including seven tophandlers. But for Wal-Mart they just take the cans off and throw them on the ground. That way they need fewer clerks. Cans headed for Atlanta, Dallas, Memphis are decked and then put on rail right away. [At this point we talked about the APL terminal and the high-tech jobs for clerks.] They have the same programs here—Sparcs-Navis, but they don't use them. They still use the methods of the 1970s—chalking cans. Why? Because it's faster. They have the technology but don't use it. They don't provide the training needed to use it. Maersk paid for it but doesn't use it. They said they were waiting until the contract was settled.

Electronic systems don't work 100 percent, so you always need a backup. You need two systems. If it doesn't work, you need to be able to go back to the traditional way. You still need bodies, people. [This was borne out throughout the day. Bobby's crane stopped working twice; Craig said that was a common occurrence. And Craig's job involved fixing things that weren't working right.]

In Hong Kong they are supposed to have a fully automated terminal. But they are mainly shipping out, which is easier to do. All they do is throw cans on a ship to LA. Here we are receiving tons of stuff. We put boxes on the ground, and they have to be taken out selectively. We store them in piles six wide and four high.

There are thirteen floor runners working the terminal—seven are from Local 13 and the rest are casuals. Casual laborers are not union members, but they should be. I was a casual myself. Then my father died, and I got into the union.

Planning Room

Craig and I went upstairs to the planning room. People were sitting behind computers. One of the workers said that the high-tech additions often don't work. There are lots of failures, and the job ends up taking longer, or can't be completed at all. He showed us the computer screen. When a container comes through the gate, it pops up on the load list. They sort by port of sail and by size and weight. It's like a giant puzzle that they have to solve. It used to take longer by hand. They were using a program called SPARCS, for which they received four hours of training. This worker had been in planning for fifteen years, working here when it was Sealand. Sealand was bought by Maersk in 1999 or 2000. The transition proved to be somewhat painful.

Steve Naumovski, Manager

Craig managed to get me in to see him. Steve was manager of vessel operations. He worked for management and had never been a member of ILWU. Craig got a phone call that a crane was broken and told me it happens all the time. He went to check on it and left me to talk with Steve. Steve kept on getting phone calls throughout our conversation. Sometimes he would be on more than one line at a time. He was a heavyset, strapping person who wore casual clothes and sat in front of a computer. He had a working-class demeanor.

Steve worked for APM Terminals. APM stands for A.P. Moller, the parent company of Maersk. APM Terminals is a terminal operator. It is in charge of discharging and loading vessels. This was the Yard Department, which is like the central nervous system. The senior vice president for the whole West Coast was located in this office. They had more than thirty management level employees on the terminal. They were departmentalized but helped each other. Some of the work, such as maintenance, was contracted out.

The union planners all worked for Sealand, as did Steve. Maersk bought the international part of Sealand, and CSX kept the domestic part, which included shipment to and from Alaska and Puerto Rico. It was later bought by Horizon.

The terminal was trying strictly to handle stevedoring. As Sealand they ran the steamship line and everything else. It was still being run by the Maersk line, which had its headquarters in New Jersey. "They give us detailed directions, like the number of gangs we should use. We work as directed. The financial part of the company is in Charlotte, North Carolina. We are part of the A.P. Moller Group. We are one little branch of it, providing profit for APM. We are a terminal operator as opposed to a line operator."

I asked about cost per container lift. He said:

They negotiate a cost per lift with the customer. It can be something like eighty dollars based on a guarantee, and including union costs. The new contract increased labor costs at least 6 percent. The lease they are paying here is astronomically high. In comparison they were paying peanuts in Long

Beach. My challenge is to try to come in under budget. At Pier G we got thirty crane moves per hour and above. Here the average is twenty moves per hour—we're trying to improve it. We are still suffering from the effects of the lockout. There was a huge backup. We are still in a transition zone of getting the terminal to work smoothly.

The new cranes were 150 to 160 feet from the cab to the ground. The old ones were 89 feet. They used bomb carts for the containers as they came off the ships, and didn't try to land them on a chassis. This was for safety reasons. "We are trying for a forty-moves-per-hour operation. We are trying to break thirty. It's trending in the right direction. Increased moves should offset the rising cost of labor."

The bombcarts increase productivity. We keep track of gross productivity. The workers are paid for eight hours. We subtract down time and figure out net productivity. We are running ten cranes a day, which typically means three ships, or two Axels plus a small vessel. We have run four ships at one time. The line decides on which ship takes precedent. Right now they only have one crane on the Axel, which has to sail on Saturday.

I asked what he thought of the new contract. He thought it is good. His job is dealing with labor. He heard a lot of bitching from crane operators and saw this contract as good for them. Steadies get crane-operating jobs for five days a week. Everyone benefits. He was glad that they won't have to go through this again for six years.

Maersk Axel

Craig and I went on the magnificent *Axel*. We went down into the engine room. It was gigantic and extended down a number of floors. We climbed down ladders a couple of times, but we didn't get to the bottom. We also walked past the galley. The ship has an American crew, according to Craig. There must be special reasons for this, like where they plan to stop.

Driving around the Yard with Craig

Craig told me the work was harder in Oakland than here. The other ports had gang bosses in the 1930s and 1940s. In LA they had a foreman who worked as a gang boss, and a walking boss who worked as a longshore boss, and this division persists in Southern California. This means that two people down here do the work of one up there. Therefore the work is more intense up north, where you have to control the crane and the dock at the same time. We drove past stacks of empties waiting to be loaded.

Ship Boss

The ship boss on this day was Ron Glusac—it is a Serbian name. He was very helpful in letting Craig take time off to show me around. Ron had been a steady at this terminal for eight years. Before that he was a steady at the Long Beach Container Terminal (LBCT) for ten years. After lunch we went back to the ship. Ron stood and talked with us for a while. We talked about how one becomes a union member. The old way was that an active member would die and a child would take his book. This didn't work if the member was retired. Craig was a casual clerk when he was in college. Ron had a K card, which is for casuals. He started in 1964. His dad, who worked here, sponsored him. Union members could sponsor one person. In addition his father had pull with the union because his neighbor was connected with the PMA. The sponsorship system stopped in 1970. It was attacked under an affirmative action suit. Some people had twenty-five years in the industry before being sponsored.

Ron said that a lot of people come in through the casual hall. They put in applications and get in by lottery. At one time they took five hundred new members from the casual hall. One needs four thousand hours as a casual before one can make your book. Ron has two nephews who are now in the union. He has brothers who went to college and came to work here.

Automation

In Copenhagen, according to Ron, they have a terminal that is completely automated, including the UTRs and transtainers. There is one worker in a tower who works four hammerhead cranes. It is said that they will be able to do that here in a few years. But Ron was skeptical.

They have a new system that is run via satellite, and it tells you the location of every can in the yard. The goal is to have no one at the gates. They will be all automated and run by a clerk in a tower.

It is so much faster than it was in the old days. We will see big changes in the next few years. TraPac has a new system—a bar code system, where each container has a bar code. They use a bar scanner. The bar codes on the cans tell you where to put them. TraPac plans to sell it to other companies. TraPac handles MOL and Dole. It may be MOL's terminal—Ron wasn't sure. The clerks are worried about these changes.

Right now there are four swing people under the crane, on dock. There is an effort to cut the number to three, or to five for two cranes. They will need more workers on deck in order to relieve them. The companies want to cut the fat. Roles are changing.

Handling Problems

Craig spent some time scrambling up to deal with some problem or other. At one point he was ready to climb on to the basket that the crane moves, but it proved unnecessary. He engages in "jury-rigging" to fix a problem. For example, if a cone doesn't come out because there is damage to the corner casting, and there are only three locks available, then he figures out what to do.

Other problems include hanging or broken lashings, which are dangerous. This can happen as a result of ocean storms. Then they climb up or jump on top to fix them. But they take safety issues very seriously because it is so easy to get hurt.

Race Issues

We heard some comments about race from ILWU members we talked with, showing that, despite changes (or perhaps because of them), all interracial antipathies have not vanished. Here are some of them:

The sponsorship system stopped in 1970. It was attacked under an affirmative action suit. Some people had twenty-five years in the industry before being sponsored. After the affirmative action suit, women were allowed in with half the hours. There were several suits. One was called the Golden Suit, and it was in 1980 or 1982. There were suits for blacks as well as women. Now everyone goes by the hours.

Apart from the hours, there is also a test to get into the union. A group of workers who were mainly black didn't pass the test and sued that it was biased. The judge accepted it, and some people got money while others got into the union. It was a high school equivalency test. We need qualified people. I don't care that they got money out of it, but I do mind that they got hours. It isn't fair. It penalizes the people who passed the test. The result was that a number of minorities were pushed ahead of their place in the queue—maybe forty, ninety, or even two hundred individuals. The judge also threw out the strength and agility test.

The union and the PMA have both continued to face suits. Blacks are causing trouble all over the ports. They are being elevated to be lash or hatch bosses. The local had to attend diversity classes. There was a multitude of complaints. The union took it to an arbitrator, but they lost. Now we have taken it to the Coast Committee. A group of blacks sued the union that they didn't get to be foremen because they were black. But that didn't work because there are lots of blacks in the union. One of the activists lost his case. But it costs a lot to defend these cases. I think they are trying to get whatever money they can from the industry.

Later in the research we heard very different stories from African-American ILWU members, a topic that Jake is studying further for his Ph.D.

dissertation. What the above individual failed to mention is that the equivalency test that all workers were required to take was a major way that white workers maintained their control on the docks. Several African-American workers confirmed that illegal copies of the tests were regularly given to white workers to study, giving them an edge over workers of color. This went on for years, and it was addressed in one of the racial discrimination suits. Without a doubt, the issue of racial inequality still exists on the waterfront and warrants further research.

Odds and Ends

Here are various topics that came up during the day:

Longshore Work: It's a good deal. You had lots of educated people working here. Craig mentioned a lawyer, a pharmacist, a school principal. Some felt that everyone owes them a living. Some were jail birds. One had robbed a Jack-in-the-Box. There were all kinds of characters at the docks. One of the terminals was known as a "con" dock for the number of convicts who worked there.

American Crews: Some smaller ships had American crews. These ships were subsidized by the U.S. government so that they could be used for the military. APL, American Lines, and Sealand had them. Some were rust buckets. They had to have been built by Americans. They went to Hawaii and back. There is only one place that still builds U.S. vessels. All the rest are gone. The small vessels could move through the Canal. You had to keep repairing them. Someone had told Craig that the hull had lots of pin holes.

Longshore Work Day: Crane operators worked as partners. They were supposed to work an eight-hour day together. Instead they tended to divide it in half, for four hours each. Or they worked day to day, with each getting a day off. Sometimes they even worked week to week.

Lashing Boss: This was Tom's job. The lashing boss took care of the lashing and unlashing and worked with a lashing crew. In contrast, the hatch boss (on this day, Craig) watched the hatch.

Steadies: Craig said that a lot of the workers are steady at a particular terminal, especially the bosses and crane operators. But only so many hours can be steady. And they can always fill in extra hours from the dispatch hall. Longshoremen have to go to the hall. Most clerks go to the hall. Walking bosses just call in, even when they work through the hall. If you are steady, you don't call in unless you want extra time. Some like to work all the time. Craig didn't work as a steady. He didn't like to keep working with the same people. And he found that cliquishness develops. He also found it less interesting, preferred the variety.

Pissing in the Wind: One interesting little tidbit I learned was that long-shore workers urinate off the non-dock side of the ship. But they have to be careful about which way the wind is blowing, for obvious reasons.

Craig's Work

Here they had a boss on the dock organizing the cargo. Up north a worker does both jobs. When it comes to loading, the ship boss job becomes more critical. Craig benefited from the class action suit in terms of becoming a union regular, because he had worked enough hours as a casual. I asked if it is scary to climb up the piles of containers. Sometimes it is, when they are six high, and he has to work on the edge. When it is windy, he lies down to do the work.

Discussion

One thing that amazed me about this day was the speed and intensity of the whole operation. Containers were flying off the ship at a rapid rate. UTRs were lined up and busy driving them away. The turnover must be enormous, and keeping it all straight seems like a formidable task. Another thing that impressed me was the way the whole operation is run by the union. Management is not in evidence. Steve was the only manager I saw, and he was holed up in an office. The ILWU members are truly "the lords of the docks."

Third, technology seems like a false savior. There are just too many glitches that require human intervention. Management keeps hoping to escape this, but I was left with the impression that it isn't possible. Finally, I loved being down there. What an incredible hub of international commerce! It is truly awesome.

The 2002 Lockout

In September of 2002, the PMA locked out the ILWU longshore division for ten days, costing an estimated $2 billion a day in lost revenue for the economy (this is according to Cohen 2002, a PMA-sponsored study. For a rebuttal from the ILWU side, see Hall 2004). The lockout was prompted by a series of failed contract negotiations between the ILWU and the PMA. These negotiations were also significant in that they marked a major effort by an alliance of shippers and carriers to weaken the ILWU. Former president and CEO of the PMA, Joseph Miniace, was an instrumental player in the 2002 attack on the ILWU. Miniace was hired as president of the PMA in 1996 for the purpose of taming the ILWU (Olney 2003).

Before Miniace's reign as president, the PMA did not have much control over the workers. In the 1999 negotiations, the PMA wanted to discuss technological innovation on the docks, but the ILWU got it pushed back until the next contract negotiations in 2002. During the 1999 negotiations, the ILWU engaged in a very effective work slowdown since strikes had been outlawed under the recent agreement. In the subsequent years, Miniace outlined a plan to stop such actions in the future by conducting numerous surveys on the docks to determine what "normal" productivity looked like, to catch the union in slowdowns.

The PMA was seeking concessions from the union that would allow the employers to introduce labor-saving technology in the form of IT to increase efficiency at the expense of union jobs. This significantly affected certain clerk positions on the waterfront, with job losses reaching upwards of six hundred. In the past, clerks literally used to mark the docks with chalk indicating where containers should be placed. The process of tracking cargo involved a mess of paper that had to pass through several different hands. Today, this has been replaced with computers and on-site scanning of cargo. Much of this change in technology is a result of the practices of giant retailers and their demands for ultra-efficient tracking of their goods.

This shift in IT also led PMA members to want to rid themselves of dealing with ILWU clerks. They began outsourcing the processing of information off-site, even overseas; SSA, one of the most anti-union of the PMA employers, moved some of its work to Salt Lake City. While the PMA certainly does want control of the documentation of goods throughout the docks for reasons of efficiency, it also has a lot to do with political control. Holding the information related to cargo flow is a key ILWU right under the current contract. In the eyes of the employers, it is imperative to gain control of this function in order to weaken the ILWU's power on the docks.

During the negotiation process, the PMA accused the ILWU of engaging in a work slowdown. Under the coastwise ILWU-PMA agreement, the ILWU is barred from striking unless there are imminent health or safety issues. Rumors circulated that the government was intent on bringing the ILWU under the more restrictive Railway Labor Act, which would weaken the union's power in the ports (Olney 2003).

After ten days, President George W. Bush invoked the Taft-Hartley Act and forced the ports to reopen. This was the first time in the history of the United States that Taft-Hartley was invoked during an employer lockout. Previously it was only used to end strikes (Olney 2003). The Taft-Hartley

Act's eighty-day "cooling off" period prohibits the lockout of the workers as well as the right of the union to strike or to initiate a slow down. It stipulates that workers must work at the "normal work rate" while the parties continue to negotiate over the contract. Under the Taft-Hartley Act, the president can declare a national emergency if a lockout or strike is deemed to jeopardize national health or safety. In this case—largely due to the lobbying interests of mega-retailers—the "national emergency" became equated with lost profits for billion-dollar corporations under the guise of post-9/11 security concerns.

West Coast Waterfront Coalition

In addition to the PMA, shippers also played a crucial role throughout the 2002 lockout. In 2000, a group of shippers, mainly composed of retailers, formed the West Coast Waterfront Coalition (WCWC), now known simply as the Waterfront Coalition, or TWC (www.portmod.org). The ILWU believes that the WCWC was formed by former PMA president and CEO Joseph Miniace, but according to its founder and executive director, Robin Lanier, it was her brainchild. Lanier had worked with the major retailer organizations, especially the International Mass Retailers Association (IMRA) before developing the WCWC, and she said that she used her former contacts to pull the initial participants in the WCWC together. Regardless of its precise origins, the WCWC was originally made up of giant retailers and shippers, including Wal-Mart, Target, Home Depot, Maersk, Mattel, Toyota, and Payless Shoes, along with at least two dozen other powerful business interests (Olney 2003). For voting privileges, members must pay $4,500 a year to support the lobbying and public relations efforts undertaken in the interests of the members.

TWC's mission statement indicates that they are "a group of concerned business interests representing shippers, transportation providers, and others in the transportation supply chain committed to educate policy makers and the public about the economic importance of U.S. ports and foreign trade," while promoting the technological advancement of the ports (www.portmod.org). While this may seem to reflect a rather mundane set of interests, it became clear during the negotiations over the 2002 contract that the WCWC was more than just a group of "educators." The WCWC placed a great deal of pressure on the Bush administration, prompting cabinet members to meet with them. Assistant to the President for Homeland Security Tom Ridge contacted ILWU President James Spinosa, warning that any disruptions after the contract expiration would undermine national interests.

After six months of tense negotiations, the ILWU and the PMA agreed to a new six-year coastwise contract. Under the new agreement, the PMA would be allowed to introduce new modernizing technology and practices to accommodate the higher demand on the ports. The "technology framework" clause of the contract called for the implementation of "bar code and optical scanners, GPS systems, Internet solutions, remote handheld devices, information sharing tools." Most of the technological devices introduced under the contract jeopardized marine clerk employment. In exchange, the ILWU received enhanced base pay, improved health benefits, and better pension plans (PMA 2003). While in the end the contract was seen as a victory for the ILWU, it came with the cost of fewer jobs for longshore workers, especially marine clerks.

Since the lockout, the leadership of the PMA has changed. Miniace has since been replaced by Jim McKenna, according to a *JoC* article entitled "Miniace, PMA Sue Each Other" by Bill Mongelluzzo (10/26/04). In August of 2004, Joseph Miniace filed suit against the PMA, alleging that the PMA owed him over $1 million in unpaid bonuses and severance pay. The PMA countered that they fired Miniace because he had allegedly plotted to defraud the PMA of nearly $10 million in insurance benefits. Wrote Mongelluzzo: "Miniace left the West Coast waterfront employers with a template for introducing technology and increasing productivity. More than that, he instilled employers with a new attitude about their relationship with the powerful ILWU."

The Future of the ILWU

The last round of negotiations bought the union some time—six years, to be exact. Its leadership recognizes that even though it survived this round and maybe even made some gains, the determination to cut them back, particularly on the part of the shippers, is far from over. The union recognizes its need to shore up its position. This includes the development of a strong organizing program, led by Peter Olney, director of organizing.

The overall position of the ILWU is, in general, an exception to our account of how the logistics revolution is impacting logistics workers. The ILWU has not suffered from contingency, racialization, diminished influence, or declining wages and working conditions. The reasons for this lie partly in its position in the supply chain and partly in the union itself and its strong traditions. We are inclined to believe that the second factor is more important. One can conjecture that a port trucking strike or a railroad strike that truly shut down the flow of containers would be as devastating to the big shippers and carriers as a dock strike would. So it appears that the union's long history of solidarity and strong institutions are essential to its success.

Still, the foes of the ILWU are formidable, and they certainly are not going to simply accept the status quo. We anticipate continued efforts to weaken the union. Apart from maintaining its own vision among the union's membership—and we heard plenty of complaints that this is deteriorating, especially in Southern California—we think that the development of strong ties with related logistics workers and their unions, who can then all work together in moving the freight, could be a critical component in the survival of all of the unions at the ports.

CHAPTER 8

Landside Workers

Moving inland from the waterfront, we can ask: How have railroad workers and port truckers been affected by the logistics revolution? Have they too experienced increased contingency, racialization, weakened unions, and deteriorating wages and working conditions? If so, how have the workers and unions responded?

RAILROAD WORKERS

A Brief History of the Railroad Unions

The centrality of rail transportation to the nation's economy, especially in the early years of the country's economic development, helps to explain the considerable militancy among early railroad workers, and it has also shaped the legal regime under which they labor. Unions emerged in the railroad industry shortly after the Civil War. The workers formed craft unions around their occupations. Until World War I, only a minority of railroad workers belonged to unions, but during and after that war, membership grew significantly and continued to grow. By 1973, almost 80 percent of the workforce were union members (Lieb 1974, 26–27).

Some consolidation occurred among the unions when the United Transportation Union (UTU) brought together conductors, brakemen, firemen, enginemen, and switchmen; they represented one-quarter of the industry's workforce. The other major operating union is the Brotherhood of Locomotive Engineers (BLE). Despite consolidation, there remained many small unions, which made it difficult to reach agreements with management (Lieb 1974, 27).

Before 1973, collective bargaining generally involved each union nego-tiating separately with its particular employer. But that year, a major change occurred. The National Railway Labor Conference (NRLC), the bargaining arm for the employers, persuaded fifteen unions to bargain together, leading to a settlement of a variety of outstanding issues in a timely manner (Lieb 1974, 27–29). In 1971, the UTU had responded to a breakdown in negotiations with selective strikes against chosen carriers, which proved more effective than forcing a national agreement. It was also a strategy that was less likely to lead to emergency legislation by Congress, since the strikes only had regional rather than national impact. However, selective strikes weakened the position of the NRLC, which began to fall apart. The 1973 agreement countered this, strengthening the NRLC (Lieb 1974, 29).

Government Role in Rail Strikes

The railroads were the country's first big business, and they were viewed as being of vital importance to the nation's economic health, as we have seen. This meant that labor unrest could be a serious problem. When workers formed unions in the nineteenth century, the railroads tried to crush them. They blacklisted union organizers and forced employees to sign yellow-dog contracts (agreeing not to join a union). Both sides engaged in violence. Various laws were passed by Congress to ease the tensions, but neither side accepted them (Lieb 1974, 36–38).

Forbath recounts the history of the use of court orders against railroad strikers, the first of which occurred in response to massive strikes in 1877. Because some bankrupt railroads were put in receivership, federal judges claimed they had the right to intervene, since they were already in charge. This set a precedent for the use of injunctions to crush strikes in other industries (1991, 66–79).

Then, in response to the Great Burlington Strike of 1888, the courts dropped the requirement of bankruptcy and receivership and simply enjoined the railway workers' refusal to handle cars from struck lines. The railroad brotherhoods had provisions in their constitutions to boycott lawfully struck railroads, but the courts claimed that such boycotts were forms of illegal discrimination in interstate traffic.

The Sherman Antitrust Act of 1890 was also used to counter strikes. Lawyers for the railroads were able to obtain injunctions against primary strikes. The theory was that by striking, rail workers were engaging in illegal restraint of trade (Forbath 1991, 71). However, some federal judges offered an alternative approach to sheer repression, directing the railroads to confer with their employees to arbitrate the conflict in a more equitable manner.

The Pullman Strike of 1894 was called by the American Railway Union (ARU), an industrial union led by Eugene Debs, to overcome the divisions among the craft brotherhoods and their exclusion of large numbers of unskilled railroad workers. This strike proved to be a major showdown between conservative and liberal forces. Federal judges issued almost a hundred decrees prohibiting the ARU and other unions from "threatening, combining, or conspiring to quit in any fashion that would embarrass the railways' operations" (Forbath 1991, 75). They also issued injunctions against the refusal to handle cars from other struck lines and forbade attempts to induce fellow workers to support the strike and boycotts.

The craft unions disapproved of the ARU, condemning its efforts to create an industrial union and calling for a more cautious approach. Although the ARU was destroyed, the railroads realized that they could cut deals with the craft unions in the AFL to create labor peace in exchange for union survival. The masses of less-skilled workers were left out of the bargain. The AFL leadership came to the conclusion that "class-based strategies and industrial ambitions were too costly and self-defeating" (Forbath 1991, 78). The brutal repression that had won the day was now also endorsed by the U.S. Supreme Court.

In 1926 the Railway Labor Act (RLA) was passed. It was amended in 1934 to create the National Mediation Board (NMB) and the National Railway Adjustment Board (NRAB). The purpose of these boards was to avoid work stoppages and to promote collective bargaining and mediation. If a strike was called and the NMB thought it could lead to a national crisis, the president could ask Congress for emergency legislation to stop it, a practice that was used extensively (Lieb 1974, 40–41). The RLA was used as a model in constructing the National Labor Relations Act (NLRA) of the New Deal and its accompanying National Labor Relations Board (NLRB), but these institutions are not as harsh toward labor than the RLA.

Racism in the Railroad Unions

Unions in the railroad industry were notoriously racist (Foner, 1974). Bernstein (2000) makes a compelling case that, not only were the railroad brotherhoods discriminatory and exclusionary toward African Americans from the nineteenth century until the mid–twentieth century, but the government-created labor relations regime also supported the white unions against African-American railroad workers. By giving recognition to the white unions, the RLA increased their power to exclude African Americans.

Both the unions and the state collaborated in racist policies towards African-American railroad workers, with devastating results for the African-American workers who managed to hold these relatively well-paying jobs.

When African-American workers finally won some rights in the 1950s, the railroads had lost many of their jobs: "By the time railroad unions revoked their color bars in the 1960s, overall railroad employment had declined dramatically, and few railroads were doing much hiring" (Bernstein 2000).

The Impact of the Logistics Revolution on Railroad Workers

As mentioned in chapter 5, the railroad industry has been significantly affected by deregulation. The most apparent change as it relates to labor has been the steadfast commitment to reducing the railroad labor force. Today's railroad workers number around a quarter-million—a sharp decline from their peak in the 1930s of over 2 million workers (DeBoer and Kaufman 2002, 70). In 1930 there were 1,488,000 Class I railroad workers. But since midcentury, every decade has shown a decline: 780,000 in 1960, 566,000 in 1970, 458,000 in 1980, and 216,000 in 1990. The number is still falling. For example, it was 155,000 in 2003 (American Association of Railroads 2004, 56).

This decrease in the railroad labor force has been made possible by the industry's adoption of labor-saving technologies. Similar to the longshore industry, automation and information technology (IT) have altered the landscape of the railroad industry. Today, there are fewer freight trains, but they are longer and heavier (Talley and Schwartz-Miller 1998). With double-stacking of containers on rails taking off in the 1980s, the average gross tonnage moved by trains has increased. Accompanying this shift toward longer trains has been a move to cut costs in other areas, especially in crew size.

Today, trains typically go on much longer runs without changing crews, which reduces the need for train and engine employees and has contributed to the overall decline in working conditions for railroad crews. Central to the reduction in railroad labor has been a decline in working conditions. Federal labor protection programs have been eliminated as part of the deregulation program (Talley and Schwarz-Miller 1998, 129–30).

Union membership has remained high, but density has fallen somewhat, from 83 percent in 1973 to 74 percent in 1996. Weekly earnings (measured in 1983/84 dollars) rose to a high of $507 in 1983 and have fallen since then to $470 in 1996 (Peoples 1998). The bargaining power of railroad workers has declined as a result of deregulation. The 1985 industry-wide contract negotiations were a turning point, when employers gained power and workers lost it. Pay increases were diminished, as was the standard cost-of-living adjustment provision, and a two-tier pay system was instituted (Talley 2002).

Under both the Reagan and George H. W. Bush administrations, a series of recommendations were issued by the Presidential Emergency Board, in 1985 and 1991, to investigate ongoing labor disputes in the railroad industry. In 1991, the railroad industry sought 20 percent wage reductions. This went to arbitration, where a settlement was reached over labor's opposition.

In terms of earnings, total compensation for railroad workers rose from $4.9 billion in 1960 to $6.4 billion in 1972, even though employment had declined by about 250,000. Hourly wages rose from $2.66 in 1960 to $5.03 in 1972, when the average hourly wage of manufacturing workers was $3.81. This gain in wages for railroad workers was achieved by the unions in exchange for an agreement to modify the work rules over time (Lieb 1974, 19).

Since deregulation, nominal wages have steadily risen, from $9.22 an hour for operating employees in 1980 to $14.53 in 1993. However, using a detailed mathematical analysis, Talley and Schwartz-Miller found that weekly earnings for engineers fell after the passage of the Staggers Act in 1980 (1998, 138–51). In a more recent article, Talley (2002) reports that the union weekly real wage for railroad engineers dropped from $656.43 during regulation to $610.50 in the deregulation period, or a drop from $14.01 to $13.03 per hour. This decline can be attributed in part to an increasingly conservative Congress that is more supportive of industry employers than workers (Talley and Schwartz-Miller 1998, 131).

Impact of Intermodalism on Railroad Workers

We spoke with Tim Smith, who serves as a member of the California Legislative Board for the Brotherhood of Locomotive Engineers (BLE). He said: "Intermodal shipments have changed railroading as we know it." The railroads used to use boxcars. Now they use piggy back (for truck trailers) and containers (double-stacked). "The railroads don't make as much per container as they did per boxcar," said Smith, "but they make it up in volume."

Tim said that intermodal has had a severe impact on railroad labor. When he started working as an engineer in 1972, covering the route from Roseville, California, to Sparks, Nevada, over the Donner Pass, seven people worked a train. Today they have two—an engineer and a conductor, and the trains are bigger and heavier. Changes in technology have played a role in this shift, but they often have been imposed with insufficient training. "This has to do with the modern motto: do more with less. They want to trim down, be lean and mean." This change has affected the retirement system, since fewer workers are paying into it. They have a third fewer workers paying into it, and a third more workers ready to retire. On the other hand, the new technology does accommodate smaller crews, and the equipment is a lot better.

We explored Tim's opinions about the Union Pacific versus the BNSF. He said:

> The UP is one of the most cutthroat organizations I have ever seen. We were sickened by their takeover of the SP [Southern Pacific]. Not that the SP deserved rewards for sainthood, but they weren't as bad. The UP is one of the most arrogant organizations. They won't talk or settle. You have to force them to deal with you. You have to hold their feet to the fire. They like to save money on any dispute by dragging it out. The BNSF is basically made from the same cloth. But since the Cajon accidents and deaths of recent years, they have jumped on the safety issue. I've applauded them for that. They are turning a corner, and taking care of some problems.

Deteriorating Conditions

We cannot be sure whether conditions of railroad workers today are a product of the logistics revolution or deregulation or some other factors. But there is little doubt that railroad workers have lost ground in recent times. The biggest factor seems to be the drastic cutback in staff by the railroads, leading to grueling schedules and dangerous fatigue on the part of workers, and occasional accidents.

Tim Smith of the BLE talked about this: "With the decline in crew size, there is more fatigue, and less people to help if an issue arises. Before, you could get help if you needed it. Now, if you have switching to do, you have to do it yourself. There are too few workers. The railroads are taking a risk, especially if the conductor or the engineer is young and inexperienced. They have cut us down to the quick."

According to Smith, some aspects of the work have gotten worse, and some have improved. On the deterioration side, fatigue is a big issue: "This was one of the first industries to operate 24/7." At the time of the interview (June 2002), there was a bill before Congress, HR 4761, that aimed at dealing with fatigue because of a spate of railroad accidents in which fatigue appeared to be a factor. Smith said: "The carriers keep saying: 'We will work with labor and find a way to resolve it.' But they haven't done it yet, and it's been an issue for years. . . . When you are done with work, you are supposed to be off duty for eight hours. That is the standard of rest mandated by the federal government. But it doesn't take into account that the worker may have a one and a half hour commute time to get home. Then he gets called one and a half hours before he is required to come back to work. So he may only get three and a half hours of rest or sleep."

Smith went on: "The carriers are completely focused on the bottom line. They don't want to resolve these issues. We say that, for them, 'Safety is for sale.' There has been a proposal for a 10-5 rule, or a 7-3 rule, where they work ten days and are off five. This would be safer, because the men and women would be more rested. The NTSB [National Transportation Safety Board] says that fatigue is a major problem in accidents. They put out a recommendation to alleviate it three years ago, but the railroads have done nothing."

Accidents provide a small window on railroad working conditions. On April 23, 2002, a BNSF freight train crashed into a Metrolink passenger train in Placentia, California. Testimony in the resulting legal case revealed some of the conditions faced by the engineer and conductor of the freight train. According to a *Los Angeles Times* newspaper article titled "Lawyers Cite Fatigue in Fatal Placentia Rail Crash," by Dan Weikel: "Industry experts say that because of long hours and constantly varying starting times, engineers and conductors often don't get much sleep, which can lead to lapses in judgment and slow reaction times while at the controls of locomotives" (6/12/05, B3). Here is part of the testimony of Dean E. Tacoronte, the conductor on the train, as described by the *LA Times:* "The evening before the crash, Tacoronte stayed at a San Bernardino hotel with his wife, whom he saw infrequently because of his work schedule and the fact that their home was in Needles, near the Arizona border. He said he had virtually no sleep before going into work. At 11:30 p.m., he was told to report to work in Los Angeles three hours sooner than expected. After reporting at 2:30 a.m., his train's departure was delayed almost five hours, during which time he took a ninety-minute nap in the cab of the locomotive."

Tacoronte's schedule reveals that he had varying starting times for work that did not allow for the establishment of a pattern of rest. From March 17 to April 14 he worked nineteen days straight. After three days off, he worked six straight days before the crash. He often had eight to ten hours off between shifts, but part of that time was used for commuting and preparing for work.

Weikel presents a chart that gives Tacoronte's schedule in March and April 2002. Here is a list of some of his starting times: 5 p.m., 11:45 a.m., 12:15 p.m., 12:30 p.m., 7 p.m., 10 p.m., 5 p.m., 9 a.m., 3:45 a.m. and so on. For example, on March 21, he started work at 7 p.m. and worked until 7 a.m. the next morning. He then had to report to work at 10 p.m. that night (March 22) and worked again until 7 a.m. on March 23 and then had to report back to work at 5 p.m. that evening. This last ten-hour break had to include driving back and forth between home and work, as well as eating, sleeping, and general living. In his deposition, Tacoronte said that "everyone knows you don't get much sleep" working for a railroad. Engineers and conductors, he said, are constantly "in a zone" of trying to stay awake and do their jobs as safely as possible.

The engineer, Darrell W. Wells, gave a less extensive deposition, but his schedule showed that he had many ten- and eleven-hour shifts, mostly during the night and early morning. He complained to investigators about the quality of sleep that train crews get, saying that he would like to see more of a set schedule "instead of working seven days a week, 365 days a year, and having to beg for time off."

We interviewed Ray Enriquez, engineer for the Union Pacific and legislative representative to the California State Legislative Board for the BLE. We met with him at his modest home in Whittier. Enriquez has a standard route, between the East LA rail yard and either Yuma, Arizona, or Yermo, California. Here are some of the things he said about schedules and fatigue:

> Work schedules are random. You never know when you will be called in. It plays havoc with your family life. You can't plan for anything. You don't have any friends except the ones who live right near you. If you need a day off to take care of personal business, they can deny you. We are forced to become liars. They can't force you to work if you lay off sick, so guys call in sick. We are supposed to get five personal leave days a year, but they can deny that request, so people use sick leave to get their personal days. The policy is that you are available 80 percent of the year. The year is divided into ninety-day chunks, and if you work less, you can be subject to discipline. Me and my wife don't have kids, but those who do miss their kids' ballgames and birthdays, or anniversaries.

Enriquez described for us the system of railroad hotels. A train may go from Long Beach to Chicago. They will divide it up into runs. One may go from the port to the East LA yard. The next may go from East LA to Yermo (ten miles east of Barstow). When you get to Yermo, you sleep over, and then drive another train back to East LA the next morning. UP recently built a new hotel. Before that the hotel was like a prison. It was right in the rail yard. The diner was a grease pit. The rooms were tiny and made out of cinder blocks. "The only thing missing was bars on the windows." The new hotel is better, but it's right next to the I-15 freeway, so if you are on that side it is hard to sleep.

Enriquez teaches about hazardous materials handling for rail workers at the George Meany Center. He talks with a lot of different rail workers, and they complain about the places they have to stay. When you get off the train, he says, you are "tied up." You are not at home, and you are not paid. They will not pay you for sixteen hours away from home. After sixteen hours, they have to start paying. You can spend more time away from home than at home.

Conditions have definitely worsened. He has talked to older people who tell him this. "They make you do more work for less money." And they provide less training. In 1998 UP hired a lot of new people, and they did not give them proper training. Enriquez was hired before this, in 1993.

At that time the new people would learn the job from the "old heads" who had seniority. "They would teach us how to stay out of trouble and be safe."

Tim Smith confirmed Ray's account. He said that the divorce rate is high in this industry because workers spend most of their time away from home. In the course of a week they may spend as much as 132 hours (out of 168) away from home.

Rail Unions Today

According to Enriquez, the union is weak. "We can't strike, partly because of the RLA and partly because we can't get everyone on the same page. People don't have faith in the union any more." They also get faced with court injunctions to get back to work. The disunity is partially based on different pay systems. Someone with high seniority will get $330 a day, so he will have no incentive to slow down.

Each railroad has its own locals or divisions, as they are called in the BLE. The Union Pacific had division 660, and the Southern Pacific had divisions 5 and 56, so the merged company has 3 divisions. This did not go smoothly. The BNSF has its own divisions. One of them is 662. However, the groups of railroad employees do have common committees.

Here is Tim Smith's account of the weakening of the railroad unions:

> The unions have been weakened. For example, the railroads now have remote control technology, which you can wear on your belt. There is nobody in the cab. You can operate the train from the ground. And we've been denied the right to strike. The carriers spend millions and millions on technology to get rid of jobs. We protested. We went to a district court judge. She defined it as a "minor dispute." If we have a strike or slowdown or sickout, we will face the judge's wrath. We can't protest. If we do, they will throw people in jail and fine the union for huge amounts.

Smith thinks the judges are on the take. "The carriers have a lot of money to throw around. Labor can't strike. We can't even sit down at the table. There is no level playing field. If we have a grievance, the employer immediately calls for arbitration."

Smith told us about one engineer who was working a particular route in Southern California. In 1985 he was making $210 for the run. Now, for the same run, he makes $220. So he has had a gain of $10 over the last seventeen years. "Agreements have been watered down. Now they are trying to get us to pay for health and welfare. This used to be a good job, but it isn't any longer."

There appears to be considerable conflict between the two major railroad unions, the BLE and the UTU. According to Smith, the UTU is now out of the AFL-CIO. They were forced out because they had been trying to take over the BLE for years. The BLE complained to the AFL-CIO, which invoked its anti-raiding policy and accused the UTU of raiding. The UTU backed out of the AFL-CIO in 2000, partly to avoid the fines they were being charged. (Note: The authors have not heard the UTU side of this story.)

Since then the BLE has affiliated with the Teamsters (the IBT), which has strengthened them. At the time of the interview with Tim Smith (June 2002), the IBT had 1.2 million members, while the BLE had 39,000. The UTU had over 100,000 members, making it the largest rail union.

There is a National Carriers Conference Committee (NCCC), which represents all of the Class 1 railroads and engages in pattern bargaining with the unions. According to Tim Smith, the UTU is carrier-friendly, willing to trade away jobs: "They have an unholy alliance with the carriers." For example, they made a deal under which they would control the workers who use belt pack (remote control) technology, even though these workers would fall under BLE jurisdiction. Said Smith: "Ideally the railroad unions would all get together and decide on what they want in the agreement. But the UTU acts like a rogue union, and cuts a backroom deal with the NCCC beforehand. Then the NCCC comes to the other unions and says, here is the Pattern Agreement. The other unions protest, leading to arbitration, and they generally lose. So it ends up that the NCCC won't negotiate with the rest of the unions. The belt-pack agreement that the UTU signed will cost about two to four thousand jobs."

Assessment

It seems fair to say that the logistics revolution, including deregulation, has had a negative impact on railroad workers, though not as bad as for some of the other logistics workers. Although the industry remains unionized, the unions have been weakened. On the whole, the work has not been made contingent or outsourced, nor has it been racialized. But jobs have been reduced, pay has declined, and work conditions have deteriorated.

PORT TRUCKERS

A Brief History of Trucking Unions

Long haul trucking arose, in part, in response to the power of railroad unions, though surely its higher level of flexibility would have caused it to thrive anyway. The two industries developed at different times and under different political circumstances. Of course, the union that developed in this sector is the mighty International Brotherhood of Teamsters (the IBT or just the Teamsters). They are an interesting case because trucking does not seem like a sector that would lend itself easily to unionization. The industry consists of many small companies and individual contractors—hardly the organizing ideal of the large factory, where workers get to know each other and form a common, oppositional culture. Yet the Teamsters grew to be the biggest, most powerful union in the country for a period. How did this happen?

As indicated by their full name, which evokes the era of horse-drawn wagons, the International Brotherhood of Teamsters, Chauffeurs, Warehousemen, and Helpers, is an old union. It evolved from the Team Drivers' International Union, which was founded in 1880. In 1903 the AFL helped to overcome jurisdictional disputes among Teamster locals by promoting the development of a single international union (Garnel 1972, 34–37).

Daniel Toben was elected president of the international in 1907, taking over an organization with "a heritage of deep internal conflict, chronic secessions, and equally frequent reaffiliations" (Garnel 1972, 37). Nevertheless, he managed to remain president of the IBT until 1952, playing a critical role in developing national unity in the union. Teamsters locals suffered from collusion with the employer, extortion, and other forms of racketeering, partly because of the fiercely competitive nature of the industry. Sometimes they acted as the enforcing arm of an employer association, and sometimes they used physical force to "punish" competitors for breaking rate-setting agreements (Garnel 1972, 38).

Given the strategic position of trucking in the larger economy as a process that most goods must pass through and given that transportation costs are a small percentage of the total value of a commodity, businesses would rather bribe the drivers than risk having their flow of goods cut off. Local governments opted not to intervene or received payoffs, allowing for the development of racketeering in the industry (Garnel 1972, 38). Violence was also commonly used by union members. These features encouraged the development of strong Teamster Local autonomy and a weak International (Garnel 1972, 40).

By the early 1930s the Teamsters had a secure position in only a small number of cities in the West, especially San Francisco, Oakland, and Seattle. The freight locals there managed to achieve high wages and good working conditions and had a stable understanding with their employers, who respected their power. The union was militant in demanding concessions but ideologically conservative. For example, at their 1935 convention they barred Communists from membership. They rarely engaged in strikes; the leadership did not like to use them, and especially opposed sympathy strikes and general strikes—in part because they were so often called on to support the strikes of others because of their pivotal position in the process of production and distribution. Unofficially, truck drivers often helped strikers by refusing to cross their picket lines (Garnel 1972, 61).

The next Teamster leader after Toben was David Beck, who started his career in the Pacific Northwest. He was an ardent supporter of the free enterprise system, and of management-labor cooperation, but he believed that the highly competitive and low-margin trucking industry needed to be stabilized by limiting competition. This could be achieved, in part, by equalizing wages, hours, and working conditions—or taking labor standards out of competition. He also tried to raise the barriers to entry for owner-operators into the business, since they tended to undercut other truckers. Meanwhile, he was fiercely anticommunist and a strong opponent of the CIO, putting him in direct conflict with Harry Bridges (Garnel 1972, 67–77).

By 1940, interstate motor carriage had developed, and the Teamsters were able to form multi-state bargaining units. James Hoffa played a critical role in centralizing the Teamsters' bargaining, leading to nationwide contracts. As often happens, the unity of the workers led to the organization of the employers, who formed the Trucking Employers Incorporated (TEI) in 1970 in order to be united in their bargaining with the union (Leib 1974, 31).

By 1971, the Teamsters had a membership of more than 2 million, making it the largest labor organization in the country. By this time, twelve thousand trucking companies, including almost all federally regulated motor freight lines, had Teamster contracts. The Teamsters are an industrial union, despite their history as members of the AFL. They organize all workers in an industry regardless of trade or skill, in sharp contrast with the railroad unions. The union was able to transform truck driving into a relatively high-paying occupation with decent benefits (Lieb 1974, 30).

The Teamsters faced political problems. In 1957 they were expelled from the AFL-CIO on allegations of corruption. As is well known, Hoffa became a target of the Kennedy administration, and he served an eight-year prison term for stealing from the union's pension system and for jury tampering (Lieb 1974, 30). Despite these problems, the union continued to grow. From the time it was expelled from the AFL-CIO in 1957 to 1969, the IBT grew by 36 percent, while the national growth rate of unions as a whole was 12 percent (Lieb 1974, 31).[1]

---

[1] Unfortunately, we were unable to find studies of racism in the IBT in the period before the logistics revolution, and we must also admit that we did not look very hard. It would be extremely surprising if racial problems did not exist.

The Effects of the Logistics Revolution on Truck Drivers

The trucking industry was deregulated with the Motor Carrier Act of 1980, leading to a reduction of ICC regulation of the industry. Restrictions on entry were lightened and discount rates were permitted. As a result, the number of trucking firms increased dramatically, more than doubling by 1987. The non-union TL (truck load) sector grew rapidly, while the unionized LTL (less than truck load) sector declined in numbers. The driver work force grew from 1.1 million in 1978 to 1.9 million in 1996, while union jobs and IBT membership shrank. Regulation had also supported national bargaining, as represented by National Master Freight Agreements (NMFA), but with deregulation, more trucking companies withdrew from these agreements (Belzer 2000; Talley 2002).

Both railroad workers and truck drivers lost bargaining power after deregulation, but the truckers lost power much earlier than the rail workers. By 1982, the NMFA contract froze wages for three years and set up new work rules to make union trucking companies more competitive with non-union firms. In 1985 the NMFA set up a two-tier wage system that discriminated against new hires. And in 1988 the contract set up Employee Stock Ownership Plans (ESOPs) that effectively resulted in wage cuts (Talley 2002). Summarizing the effects of the regulation and deregulation periods on numbers and wages, Talley (2002) found that truck drivers grew from an average of 919,000 during regulation to 3,911,000 under deregulation. Weekly real wages fell from $579.21 to $502.86, and hourly wages dropped from $12.07 to $10.66.

Port Drayage: The Shift from Union to Non-Union

Port drayage is a small subsector of the trucking industry, as we discussed in chapter 5. How was this sector affected by deregulation?[2] Before deregulation, port trucking was a unionized sector, under the Teamsters. In Southern California, IBT Local 692 was in charge of the port drivers. Wage increases could be passed on by the drayage companies by requesting price increases from the ICC or the California Public Utilities Commission. Before deregulation, union drivers made around $12.50 per hour and received about $10 an hour in fringe benefits.

Deregulation changed the dynamics of the industry completely. It gave power to the shippers, while the carriers lost power. When a carrier said it would institute a rate increase, the shipper would refuse and seek out a carrier at a lower price. New companies entered the California

[2]Deep thanks to Ruth Milkman for sharing her research on this period. Her work provided great insight into what deregulation did to port trucking.

market, ready to undercut established practice. Competition intensified dramatically.

Among the new entrants were so-called owner-operators. These were individuals, or micro employers, who owned a truck or two, and were available for employment outside of the union structure. We interviewed Ernesto Nevarez, an activist in the port trucker community, on three different occasions in early 2002.[3] Here is how Nevarez described the transition:

> The process started in the late 1970s, with white drivers who left the union and bought their own trucks. They were making good money. Some netted $43,000, and some even $60,000. It was an overnight free-for-all. They were the first generation. Then came a second generation. They weren't in the union like the first generation. They weren't Latinos either. They came in between 1980 and 1982. They were willing to work for 10 percent less than the others. They had no communal value system like the old unions guys had. The workforce grew by 20 to 30 percent. You could still make a decent living. Then in 1983 and '84 you have the Central American conflicts. In 1983, 5 to 10 percent of the work force was Central American.
>
> The main incentive for getting into trucking was that you didn't need a green card or an I-9 form. You could make ten to twelve dollars an hour. It was a natural marriage. There was no law, no enforcement. The immigrants worked their asses off and brought down the standards. They didn't mind a thirty-six-hour tour of work. The expansion of landbridge at this time led to the exodus of the first and second generation, and the rise of the Central Americans. A padrino would bring you in. These were the caciques. [The term *caciques* is used to describe the worst employers in the harbor drayage business.]

Gradually this shifted to an immigrant occupation, as mostly white native-born drivers left the industry and Latino immigrants entered. The drayage companies shifted to employing more owner-operators (or independent contractors), displacing union drivers. This led to a proliferation of smaller firms, resulting in cutthroat competition. The basis of pay shifted from an hourly wage to pay by the load. A transition period occurred, when the companies double-breasted, meaning that their companies had union and non-union parts. But gradually the union was ejected from the market, with only minor exceptions (Milkman and Wong 2001).

According to Nevarez, by 1985 the IBT had lost the harbor. They called a strike on the West Coast, and it flopped. The Central Americans did not

---

[3]Manuel Barrajas, then a graduate student at the University of California, Riverside, and currently a professor at California State University Sacramento, helped with these interviews.

want the union because of the green card issue. "The Teamsters thought they were still living in the 1970s, when people wouldn't cross a picket line," said Nevarez. "They blamed the Latinos." In 1984 the industry was half Latino and half white. The whites saw the Latinos as an enemy that was undercutting them at certain companies. Unlike the Latinos, white drivers knew they had some rights; they wouldn't work thirty-six hours straight. Many whites left port trucking after 1985, while the Latino presence doubled between 1984 and 1986. They expanded by selling trucks to their relatives. After 1985, the employers were able to lower the rates. "The employers thought they were doing the immigrants a favor by employing them," said Nevarez, even though the pay was low and port trucker families had to struggle to survive.

Independent Contractors

Port truckers are contingent workers. Instead of having steady employment, their work has been outsourced. They appear to be independent small businesspeople who arrange to do work for a drayage company as an independent contractor. They get paid a lump sum for the job and have to take care of all of the costs of the job themselves.

Monaco and Grobar (2004), who conducted a study of port truckers in Southern California, describe the job situation of the drivers. Despite the term "owner-operator," the port truckers do not operate as independents with their own authority. Rather, they contract with harbor drayage companies. The companies usually do not directly employ a staff of drivers but instead serve as brokers who contract with the drivers to move the containers. The company dispatches the drivers to a port terminal for dropoff or pickup, using chassis owned by the steamship lines. The drivers are paid a standard fee depending on the length of the haul.

This system appears to us to depend upon a kind of legal fiction. The drivers really work as employees of the drayage companies, and their pay per job is the equivalent of piece rate, reminiscent of the early days of industrialization. That they own (or lease) their tractors is the equivalent of having a worker provide some of his or her equipment. These features are common in the garment industry, where workers are paid by the piece and sometimes must bring their own scissors or specialty parts of the sewing machine. The legal arrangement is partly fictional because sometimes the truckers sign exclusive employment agreements with their trucking company "employer." The independent contractor status of the port truckers is of benefit not only to the drayage companies but also up the line to the steamship lines who employ those companies and eventually to the shippers, whose transportation costs are cut by the low pay and poor working conditions of this group of workers.

Bacon describes some of these benefits to the employers:

> Every morning, harbor truckers bid for the right to pick up a container. . . .
> If the dispatcher gives them the load, they then wait for hours in front of
> a terminal to pick it up or drop it off. Dozens of rigs in huge lines, their
> motors idling, stretch for miles in front of the gates to the docks before they
> open every morning, in ports from coast to coast. By day end, most drivers
> have put in as many as 16–18 hours. Because they're owner-operators, these
> workers have no rights under much of U.S. labor law, including the right to
> overtime pay. They're not covered by wage and hour protection, since they
> supposedly work for themselves. They have Workers Compensation Insurance,
> to cover workplace injuries, only if they buy their own policy, an expense
> most can't afford.
>
> Most important, the National Labor Relations Board says they're not
> workers at all, and therefore aren't covered by the laws that protect the right
> to form unions. In fact, the Federal government says that if drivers even try
> to agree with each other on a price to charge the shipping companies for car-
> rying a container, they're in violation of the Sherman Anti-Trust Act, passed
> originally to restrain monopoly corporations. The fines and jail time they
> might incur by violating the Act would break any self-employed truck driver.
> ("Who Murdered Gilberto Soto?" 1/28/05, www.ilcaonline.org)

Let us look at these features more closely. The cost of waiting in long
lines at the port terminals and the cost of congestion on the roads must be
borne by the drivers themselves, since their employers incur no penalties
for their wasted time. It is up to the driver to make up the lost money by
extending his (or, in a tiny minority of cases, her) hours, so as to squeeze
in another trip. This leads to a form of self-exploitation that is typical of
sweatshop conditions (see Belzer 2000).

Meanwhile, as Bacon points out, even though the truckers are employees
in everything but name, they receive no protection from the Fair Labor
Standards Act, which governs wages and hours of work. For example,
their hours of work can extend way beyond the mandated eight-hour day
or the forty-hour week without their receiving overtime pay. Moreover,
they receive no benefits whatsoever: no vacation pay, no sick leave, no
pension, no health care coverage. These must all be covered by the drivers
themselves.

That they are considered to violate the antitrust law if they form a union
(because this would be seen as colluding to set prices) is especially ironic
given that the steamship lines have been granted limited antitrust immunity to
suggest rates through the conferences. Giant multi-billion dollar companies
can combine to agree upon rates, while micro-enterprises are considered to
be law violators. The effect of this misapplication of the law is to threaten

not only the drivers but also the union. If, for example, the IBT tries to organize the truckers, it can face massive fines for violating antitrust law. Since this has, indeed, happened, the legal fiction forces the union to seek devious means of organizing.

Conditions in Southern California Ports

Monaco and Grobar (2004) conducted a survey of 175 port truckers in 2004. This research is very revealing about the situation of the port truckers. Here are some of their findings: Most of the port truckers are engaged in three types of hauls: landbridge (that is, taking the container to a railhead), Inland Empire (driving the container to a warehouse or distribution center in the Inland Empire), and local delivery (which can be to the warehouse of a local company or to a facility, where the container's contents are transloaded to domestic containers and trailers). About 20 percent are engaged in long haul trucking. The Inland Empire trips are the most common.

Eighty-seven percent of the sample are "owner-operators" or independent contractors. This compares with 10 percent among truckers nationwide. They are paid by the trip, and they work long hours to maximize their income. The median hours per day is ten, and some worked as much as fourteen hours. The average number of trips per day is a little over three. The average length of their last trip was 4.6 hours, 2.6 of which was spent waiting in line.

The median amount they received per trip was $65, and the median daily pay was $200. But the drivers have to pay for the truck and its maintenance, insurance, and fuel. Taking these costs into account, the median driver earned about $25,000 in 2003. This is lower than the figure for national owner-operators and for non-union drivers. Of course, it is much lower than the pay of union drivers. Needless to say, there is a distribution of annual earnings among the port truckers, from around $10,000 to $55,000. However, they have no retirement plan, and only 10 percent have health insurance.

The workforce is overwhelmingly Latino, at 92 percent, pointing to racialization. This does not mean they are mainly undocumented, however. In fact, 11.4 percent were U.S.-born, and 57 percent are U.S. citizens. Monaco and Grobar did not ask about immigration status, but we have heard anecdotally that the percentage of undocumented immigrants among the drivers is low. Even though the vast majority are Latino, Latino truckers still earn more than $11,000 less per year than non-Latino drivers.

Some of the port truckers may prefer to be independent contractors. There is the promise that through hard work and putting in extra hours, they might be able to make some money and move up and become a real independent business owner. Of course, this calculus often fails to take account of the expenses the drivers face as independent contractors. Another advantage of the status lies in the fact that one does not need a formal education or to speak English. One-third of the drivers in the survey had not completed a high school diploma. If they were employed directly by the drayage companies, they might face language and education barriers.

Still, we have attended port trucker meetings and followed the Internet chat room "Truckers Unite!"; we have noticed that many of the drivers are well aware that their status as independent contractors is a sham. They would much rather have a decent job as employees, with steady pay, benefits, and a union contract. True, these workers are most likely to be the most experienced and politically sophisticated. Undoubtedly there are some who carry the hope that "owning their own business" is the route to success in the United States.

Monaco and Grobar (2004) discuss the benefits to the drayage companies of the employment status of the port truckers. They do not have to invest capital in trucks. They are protected from variations in the cost of insurance and fuel, which must be borne by the drivers. They avoid having to pay benefits and do not face unionization.

Dysfunctions of the System

It is clear that the drayage companies, the steamship lines, and the shippers who employ them all benefit from having a low-wage, non-union, exploited sector in the port truckers. The employing companies at every level are able to externalize various costs onto the drivers, who must pick up the slack in a "flexible" system. Meanwhile, there is little incentive to improve things, since the system makes their labor so cheap.

Nevertheless, there is widespread recognition in the industry that this is not a healthy system. We found considerable sympathy for the drivers among many of the people we interviewed. Indeed, we learned of the book *Sweatshops on Wheels*, by Michael Belzer, from Patty Senecal, owner of a drayage company.

The dysfunction is evident not only in the low wages for drivers but also in other side costs. The drivers tend to buy old trucks, because that is what they can afford, and that increases the likelihood that the vehicles will have pollution problems and will be more accident-prone. Adding to this is an incentive to put off maintenance because, again, the drivers usually can not afford it.

The long wait in line at the terminals, where diesel is being belched into the air, contributes to the pollution problem. True, this issue has received legislative attention—pushed by the Teamsters.[4] Assembly Bill 2650 was passed, over considerable opposition, calling for the fining of terminal operators if trucks had to idle outside their gates for longer than thirty minutes. Any offender could get out of the fine if it set up an appointment system or extended their gate hours, and some opted for these solutions. Moreover, there was little funding available to enforce the law, so Monaco and Grobar (2004) conclude that it had little ultimate effect. They found that on average, 48 percent of trip time is spent waiting to get in and out of the port.

Another law that was passed on Teamster initiative was a chassis road-ability bill. The problem here is that the chassis are owned by the steamship lines, but if there was something wrong with a chassis, the Highway Patrol would fine the driver. The law pushed responsibility for chassis safety back onto the chassis owners, which presumably served as an incentive for keeping them in better shape.

All of these dysfunctions of the system, despite the efforts to fix some of them, have led to militance among the drivers, to organizing efforts by unions, and to occasional driver shortages. As we have said, industry participants bemoan the fate of the truckers and wish the system were different, but they feel that they cannot be the first ones to change it. However, they all seem to agree that unionization by the IBT, or worse still by the ILWU, would be a grave mistake. And government intervention is also to be avoided, if possible. They see the problem, but they do not want to find a solution that would cost them anything.

One effort to improve the situation of the port truckers was to extend gate hours through the OffPeak system, administered by PierPASS. The main purpose of this innovation was, of course, not to alleviate the situation of the truckers but to deal with the rising congestion as the influx of imports continues to rise. However, there was a side hope that the port truckers would be beneficiaries of the change because lines would shorter and they would be able to fit in more hauls per day, thereby raising their incomes.

Much to the surprise of the planners, port truckers were not thrilled with the new arrangement. For one thing, they are not paid extra for working at night. And the option of working at night means working more hours per day and spending less time with one's family. From the drivers' point of view, this is not a good deal. In a *Los Angeles Times* article entitled

---

[4]Local Teamster port trucker organizer Gary Smith is responsible for devising some of these legislative plans, although he has not received public recognition for doing so. He worked with the California Trucking Association (CTA) to get the bills passed so that they did not face likely failure if they were labeled as Teamster legislation. He also worked with environmentalists and a sympathetic state legislator (Lowenthal).

"The Ports' Short-Haul Truckers Endure Long Hours, High Costs," Ronald D. White described the situation of drivers after PierPASS was instituted. On average, a port trucker could expect to earn about $50 for hauling a full container and $35 for an empty, but that money also covers the time for pickup and delivery. A driver could expect to collect $340 in gross income if all went smoothly, but it often does not (11/21/05, C1).

White interviewed some of the truckers and found they had numerous grievances. One driver, who was 51, experienced problems with his night vision. He found it more difficult to get work during the day, so sometimes works 12 to 16 hours just to make $300—enough to make a profit. Another trucker drives a truck with 500,000 miles on it, 200,000 of which were added by him. He spends at least $1,200 a month on fuel for a vehicle that gets five to seven miles per gallon. He has to pay $7,000 in insurance a year, which does not include maintenance. It is conditions like these that are leading more port truckers to leave the industry, causing concerns about a driver shortage. The most recent expense has been the 2006 spike in gas prices, which has not helped matters.

Union Organizing Efforts

We can divide the port truckers' efforts to organize into three phases: independent organizing by the drivers themselves, the organizing effort led by the Communications Workers of America (CWA), and the Teamsters' port trucking campaign.

Independent Organizing. As mentioned above, we spent a number of hours interviewing Ernesto Nevarez, a dedicated activist in the port trucker cause. Nevarez knows a lot about the history of the drivers. We have only been able to provide a brief sketch here of everything that he talked about.

According to Nevarez, who is a Chicano, about 90 percent of the port truckers are Central Americans and 10 percent are Mexicans. "The Central Americans are assimilating, but not into mainstream culture. Rather, they are assimilating into Chicano culture. They are becoming Chicano activists." Nevarez estimated that no more than 15 percent of the drivers are undocumented, since they face licensing requirements and checks by the Department of Motor Vehicles. He speculated that about 15 to 20 percent had special amnesty waivers coming out of U.S. programs for Central American refugees. The majority, around 70 percent, have green cards or are citizens. Nevarez claimed that many of the drivers were recruited from Central America; the trucking companies sent recruiters in the early 1980s, telling the recruits they did not need immigration papers because they were independent contractors.

The Central Americans keep in touch with the homeland through ham radios. They also listen to El Cucuy de la Mañana, a radio disk jockey from Honduras. "He is listened to by all of the Central Americans, and he reaches the harbors all over the country," said Nevarez. "The community finds out about every strike and action right away."

Nevarez said that the Central Americans bring their culture of civil unrest to the port trucker struggles. He described them as being similar to Palestinians, steeped in generations of conflict. They include a variety of backgrounds, including former professors and ex-military people. The Central Americans are transnational. They use a system of cooperative financing called Cudena, a type of rotating credit association. If a truck breaks down, it costs nine thousand dollars to fix, so the group raises the money to help the driver out. This practice helps to create solidarity.

Various organizations were developed by the drivers, including TUTA (Troqueros Unidos de Transporte Asociados), WRTU (Waterfront Rail Truckers Union), and LATA (Latin American Truckers Association). These groups would strike. TUTA, for example, was formed by Central Americans in 1984: "It was a kind of self-help, benevolent association that helped families with funerals and things like that. They had a great leader—Stanley Paniago. TUTA charged members ten dollars a week, so it had resources. TUTA claimed it was an association, not a union, to avoid the owner-operator problem."

The WRTU emerged in 1986. Nevarez said it was considered a "white boy's union" because it was run by Jerry Bakke—a good guy, in Nevarez's view. TUTA had isolated itself by focusing on only one company, H&M. According to Nevarez, lots of people joined the WRTU. Milkman and Wong (2001) report that in the summer of 1988, the WRTU held a two-and-a-half-week strike over the problem of long waiting periods.

Nevarez described another strike in 1991:

There was a strike by the WRTU. It involved Lorenzo, Carrasco, and La Negra Tomasa. It was at ATCO Associated Transport. The owner's checks were bouncing, and the guys didn't get paid for two weeks. Then the company closed. Ten to twelve guys pulled out loads, for J. J. Newbury's and McCreedy's, and parked them. The police came. We said it was a labor dispute and we wanted our money. These guys were all radicals. They were "La Mara"—the gang, the main guys. Everyone got a container and parked it. About forty to fifty guys from the WRTU met and guarded the containers. One of them was Rios, who was a Brown Beret [a Chicano activist group]. This all happened in Gardena. After eight days, they got calls from the owners of the containers, Newbury's and McCreedy's. The guys figured they were owed a hundred thousand dollars. The companies came up with seventy-five thousand dollars, and the containers were released to another trucking company.

Nevarez described an important source of worker solidarity:

> The Latinos were united here [in the United States], despite incredible divisions in their homelands. They united around labor struggles. In 1991 there was a strike at H&M. The union depended on the workers' bonds to their home towns. They kept in contact via two-way ham radios. The guys would get reputations, like that they had killed five people. There was a fear that your family back home would get a visit if you crossed "la union." You had to play by the rules of the organization in this home away from home. Sometimes you had Somocistas and Sandinistas together, but they had to put that aside. They all felt attacked by *la Migra*, the employer, and those using the employer.

The 1993 strike, which lasted eleven days and was sparked by a rise in diesel fuel prices, upset world trade, according to Nevarez. The strike was against a trucking company named CalCo: "It was a strike without leaders. They put a dozen people in jail. At the time, Bob Curry, owner of Cal Cartage [a major drayage company] owned about 85 percent of the trucking companies. CalCo was owned by a Korean, Chong Suh. The protest here affected people in Korea right away."

According to Milkman and Wong (2001), LATA emerged as a result of this strike. Nevarez said that LATA was connected with TDU (Teamsters for a Democratic Union), the reform movement in the IBT that led to the election of Ron Carey as Teamster president; the group is further to the left, politically speaking, than the current IBT leadership. While TDU had some strength in the Pacific Northwest, it was weak in Southern California, putting LATA at odds with the more traditional Teamster leadership.

The CWA Campaign. The CWA got interested in port trucker organizing in 1994, according to Nevarez, during a period when LATA was strong. In 1995 the CWA began pumping money into the campaign. In Nevarez's view, the CWA effort was orchestrated by the ILWU, and its goal was to keep the IBT out. But Milkman and Wong (2001, 2006) have a different view. According to them, in the mid-1990s, the truckers made a bid to affiliate with CWA Local 9400 (telephone workers). The union recruited during 1995 and 1996. They began with fifteen workers, but the group grew to contain thousands. They started with a series of demonstrations. In October 1995 they organized a giant caravan of trucks from the port to downtown, receiving a supportive resolution from the city council. In February 1996 they did a similar convoy in Long Beach. The CWA made several political efforts to challenge the legal definition of independent contractor, but were not able to succeed.

Then, under CWA leadership, the drivers went on strike in May 1996. They pursued a two-pronged strategy: they struck for union recognition against a dozen or so trucking companies with traditional employment, and they created a company called TMA (Transport Maritime Association), owned by Donald Allen, which would hire the truckers as regular employees. This would allow them to organize a union legally, and TMA would recognize them as union drivers and members of CWA Local 9400. The TMA would lease to conventional trucking companies. They would create a new dispatch system. Over four thousand truckers signed up.

The "strike" consisted of declining to work with the standard companies and signing up with Allen. This was by far the most effective of the strikes of the 1980s and 1990s. It received extensive support, both from the community and from other unions. The steamship lines responded by rerouting some ships. They won court injunctions, barring mass picketing at the terminal gates. The trucking firms refused to employ TMA drivers. They began recruiting replacement workers. Allen threatened to operate as a rival company instead of a labor-leasing company, but this must have fizzled.

The campaign was dogged by unforeseen problems. One of the top CWA leaders suddenly had a heart attack. Allen lacked the capital to carry out his promises. The trucking companies refused to do business with him, and the TMA collapsed. Nevarez's viewpoint is that the truckers want to use the unions for their own purposes and do not want to be the objects of their organizing drives. In other words, they have a sense of their own importance, autonomy, and power—they are hardly the passive recipients of the organizing efforts of others.

The Teamster Campaign. The IBT has been running a port trucker organizing campaign for the last few years.[5] The campaign is being run by the Port Division of the union (see www.teamster.org/divisions/_port/port.asp). We participated marginally and briefly in this effort when Gary Smith was the local Teamster organizer. We shall not describe the campaign in depth here. Essentially the idea is to organize port truckers throughout the country and bring them into the IBT.

The Teamsters have developed a Port Driver Bill of Rights, which is available on their website. Here is a brief version of the points it makes:

---

[5]Hal Leyshon (2001) has written an excellent study of port trucker organizing efforts in the ports of Seattle/Tacoma, where the Teamsters of a TDU-led local (Local 174) ran an impressive organizing drive. Leyshon thoroughly analyzed the situation of the port truckers and their efforts to organize—unsuccessfully, it turned out.

Port Drivers have certain fundamental rights, including the right to:

- Earn a fair wage to support themselves and their families;
- Health benefits for themselves and their families;
- Pension benefits;
- Compensation for all the time it takes to do the assigned work, including waiting time, maintenance and repair time, and time taken moving containers within the port;
- Safe and road-ready equipment at time of dispatch;
- Properly labeled containers, of a safe weight for transport over public streets and highways . . . ;
- Information on the contents of the containers they haul . . . ;
- Ironclad whistleblower protection for reporting the use of the same container to transport food products after toxic or hazardous materials without the container first being decontaminated;
- The right to refrain from cleaning out containers that have transported toxic substances or hazardous materials. . . . It is work for trained professionals;
- An environment free from all forms of harassment, discrimination, retaliation, and oppression; and
- Freedom to organize and form a union without the interference of employers.

This list demonstrates many of the types of unfair treatment that the port truckers face. Because of their independent contractor status, the union has felt that it has to find a way around a direct organizing drive. On the IBT website it states: "The Port Division is currently working with anti-trust lawyers to develop a legal strategy to organize the more than 40,000 owner-drivers who haul containers and bulk cargo in our nation's ports." One approach has been to try to get legislation passed that will allow independent contractors to join or form unions. In California, Senate Bill 848, introduced on behalf of the Teamsters by State Senator Joseph Dunn, aimed at extending antitrust immunity to owner-operators so that they can join unions, but Governor Arnold Schwarzenegger vetoed the bill in September 2005.

As we have already noted, the union has managed to get some pro–port-trucker legislation passed, including a law to fine terminal operators for long waits by truckers outside their gates and chassis roadability legislation to make the owners of the chassis—the steamship lines—take responsibility for fines arising from defective chassis. Meanwhile, the IBT has formed an alliance with the ILWU and the ILA to cooperate in organizing the port truckers. An important aspect of this alliance has been the effort to settle jurisdictional problems among the unions. The ILWU has drivers among its members, but they tend to have work that is limited to the docks. The IBT, on the other hand, claims control over the drives that come to and leave the terminal through its gates.

We have heard criticisms of the IBT efforts, including the fact that very few organizers have been assigned to it. The result is that there has been a lot of negotiating at the top (between the union and the companies) without much involvement by the drivers themselves. This has led to some anger by the drivers toward the union and even to some efforts to organize outside of it.

At the time of writing (early 2007), the IBT had resigned from the AFL-CIO and joined the new Change to Win union federation. The port truckers campaign got a boost from this new alliance, and Change to Win leaders were working with the IBT to make a success of it. We shall see what happens.

Assessment

In terms of our predictions about the effects of the logistics revolution on logistics workers, we find that the port truckers have suffered the full brunt of the impact. They have been made into contingent workers (by being defined as independent contractors), the job has been deunionized, the immigrant workers have been racialized as immigrant Latinos, and wages and working conditions have fallen.

Let us dwell for a moment on the racialization aspect. As we have stated, there is some sympathy for the port truckers as an obviously poorly treated group. And yet, we suspect, that they are Latinos as well as immigrants leads to a certain lack of ardor in fixing the situation. Undoubtedly this gets rationalized—"they are better off than they were in their country of origin," "they aren't citizens so they don't deserve equal treatment," "they brought this on themselves," and so on. We suspect that if they were white, calls for reform would be much louder and more sustained. Instead, because they are "only" Latino immigrants, their poor condition is tolerated, especially since so much money is saved this way.

There is an interesting dynamic with the ILWU regarding the racialization of the port truckers. On the one hand, some employers are quick to point out that ILWU members make so much more than the drivers. The implicit point is that the longshore workers make "too much" money and that if they made less, the drivers would be able to make more. We imagine the ideal, from this point of view, would be to ratchet down ILWU wages considerably, raise port trucker wages a little, and end up with lower labor costs in general. In other words, they would want to average downwards.

On the other hand, among workers themselves, there is some bad blood between the ILWU and the drivers. Port truckers complain that ILWU clerks treat them discourteously or take breaks, leaving drivers to wait in long lines. Drivers feel that they face some racism from ILWU members. And the truth is that some ILWU members do blame the immigrants for the downfall of the union in the ports (IBT). They feel that the immigrants came in and undercut the union, driving out the (white) union drivers. So, the sentiment goes, the Latinos have no one to blame but themselves, and they can't expect solidarity from good union members now that they want to organize. These may not be the dominant feelings, but we heard these kinds of attitudes during our research.

In conclusion, both railroad workers and port truckers have lost ground as a result of the logistics revolution. Its impact on them has been different. The truckers have been made into contingent workers, whereas the ranks of railroad workers have been slashed by the thousands. Unions have lost strength in both industries, but the decline is much more severe for the truckers. Racialization is more prominent among the truckers. But both groups have suffered from declining wages and working conditions, albeit more severely for the truck drivers. Labor, as represented by these two groups of workers, has been hurt by the logistics revolution.

CHAPTER 9

Warehouse and Distribution Center Workers

Our final group of logistics workers is employed in warehouses and distribution centers. What has happened to them as a result of the logistics revolution?

A BRIEF HISTORY OF WAREHOUSE UNIONS

One set of warehouse workers was connected with the waterfront. These workers handled the cargo that was brought on and off the ships. Out of the 1934 maritime strike and the formation of the ILWU came efforts to organize. In August 1934 the Weighers, Warehousemen's, and Cereal Workers Union Local 38–44 in San Francisco became active as part of the ILA and started an organizing drive, which was supported by the longshoremen. It later became ILWU Local 6 (for more information on this history, see www.ilwu.org).

In 1935 the union began its "march inland" to organize warehouse workers, especially around Sacramento (Schwartz 1978). They later became ILWU Local 17. By 1943, about 85 percent of the warehouse workers in Sacramento belonged to the new union. The ILWU (affiliated with the CIO) and the IBT (an AFL affiliate) fought over warehouse union jurisdiction. Teamster chief Dave Beck threatened to boycott the coast to pressure the ILWU to give up its inland warehouse members, but the effort failed.

The division between the unions was healed when James Hoffa succeeded Beck as IBT president, and in 1958 the two unions began to cooperate in contract negotiations in Northern California for their respective warehouse units. In 1960 they agreed to joint negotiations and coordinated strikes, which led to improved wages and working conditions.

In Southern California, warehouse workers were organized in ILWU Local 26. This local was able to build a secure organization, improve wages, and combat racial discrimination in the time before the logistics revolution.

WAREHOUSE WORKERS IN THE INLAND EMPIRE AND THE LOGISTICS REVOLUTION

At least ninety thousand workers are employed in the warehousing sector of the Inland Empire, according to John Husing. The figure is not precise, because companies select their own industrial classification code (SIC) in reporting their employee numbers to the state's Employment Development Department (EDD), which Husing uses as his source. For example, some retailer DCs may classify themselves as retailing rather than warehousing.

Another approach is to use the number of DCs and their size as a basis for estimating the size of the employee population. A simple rule of thumb for the number of workers per DC is to divide square footage by 2,000. For the newest, most technologically sophisticated DCs, the figure may be as high as 2,200. Adding up the square footage reported by the real estate agencies in Ontario, Chino, Rancho Cucamonga, Fontana, and Mira Loma, the total comes to 183 million sq. ft. Dividing by 2,000 gives us 91,500 workers. True, some of this square footage may not be warehousing space; perhaps some of it is being used for other industrial purposes. Still, given the convergence of the two systems of estimating, we feel fairly confident that the 90,000 figure must be fairly close to the mark.

The cost of labor in the Inland Empire is about 5 percent lower than it is in Los Angeles. There may be several reasons for this disparity: educational standards are lower, the cost of living is lower, workers are generally young and get paid starting wages, there is a shortage of alternative jobs, unions are weak or nonexistent, the labor force is heavily Latino and suffers from some discrimination, there is a lack of political representation at the local level for the Latino population (which precludes demands for improved labor standards), and there is pervasive use of temp agencies and employee leasing firms.

According to Steve Harrington of the DMA, the number of workers per warehouse has decreased with technology. Computers perform the task of inventory control. The work force gets divided between skilled labor for people who can handle computers and physical labor that can be done by anyone off the street.

Harrington pointed out that wages for warehouse workers were climbing because of a shortage of labor due to the rapid local growth of the industry. The average warehouse wage used to be eight to ten dollars per hour, but it had risen to ten to twelve dollars. Moreover, it is possible to move up through the ranks, become a foreman, and make forty thousand dollars a year. "You can make a career in this business."

Harrington also told us that the County of San Bernardino has a jobs development program that helps welfare recipients and the unemployed to find jobs. A warehouse can present them with criteria for potential employees. Typical criteria for a warehousing job would be: a high school diploma, no felonies, and previous experience. Some employers require some basic math skills. This local program pre-qualifies workers, handling recruitment and interviewing. It saves the DCs money: they do not need to advertise or hire a human resources (HR) person. The DC only has to do the last interview. Also, the program pays half of the worker's wages for the first three months, to cover training. The program will also provide on-site training and startup clothing for the workers, such as special shoes.

We asked Harrington about the workforce composition in terms of gender, age, and ethnicity. He answered as follows: "There are women in the warehouses. The days of no women are over. Generally, the employees reflect the demographics of the area. There are lots of Hispanic workers. I don't think they are undocumented except maybe in the smallest places."

Student labor is also sometimes employed in the DCs. Harrington started this way himself. UPS has a major program for students. They pay ten dollars an hour and provide benefits after ninety days. They also pay three thousand a year towards their college education. But "they really work those kids hard." In general students are an element in the work force. You can get away with paying them eight dollars an hour.

TEMP AGENCIES

The growth of DCs in the West End of the Inland Empire has stimulated a related industry, namely the temporary employment industry. While temp agencies supply labor to other sectors as well, there is no doubt that temp agencies have grown in importance in the Inland Empire, a major reason for which is the growth of distribution centers in the region.

Shirley Patrick, who works for a small temp agency called York Employment Service in Ontario, was the first person we interviewed on this topic, and she proved very helpful to us. When we asked her how the development of DCs in the area had affected the temp business, she replied, "The economics of this area is driven by temp agencies."

Patrick explained that the big warehouses use temp agencies for the following reasons: "They are all cross-docking operations out here. They have peaks, like Christmas and Halloween, so they like to use temp agencies to deal with the ebb and flow in demand. Also, they give us the liability—we are responsible for the workers' comp. They also do not have to hire an HR person for fifty thousand dollars. And they do not have to wait when they need workers at a moment's notice." Patrick said:

> The DCs lucked out by having the temp agencies available. They can call for a replacement worker many times a day. If a trailer has just backed up, they can call and get workers. We cover workers' comp, Social Security, and bonding. We have total responsibility for the worker. If there is an accident, we take care of it. We prepare an invoice to cover how much he has worked—say four hours or three days. The liability is all ours. It saves them a lot of money. And they don't have to cover unemployment insurance. We are the responsible employer, while they direct the workers.

About 60 percent of York's business is with warehouses, and the remaining 40 percent is for clerical workers. They do not want it higher for DCs. They like to have some smaller accounts, because if you have too many of yours eggs in one big account, and that business goes belly-up or shifts to another agency, you are in deep trouble. "That's what happened to Western Temp, which went bankrupt. They had everything in one big account."

Temp agencies are so important because they provide flexibility. There are 270 of them in the Ontario area, and the numbers have been growing because of the DCs. It has become a cutthroat business. "We are up against Select, Manpower, Kimco, Addeco—all national companies. We are just one company. We have to mark up to cover our costs. But those big companies provide less service."

"We won't wallow in the mud." Patrick said this several times. She meant that they will not get into a bidding war with these big companies. "We make a good honest bid, and try to stick with it. We may be a little flexible, but we will not wallow in the mud. The big companies come in lower. Many of them are self-insured. They pay into a pool for workers' comp, which cuts their costs."

She started working here around fifteen years ago. There were only a few agencies in the area then, and a lot less mudslinging. "We would form relationships with the other agencies, and we would help them fill their positions if they ran out of people. It still happens among the smaller agencies, but we would never call the big ones."

We asked Patrick what proportion of the DCs relied on temps. She could not give a clear estimate, but thought it could be around 60 percent. The remainder have an HR person. "Party City uses all temps (forty of them) except for management. Skechers, with its five huge warehouses, uses all temps. So does Kmart, which pays them $6.75 to $7.00 an hour. Wal-Mart is similar. They also pay minimum wage or close to it." She continued: "We won't work with companies like that. It is too labor-intensive for us to deal with minimum wage. This is because the agency gets a percentage markup, which is, of course, lower the lower the wage. It's hard on the office staff, and it doesn't pay. The big DCs go to the big agencies, and vice versa. Select had Kmart, and has Wal-Mart."

If there is a suit over an accident, it comes to the temp agencies. Consequently, her company always looks at the warehouses before it accepts them as customers. For example, Sports Chalet has a dirty and dangerous warehouse, filled with clutter. "We check out all of our customers," said Patrick. There were two small accidents at Party City. York staff had to go over and investigate and file a workers' comp report.

The temp agencies establish relationships with their DC customers. We asked if the workers tend to leave the agency for a more permanent job in the DC, if they can find it. "They are supposed to do six hundred hours with the agency," said Patrick. "But sometimes the DCs want to siphon off the stars. We will sometimes bend the rules and let them do this, in order to keep their business." The workers have to be over 18 years old. They are not especially young, Patrick said. Some are in their thirties. "Because we do a lot of intermodal work, they have to be over 18, because that is defined as interstate and so comes under federal standards."

We also asked her about ethnicity and gender in the workforce. Everyone who works for York has to be fluent in English. Some agencies specialize in Spanish-speaking workers, like Alta Staffing. Halco has some Spanish speakers. The warehouses hire lots of "Hispanics"—over 50 percent, which reflects the surrounding population. Patrick says: "I can honestly say we only look at qualifications. We don't look at size, ethnicity, gender, religion, et cetera. We try to match the person to what the employer wants. Our customer pays the bills, and we want to please him." She sends women to unload trucks, as well as men. They have a set of people who work for them, and turnover is low.

We asked about unions. One or two of the companies are union companies, so they are union in their DCs as well. An example is Oromco, which is a light-fixture company. When the agency is dealing with a unionized company, it abides by the contract. Patrick said: "A company is either union or not throughout the country." For example, Phillips Industries had a DC here. When there was a union campaign, they closed and left California. She said they would not cross a picket line with their temps. But rather than coming from a position of solidarity, Patrick sees the IBT as big bullies, and she wouldn't put her workers in a hazardous position.

Another viewpoint on temp agencies came from Patricia Goodwin and Joan Acosta, who work for Preferred Personnel, one of the top agencies in the Inland Empire. Goodwin and Acosta said that the warehousing industry uses temps because of the uneven demand for labor. There are peaks and valleys. "The DCs just want to pay for the labor they need. They often call us at the last minute. A container is due to arrive at the port the next morning, so they will call and ask for twenty or more temps the next day. Or containers can be hung up at the port, and then all arrive in a clump."

According to these women, every warehouse uses temps. They will have permanent staff, but a major part of the workforce is the temps. The temp workers themselves vary in permanence. Some are not looking for a permanent job. For one of their customers, Worldwide Dreams (which handles accessories, like purses) the agency provides a stable labor force of seventy people. After a time, the customer marks up the base rate, and when they have sufficient hours, they get paid holidays, vacations, and bonuses. The temp agency then charges a lower rate during these paid extras. Our interviewees see the company worldwide as a good employer. However, there is considerable variation in the quality of DC employers, according to Goodwin and Acosta.

Here is the way they characterize the relationships: "The workers are *our* employees. They are on our payroll. We pay them weekly. Then we recover the payroll from the customer. We try to get it in ten days, or at most, thirty days. [There is clearly some bitterness about this.] They are operating on our money. They don't pay COD. The DCs are not generous. They see their people as numbers. In contrast, we are fond of our workers and are happy when they get hired permanently."

In other words, there is a much closer relationship between the temp agencies and the workers than between the DCs and the workers. In a way, the temp agency is like a labor contractor whose interests are more closely tied with the workers than with the real employer. Of course, this may not be the case for all temp agencies. The big national chains may be far more impersonal.

Kay Aguilar, who is employed by Team One, a national temp agency, works full-time at the Target DC in the Inland Empire. She spoke about the industry in general as well as her own situation. According to Aguilar, about 75 percent of the DCs use temp services, but that does not mean that all of their workers are temps. They use temps for different reasons, with seasonality as the main factor. They use temp-to-hire when they are short on HR support, but the main reason is flexibility. A big advantage in using temps, according to Kay, is cost containment. The DCs do not have to run ads or hold interviews.

Aguilar said that the temp business is very competitive. "The margins are bad—they aren't reasonable. Making them worst is the fact that the temp agency has to cover workers' comp, FICA, unemployment insurance, and state and federal taxes because they are the employer." A workers' comp accident will raise your costs, so Aguilar's company tries to avoid them. They try to place workers in safe environments only, they build safe work habits, they give safety orientations, and they pre-screen to make sure that workers have not filed workers' comp cases in the past.

To sum up, we were given a number of reasons for the use of temp agencies by the DCs: It provides flexibility to deal with fluctuations of season and the arrival of cargo. It enables the company to avoid having to hire an HR director and all of the other associated costs of recruiting employees. It serves as a form of pre-screening for regular hires. The temp agency can make sure that the workers have a high school education and have not committed any felonies. After this first screening, the company can hire a temp for three months and see if they file a workers' comp claim. Both DCs and temp agencies want to avoid costly workers' comp claims even if they are fully warranted. They also fear that some workers game the system and file unwarranted claims. By letting three months pass, the temp agency can avoid hiring this form of "trouble maker." The workers' comp insurance is covered by the temp agency, alleviating the need for the company to cover it directly. In some cases, the temp agencies may misclassify warehouse workers, thereby paying a lower premium, which would be much harder for the DC itself to hide. Lastly, it keeps unions out.

THE WORK FORCE

According to Aguilar, DC workers need some math aptitude because they have to be able to count to build pallets. However, the most important requirement is dependability. Her temp agency does a reference check and a background investigation regarding thefts. They want to make sure that the workers have not committed any felonies. They want them to have a GED. They need to be able to learn to use a hand-held electronic instrument. Some DCs want the temp agency to look for a clean driving record, because they will have to drive a forklift.

Temp workers are mainly young, according to Aguilar. They are just getting their foot in the door. When they are older, she feels leery, wondering what is going on in their lives. The majority are in the twenties. Here is what Aguilar said about the gender composition of the DC temp workforce: "Women are catching up, but it's about 80 percent men and 20 percent women. We evaluate the environment to see who is suitable for the job. Women are capable of standing all day. They have smaller hands and are able to concentrate. Men have big hands and shorter attention spans. It depends on culture, too. In a Hispanic environment, you can't have women lead because the men would have a fit. With Orientals, the men are like women, with small hands. They are petite."

Needless to say, we find this type of stereotyping appalling and only report it because it is obviously widely held.

As with the DC industry as a whole, the temp workforce reflects the local population. According to Aguilar, there are lots of Hispanics and African Americans. Riverside has more African Americans, as does Upland. Ontario is more of a melting pot, with Hispanics, African Americans, and whites.

WAGES AND WORKING CONDITIONS

Apart from the wage discrepancy, what are labor conditions like in the Inland Empire DCs? It is our impression that starting wages fall in the eight to ten dollar per hour range, with some notable exceptions. The Toyota DC pays an average wage of seventeen dollars an hour, making it a highly desirable place to work. It is possible that the other automobile companies follow a similar strategy, though Toyota prides itself on its exceptional standards. Opportunities for upward mobility to low-level supervisory positions are seemingly abundant, allowing workers to move up in terms of pay.

Apparently there is a labor shortage, especially of workers with the needed skills, which include reading, elementary computer skills, and the ability to handle complex machinery such as forklifts. Training programs are being developed in a number of schools in the region, which may alleviate the shortage. The work itself probably takes multiple forms, from folding clothes and putting labels on them (likely to be women's work) to driving a forklift (probably men's work). It can be dangerous work, and accidents happen. This leads to the state setting high workers' compensation insurance rates—a source of considerable grievance to the industry.

The challenge of forming a union by temp workers is intense, and this may, in fact, be the critical factor in choosing to use this form of labor. A fragmented, unorganized, depoliticized workforce certainly has its attractions. A small union toehold does exist in the area. Most important is UPS, which is organized by the IBT, though it remains a low-wage employer, dependent upon student labor. The Teamsters appear to have a few other warehouses in the Inland Empire, though we were unable to obtain a list. Some major union LTL trucking companies, also organized by the IBT, are active in the region. We heard, but were not able to confirm, that GM was opening a unionized facility. UNITE had an old Kmart DC in Los Angeles under contract, and the union has apparently organized Kmart's newer, more modern facility in the Inland Empire successfully.

LABOR STANDARDS FOR TEMPS

Aguilar discussed the issue of labor standards for temp workers, observing that the 3PLs were the worst offenders because their profit margins were so low: "They only want bodies to do the work." At Target, where she works, the temp jobs are similar to those of the regular employees. We asked Aguilar whether temp workers make as much pay as direct hired. The answer is no, confirming Steve Harrington's comments about this. The rate of pay for the temp worker depends on the bill rate of the temp agency, that is, the markup that the temp agency sets for itself. The more requirements the DC puts on the temp agency, the less the agency can pass on to the workers, and the more problems they have with retention. "Of course," said Aguilar, "we aren't a social service. We are in it to make money."

In general terms, she estimated that in 2002, the DCs paid the temp agencies about $12 per worker. The 3PLs pay less because they are only making pennies on the dollar. The "company direct" DCs, that is, the corporate DCs, pay better. At the Target DC, where Aguilar works, direct hires can start at $12.80 and go up to $17 with experience. The temps start at around $8.50, and it can go up to $9.50 and even $12. Temp workers do not receive paid benefits, though they may get options to purchase them, but most can't afford them. Team One does pay for holidays and vacations after employees have worked for them for a while.

According to Patrick, the workers get no benefits, no paid vacations, and no sick leave. The agency may pay for a holiday sometimes for a long-standing employee. But she believes that warehouse wages are going up. "Hardly any of the jobs are minimum-wage anymore. Most temp workers won't take a straight minimum wage job of $6.75 and hour when someone is offering $8 an hour." She agrees that there is a small labor shortage, of recent origins, which may be driving wages up a bit. "Toyota is the best employer, pays the most. They have a waiting list of five hundred. They provide benefits. Another good employer is Meico, which is connected with Honda."

DIRECT HIRES, PERMATEMPS, AND EMPLOYEE LEASING

We asked Kay Aguilar whether temp workers ever become permanent. She replied that the word *permanent* is a no-no, because nothing is permanent and you never know when you will get laid off. Rather, the industry uses the term *direct hire*. Warehouse workers can be employed on a temp-to-hire basis, meaning they can move from the temp position to becoming a direct hire. "The workers start as temps because the company wants to test-drive them, check them out," she said. The temp agency thus serves a kind of screening and probation role for the DC, which then selects the best of the workers. The temp agencies find that their best workers are creamed off—"but we are happy for them."

Are there "permatemps," we wondered? By this we meant people who occupy the same job endlessly but are never converted to a direct hire position. Aguilar referred to these as "payrolled" people. The DC will sometimes turn over its own employees to a temp agency to handle the payrolling and cover the workers' comp. This makes the temp agency the direct employer, since whoever cuts the check is the employer. (We define this system as *employee leasing*.)

We wondered about the stability in the relationship between DCs and temp agencies. Do DCs use one temp agency or more? Do they develop long-term relationships? Aguilar responded that there are various scenarios. Some DCs use several temp agencies as backups. They operate on JIT and have to move the merchandise. Sometimes management projections aren't accurate, and they may have to order twenty-five people to work the next day. It is hard for a temp agency to respond that quickly, so the DC will use several services. Other DCs are better organized and know a week in advance how many workers they will need. A three- to four-day lead is sufficient.

Some DCs treat the temp agencies well and others don't, according to Aguilar. Some treat the vendor as a partner, and others feel that people are expendable and don't bother to cultivate a relationship. What about Wal-Mart, we wondered? Here is her reply: "Wal-Mart uses all 3PLs to run its DCs. It uses Exel and Complete Logistics. I believe they use three temp services, including Staffmark. These agencies have a very low markup, which they try to make up in volume. But their liability is dangerous. If they have one accident, it wipes out their profits. They operate almost like a cattle market. Exel is known for employees getting a lot of back injuries. They don't provide the employees with an orientation. They work their people too hard."

It should be said here that Aguilar was working for a major Wal-Mart competitor, Target. She worked for Target full-time and saw them as a fantastic employer. Team One, Aguilar's temp agency, is a Latino-owned, California-based company that had been in business for ten years in 2002. It specialized in very large "on-sites," which means that the agency is at the DC and manages the workers. She said: "There are non co-employment issues because we manage our workers on site." If the agency is not present and an accident occurs, the DC must put it on its own OSHA log. "By being present, we put it on ours."

Apparently there are two types of temp agencies, and each has its function. On the one hand is the commonsense understanding in which workers go to an agency that specializes in temporary placements. The workers are sent to a company to work there for a limited period. Some may end up being hired as direct employees, and the use of temp agencies can provide the firm with a kind of probationary period in which potential employees are screened. This means that the "best" workers, however defined, are creamed from the temp pool into the direct employee ranks. The issue of defining "best" is important, because it may entail making sure that workers will not file workers' comp claims.

The other form of temp usage is known as employee leasing. In this case, the company turns its regular employees over to an intermediate "employment services" agency, which then serves as their employer of record. The temp agency doesn't recruit workers or supply extra labor in times of need. It simply manages the labor force for the principal company. One of the advantages of such an arrangement is that the DC can distance itself from the workers and can claim, correctly, that it does not employ them. The principal reason for creating such a buffer is probably to avoid workers' comp problems. The leasing firm takes full charge of workers' comp issues. Presumably, in these cases the DC could also avoid being the employer for union purposes. Although this situation reeks of joint employment, it seems very likely that the DCs have laid down careful legal cover to avoid any such claim.

WORKERS' COMPENSATION

There was plenty of discussion in our interviews of the role that workers' comp plays in the use of temp agencies. It was believed that temp agencies are often used by DCs to avoid having to deal with workers' comp, while the temp agencies engage in scams to try to underpay into the program. One way this can be done is by misclassifying warehouse work, which is a fairly high-risk occupation, so that the rates are lower than they should be. The temp agency has to cover workers' comp, FICA, unemployment insurance, and state and federal taxes, because it is the employer.

Shirley Patrick said that workers' comp is higher for the temp agencies. They are horrified at the expense. It costs them about twenty-five thousand dollars a year. Because it is so expensive, the temp agencies manipulate the figures. They change the workers' classifications. Each job has a classification code. They put down a less costly code. For example, clerical work is low costing, whereas warehouse work, which is more dangerous, has higher-priced workers' comp. If they are audited, the agency is penalized for fraud, and the company that uses them is also fined. But this kind of fraud is very common.

The use of temp agencies affects wages and working conditions, among other things. While the industry prides itself on reasonably decent salaries and benefits for its employees, an army of temp workers receives none of these advantages, and it works at close to the minimum wage. For example, Steve Harrington of DMA said that the warehouses typically pay the temp agencies something like $10 per hour, and the agency pays the workers $6.50 or $7. The agencies also have to cover workers' compensation, so they have little left for their margin. "Workers' comp has killed their margin. Some have folded. If an employee is injured, their premium goes up. They go out of business, reopen, and set up a new workers' comp system."

Aguilar discussed this issue:

> If the temp service does due diligence, it makes sure that the temps are placed in a safe environment. I won't place my workers in an unsafe environment. I make sure there aren't two sets of rules regarding safety—one for temps and one for others. There are bottom feeders in the temp industry that don't do that. I have seen places where one set of workers was wearing helmets and another wasn't. When I asked about it I was told, "They are just temps." The companies that behave this way are whores. They are generally mom-and-pop operations. The temp industry is notorious for them. They shut down and change their names in order to avoid workers' comp payments.

Like others, Aguilar stated that some of the temp companies cheat on their workers' comp. They do not pay in the right workers' comp group.

In sum, it appears that one of the major motives for the use of temp agencies is to avoid dealing with workers' comp. There are three mechanisms: First, the DCs employ workers as temps to check them out for several months, to make sure they won't file a workers' comp claim. The implication of this practice is that the companies feel that there is no such thing as a legitimate claim that all claims by workers are fraudulent. Second, the temp agencies take over responsibility for workers' comp payments, sometimes cheating by misclassifying employees so that they pay lower rates than warehousing requires. Third, in the case of employee leasing, the temp agency maintains a full-time staff person on site at the DC to make sure that in case of an accident, the DC itself does not have to report it. This is a mechanism for avoiding any hint of joint employment, and it also ensures that the DC has no responsibility for accidents on its premises.

Law enforcement agencies have become aware of these kinds of scams, and some investigations are under way in the Inland Empire and elsewhere in the country. We spoke with Glenn Shor of the California Division of Labor Standards Enforcement (DLSE) about it. He said that there is a lot of interest in the issue of workers' comp scams, especially with the development of DCs in semi-rural areas. County district attorneys are making inquiries about it. Moreover, Shor reported that the AFL-CIO was looking into the big temp agency Labor Ready. There are also cases in Ohio and Washington.

The investigations and cases concern the three issues we have already mentioned, that DCs employ workers as temps to check them out for several months and make sure they do not file claims (implying that the firms believe that most workers' comp claims are not legitimate); the temp agencies take charge of workers' comp for the DCs and sometimes cheat by misclassifying the employees to lower-risk and lower-rate jobs; and the temp agencies maintain full-time staff at the DCs so that the DCs avoid having any record that their employees were hurt in accidents. The DCs are supposed to have their own workers' comp insurance policies, even if they are under the umbrella of a temp agency's policy. If they do not do so, they are violating the law.

Shor said that in California two agencies get involved, depending on how the issue comes up: the Fraud Division of the Department of Insurance, and the DAs of the counties. Shor's office, the Division of Workers' Comp in the DLSE, focuses mainly on the lack of insurance: "There is existing law under the workers' comp fraud statutes that would encourage going after the DCs, and we have some special funding to do it. But these are difficult investigations, and we tend to go after easier cases."

We followed up this discussion with a conversation with Tracy Bartell, a deputy district attorney for San Bernardino County. Her job was focused on workers' comp premium fraud, where employers were cheating the insurance companies. She thought this was probably rampant among the DCs but was not certain. At the time of the interview (September of 2002), she was prosecuting a woman who worked for Adeco, a giant temp agency. A man named Thomas Stephens was hired through them as a forklift operator by DC Logistics. He twisted his knee and apparently got a deep thrombosis, but Adeco denied treatment.

Another common scam is to divide workers' pay into minimum wage and "shares." This is done by a payroll agency (which may be the same as an employee leasing company). The only check that is officially known is the wage check. The shareholder check is received separately. The purpose of this scam is to avoid paying not only workers' comp insurance but also unemployment insurance to EDD.

We also talked with Will Collette of the AFL-CIO. He was working on the labor movement's investigation of the giant temp agency Labor Ready. He said:

> The three largest industries that use temp agencies are construction, transportation, and light manufacturing. Their use is mainly driven by the need to get

around workers' comp. These three industries have the highest accident and insurance rates. Workers' comp fraud often takes the following form: A temp agency will get a five-year contract with an insurance company. They give a description of their work force but skew it in the direction of white collar office workers or gradually increase the blue collar percentage. Meanwhile they get a fixed rate. After a while the insurance carrier discovers they have been ripped off. They could sue, but generally they cut their losses and cancel the coverage.

In sum, there is a hornet's nest of problems surrounding the use of temp agencies by the DCs, some of which involve questionable legal practices.

UNION ORGANIZING

As we have already indicated, some of the DCs have a union presence as an extension of the unionization of the parent company. The IBT has a few warehouses under contract, the most important of which is the UPS facility near Ontario Airport. And some union LTL companies operate in the area. On the whole, though, the DCs in the Inland Empire are largely unorganized. Whatever purposes the temp agencies serve in terms of avoiding workers' comp, they are also a very effective tool against union organizing. Consider the challenge: If the union focuses on organizing direct hires, then the DC can strive to lessen its dependence upon them and turn to temp workers. If the union tries to organize a temp agency, then, like a garment contractor, it will be dropped by the indirect employer, the DC. You have to organize the whole *pulpo*—the "octopus," as the garment union ILG would call the entire contracted-out production system—certainly a daunting task.

Another challenge is the difficulty of singling out a particular DC or DC-operating 3PL for organizing, since it would be placed at a disadvantage relative to its competitors. This dilemma suggests a sectoral approach. In other words, the union might try to organize a clump of warehouses in one specific sector, such as auto parts or refrigerated warehousing. Of course, such an approach requires considerable resources. And some union organizers believe that it can't be done without bringing in the port truckers who, in a combined campaign with the DC workers, might be able to hold a powerful strike.

The ILWU is engaged in organizing a particular sector of the warehousing business as we write. They are focusing on the warehouses that are run by the steamship lines. This makes good sense because the steamship lines are their principal employers, and these warehouses are an extension of dock activities. We shall see how this campaign unfolds.

238

ASSESSMENT

The development of DCs in the Inland Empire is a product of the logistics revolution, so there is no substantial local history with which to compare contemporary conditions. In looking at those conditions, however, it does appear that DC workers suffer from some of the same effects as other logistics workers. Many have been made into contingent workers, with the extensive use of temps and employee leasing. They are largely racialized in the sense that they are mainly Latinos who are politically underrepresented in the region and who are paid lower wages than their counterparts in neighboring Los Angeles and Orange County. We cannot say they have been "deunionized," but certainly unions are weak and the use of temps makes unionization extremely difficult. Moreover, if part of the reason for moving to the Inland Empire was to escape LA County's unions, then one can describe these workers as having lost union protection. Finally, the more efficient, modern DCs seem to provide cleaner, less back-breaking jobs, but the number of workers per square foot has declined, so there would be job loss if warehouses had existed here earlier. Wages are low, but they may be better than they would have been without the logistics revolution, especially for direct hires. But the large temp sector works for low wages and without benefits.

CONCLUSION

In this and the previous two chapters, we have discussed the effects of the logistics revolution of five groups of workers: seafarers, longshore workers, port truckers, railroad workers, and warehouse DC workers. Let us briefly review some of the conditions faced by all five groups of workers.

— Seafarers and port truckers both have experienced a rise in contingency-based employment, racialization, loss of unions, and an overall decline in working conditions and pay.
— Longshore workers and railroad workers share some commonalities in that they are both still highly unionized, although their unions are under attack and they face job losses. Railroad workers face a harsher situation, however, since they have to deal with a decline in working conditions.
— Warehouse and DC workers in the Inland Empire have also experienced contingency-based employment, racialization, union loss, and low wages.

Nationwide, the fastest-growing sectors of the logistics industry, trucking and warehousing, have experienced rises in employment over the past twenty years, with increases of 60 and 70 percent, respectively. According to Marcy Rein, in an article in the ILWU newsletter, *The Dispatcher* titled "Desert docks and octopi: How is ILWU work changing and why?": "Union density in the fastest-growing parts of the cargo-handling industry declined steadily from 1983 to 2002. Density fell from 31 percent to 14 percent in warehousing, from 35 percent to 24 percent in trucking" in general (1/05). For port truckers, union density has been all but erased from the work-force. These sectors are also marked by the high rates of contingency-based employment and low wages. This is in contrast to the higher-paid sectors of the logistics system, especially longshore and railroad workers, who have experienced decreases in jobs.

Conclusion

Winners and Losers

The logistics revolution has, without question, brought increased efficiency to the production and distribution of goods. Products are made that are more likely to suit the precise demands of consumers. They are delivered with greater speed and accuracy and at lower cost. It can be argued that these changes have created a win-win situation for everyone. Corporations have cut costs, enabling them to be more competitive and (presumably) to improve their profitability. Consumers are able to buy the goods they want when they want them and, often, for a lower price. The clear benefits are demonstrated by the success and growth of giant retailers like Wal-Mart.

But this glowing picture is also marred by the existence of losers. The logistics revolution has not been waged without harming some actors. These include small businesses, and the "Main Streets" of some cities and towns, which have been drained of their unique character as well as their special relationship to their locality (in terms of ads in the press and support for local charities).

In fact, all the numerous criticisms that have grown toward Wal-Mart apply to the logistics revolution as well. Wal-Mart epitomizes the effects of the logistics revolution and is one of its foremost leaders. Books, movies, and television shows criticizing the company are pouring out (Dicker 2005; Featherstone 2004; Fishman 2006; Lichtenstein 2006; Norman 1999; Quinn 2000). Critical websites also abound, for example www.walmartwatch.com run by the UFCW (United Food and Commercial Workers). Hardly a day goes by without a newspaper article exposing some new scandal or containing Wal-Mart executives' defense of their firm's practices.

Among the major "losers" in the logistics revolution have been workers, as we have tried to show. We have focused our research efforts entirely on logistics workers, but the damage certainly extends way beyond them: to sales workers in the giant retail stores and to production workers both here and around the globe, who face sweatshop production in all its manifestations. Workers have lost job security, unions have been weakened, many jobs have been racialized (often by shipping them offshore to countries where workers of color suffer under systems of oppression linked to Western domination), and wages and working conditions have deteriorated.

Nelson Lichtenstein (2006) recently edited a book in which he described Wal-Mart as "a template for twenty-first century capitalism," in contrast to General Motors as the dominant corporate model of the twentieth century. His main point is that the GM era meant strong unions, wages and benefits that could sustain a middle-class lifestyle for working people, and state support for these institutions. In other words, GM epitomizes the period prior to the logistics revolution. The Wal-Mart model, which is closely linked to the logistics revolution, consists of low wages and poor benefits, fierce opposition to unions, and support for neoliberal (free market) policies here and abroad. This is a model associated with growing inequality and a hollowing-out of the middle class.

THE LOGISTICS REVOLUTION AND THE U.S. LABOR MOVEMENT

The U.S. labor movement reached its apex in the decade after World War II, when social, political, and economic configurations were very different. The "push" production system was well suited to strong trade unions. Large manufacturing plants enabled workers to meet each other and develop common cause. Manufacturers, aided by state regulation, could push increased costs out onto retailers and consumers. This enabled the firms to bear the expense of a unionized workforce. And the whole system was rooted in Keynesian economics, which supported the notion that putting more money in the hands of workers bolstered the economy. A kind of equilibrium was achieved, of big, unionized, production plants supported by institutions like the National Labor Relations Act (NLRA). The societal presumption was that unions were basically a good thing for society and should receive the full support of the law.

True, this happy picture excluded many workers, as has been well documented by writers in the "dual labor markets" tradition. While workers in the "core" or "primary" sector of large manufacturing plants, most of whom were white males, benefited from this regime, women and people of color were often marginalized. Coexisting with the big companies was a "secondary labor market" of small, non-unionized companies that depended upon arbitrary authority, lacked internal mobility opportunities, failed to provide standardized raises and benefits, and the like. Part of this division depended on exceptions in the NLRA, which left out agricultural workers, small businesses, and certain kinds of service workers from its provisions—workers who were more than likely excluded based on their race or gender.

In any case, for a variety of reasons specified in chapter 1, the political economy has changed drastically. All of the features that we have identified as the logistics revolution have taken hold, with "pull" production, increased contingency and contracting out, offshore production, deregulation, flexible specialization, and so on. These changes have meant that the characteristics of the "secondary labor market" have become more prevalent throughout the economy. Smaller, less-centralized companies, surrounded by contingency, have become the norm rather than the exception.

These important changes, it seems to us, have not yet been fully comprehended by the majority of the U.S. labor movement, or if they are understood, they have left many unions paralyzed about how to respond. They cling tenaciously to the shrinking share of the market that they can still hold on to because it retains some of the old "primary labor market" or "push" features, but they have lost bargaining power as they cannot control a particular sector any more. Too often they hold on to the state sector for partial salvation, using their political allies to pressure governments to pay union-level or "living" wages. For this reason, the most robust unionization and union growth is found in the public sector or in sectors linked to the government.

Contracting out, as we have seen, poses intense challenges for organizing, since winning a union in a contracting network too often means that the contracted firm will go out of business, as the head of the network turns to cheaper, non-union alternatives. Meanwhile, workers employed in the same network, by the same ultimate employer, rarely know of each other, and even if they do, are faced with a constantly morphing group of contracting companies. The nexus of offshore production and contracting merely multiplies this problem exponentially. Global production networks are typically secretive as well as mobile. How does one capture and bind to a union contract such a fluid entity? Again, too often, unions play it safe and focus on the few economic sectors that cannot move offshore, thereby throwing up their hands in resignation at trying to organize their industry. In part, the success of the SEIU (Service Employees International Union) in organizing comes from the fact that it focuses on the kind of services that cannot flee. On the other hand, SEIU has brilliantly taken up the challenge of organizing contracted-out sectors, for example in their Justice for Janitors campaign.

In sum, there is a way in which much of the U.S. labor movement has failed to recognize or respond to the logistics revolution. Too often, union leadership operates as if the world still looked like it did sixty years ago. Insufficient attention has been paid to the profound economic and organizational changes that have occurred. We believe that if U.S. labor is to successfully turn itself around, it cannot simply turn to organizational reform—important though that is. Rather, its leaders need to develop a new and different strategic approach to organizing that takes full account of the logistics revolution.

VULNERABILITIES CREATED BY THE LOGISTICS REVOLUTION

While the logistics revolution seems to portend the demise of the labor movement in many ways, we believe that it also carries its own, different set of vulnerabilities that make possible new approaches to working-class organization. As the concept of dialectics implies, every strength has its weakness and every weakness its strength. We need to study the new world created by the logistics revolution from this point of view. On its surface, it may appear that the logistics revolution weakens organized labor almost to the point of death. But no system is invulnerable or immutable, and current-day global capitalism is no exception. We have identified at least ten major vulnerabilities:

1. *Long Supply Lines.* The global production and distribution system associated with the logistics revolution means that products must be shipped from all corners of the globe. They must travel long distances by air and ocean transportation. As any army knows, there are dangers associated with extended supply lines because the longer the line, the more open it is to attack and the harder it is to defend. Long supply lines open up more opportunities for work stoppages than a short one. In other words, the longer the line, the more opportunities for discontented workers to rebel somewhere along it, slowing down the movement of freight.

2. *Just-In-Time.* One of the greatest vulnerabilities of global capitalism lies in a core concept of the logistics revolution, namely, the effort to keep inventory levels at a minimum and to link production as much as possible to demand. This means that the system operates with relatively small margins for errors and delays. Combining this vulnerability with the previous one, we can see that problems along the supply chain can be more than trivially costly to companies that operate on JIT principles. They may lose sales and find that they do not have the inventory they need when they need it.

A well-known case of this vulnerability was revealed in a strike at a General Motors supply plant. While this example did not involve global production, occurring within the United States, it showed the weakness of JIT because GM depended on this particular part to assemble its cars. When a strategic strike shut down the parts supplier, GM's production ground to a halt, losing the company millions of dollars and forcing them to settle the strike. This case not only demonstrates the basic vulnerability of JIT but also shows that it affords unions the possibility of engaging in a strategic work-action that is considerably less intensive in terms of resources and organizing efforts to achieve a negative impact on a much larger entity.

True, companies that rely on JIT may be able to adapt fairly quickly to such contingencies. Once they have a warning that parts of their supply chain may shut down, they can attempt to move their production and distribution around to alternatives. But still, they are likely to be very inconvenienced, and the temporary solution may be costly.

3. *Seasons.* A number of industries are subject to seasonality. This is notably true of much retailing, which concentrates a goodly percentage of its sales into the end of the year, including back-to-school through Christmas. This fact, connected to the previous two factors, again points to an unavoidable vulnerability, from an industry perspective. If it is possible to gum up the supply chain during peak season, a great deal of damage can be done to a company.

4. *Nodes.* A related vulnerability is found in the fact that almost all global supply chains must pass through a limited number of transportation nodes, such as ports and airports. These nodes are potential chokepoints in the system. It was this reality that led us to study the ports of LA/LB in the first place, since about 40 percent of all ocean-borne imports to the United States must pass through these twin ports.

This reality and its accompanying vulnerability is recognized by major shippers as well as the U.S. government. Most government attention has focused on the vulnerability of these nodes to terrorist action. If terrorists attacked a major port or airport, it could cause serious economic disruption to the country for an important period of time. This has led to policy efforts to protect against the danger, though, according to many experts, far too little has been spent on this issue. Talk of inspecting every single container for a possible terrorist threat, when the number of containers entering the country each year falls into the millions, raises concerns about interference with the free flow of commerce. Such inspections would be both costly and slow and hence are completely impractical.

But there is also awareness by the international trade community of the dangers of labor conflict that can shut down critical nodes. The ILWU lockout of 2002 is an example that led to a presidential invocation of Taft-Hartley to force the ports back open and to even more dire threats of methods to weaken the union, such as moving it from NLRA jurisdiction to the much weaker Railway Labor Act (RLA) or a ban on coastwise bargaining. As we mentioned in chapter 7, losses from the lockout were estimated in the billions of dollars.

Even without labor action, congestion has demonstrated the weaknesses inherent in a limited number of key nodes. In 2004 the Southern California ports faced a growth in container traffic that they had not anticipated and were not prepared to deal with. And continuing growth in trade with Asia will only make this problem worse.

True, shippers, carriers, and the government are seeking alternatives, as we discussed in chapter 5. But as we also pointed out in that chapter, all of the alternatives have their drawbacks. They are slower or more costly or pose the problem of constructing hugely expensive new infrastructure. Some of it might happen, and no one can predict what alternatives will be developed in the long run. But in the meantime, key nodes remain a major vulnerability, especially for a seasonal operation reliant on JIT.

5. *Unbalanced Links with Contractors.* The International Ladies Garment Workers Union (ILGWU), which merged with ACTWU to form UNITE, and then with HERE to form UNITE-HERE, faced some conditions resembling those produced by the logistics revolution long before many other unions. The women's apparel industry was one of the first to engage in systematic contracting out (the ability to shift from one contractor to the next to maximize flexibility and minimize wages), the use of piece rate and a racialized labor force both domestically and internationally, and global production and a race to the bottom, pitting countries against each other for low-wage production.

The features of the apparel industry that led it to be a pioneer in this kind of networked production system have been discussed elsewhere (e.g., Bonacich and Appelbaum 2000), but it is interesting to recognize that other major industries have come to resemble apparel production forms, leading to many sweatshop production sites around the globe.

Having to cope with contracted-out systems led some of the ILGWU organizers to learn some important lessons about how to organize them.[1] In particular, they were able to take advantage of the variable looseness of ties to contractors to pit contractors and manufacturers against one another.

The goal was to get the manufacturer to sign a jobbers' agreement under which the manufacturer would agree to work with union contractors only.

---

[1]Two contemporary masters of organizing under these conditions that it has been our honor to observe in action during their tenure at the ILGWU are Jeff Hermanson and David Young, now employed as director of organizing and executive director, respectively, for the Writers Guild of America, West, where some of the same principles apply.

Taft-Hartley contains a garment industry proviso, an exception to second-ary boycotts that allows the union to picket a manufacturer in order to get it to sign the jobbers' agreement. This is illegal for most industries, and it was only the strength of the garment unions and the obvious sweatshop problem in the industry that allowed for this exception. Still, even though the ILG had a legal advantage in being able to tie contractors and manu-facturers together and compel the latter to agree to work with union con-tractors exclusively, there are other ways to achieve the same ends. SEIU's Justice for Janitors effort accomplished a similar goal without the law on its side.

The divide-and-conquer game is played by getting some contractors to sign "me too" agreements. They promise to accept union terms if the union succeeds in organizing the manufacturer; in exchange, the union does not attack them if they temporarily stop working for that manufacturer. Of course, the flexible production system means that the manufacturer can turn to other contractors, but it takes a brave-hearted contractor to step into the middle of a labor conflict. Without strong ties to the manufacturer, why should they take the risk? So it becomes possible to peel off some of the manufacturer's contractors, leaving it in trouble. In sum, the weakness of contracting ties, normally a feature that the manufacturer can use to its advantage, can be turned into a strength for the union.

In some cases, the manufacturer depends on a core set of contractors with whom it establishes fairly stable long-term relations. Despite the ad-vantages of flexibility, there are reasons for having stronger ties with some contractors. Loyalty can pay off when there are problems of shortage, congestion, or queuing. If a firm has ties with a contractor, it can expect special treatment in time of need. The strong ties are a form of insurance. But just as weak ties create vulnerabilities for the manufacturer, so can strong ties. Strong ties contain some of the organizing advantages of big plants. They do not allow for the "race to the bottom." It is much harder for the manufacturer to shift production away from these core contractors, meaning that they are more vulnerable to a strike action.

6. International System. The system of global production and distribu-tion brings international workers together in an unprecedented manner, by linking them to the same industry and supply chain. True, there have been international linkages of this sort in the past, for example, cotton grow-ers in the U.S. south, textile mill workers in the north United States and Britain, and apparel workers in various countries in Europe and the United States. But the number of such linkages has grown hugely.

The main point is that workers around the world are employed either directly or indirectly by the same employer. This joins them in a poten-tial commonality that could be used to put intense pressure on that firm from multiple angles. That some of the major global actors are retailers

247

means that their production and distribution empires are vast indeed. They "employ" many workers of all types and nationalities under a single umbrella. Wal-Mart provides an example of such an empire. Under its umbrella are not only its direct employees: the sales workers and also the workers of its suppliers (factory workers) and logistics providers (transportation and distribution workers). All of these workers share a common "enemy," as it were, and have the potential to join together as a powerful force.

Of course, the giant retailers (and manufacturers) are very good at pitting workers against each other so that one group blames another for job loss or the decline in wages and working conditions. But, with strong and farsighted leaders, it is conceivable that labor movements around the world could find common cause in combating a shared enemy.

7. *Visibility.* That retailers play an increasingly important role in global production has implications for the role that consumers can play in this struggle. Consumers have already shown some capacity to put effective pressure on name brands, like Nike or Coca-Cola. Indeed, a whole movement has arisen, demanding codes of conduct and effective monitoring of production sites as a means of combating global sweatshops.

So far retailers have not been the brunt of this movement, but there is no good reason why they could not be. As centralized locations of multiple products, they have high visibility with consumers. Already considerable attention has been paid to Wal-Mart and its socially costly practices. The possibility of waging a successful campaign again such a giant corporation would depend on strong consumer support, building on all the experiences of the anti-sweatshop movement.

8. *Potential Allies.* The big box retailers, like Wal-Mart, have made a lot of enemies, as we have seen throughout this book, and some of these could become at least temporary allies with labor in putting pressure on them. They have been accused of destroying small businesses and the character of a community, leading to the opposition not only of the business community but also of local politicians who have an interest in preserving the cultural and business equilibrium of a community. They have faced fierce opposition by trade unions when the big box retailer threatens to undercut existing contracts with competitors.

Vendors, both locally and offshore, have expressed their anger at some of the big box retailers, and their ceaseless efforts to cut the prices and profits of their contractors. The retailers also use their power to push their vendors around in other ways that may make them consider being part of a coalition to curb the power of the retailers. These grievances could be manipulated by a union campaign that asks for a vendor to cease doing business with a retailer on a temporary basis until a resolution has been found that might even benefit the vendor. Logistics providers may share some of the grievances of the vendors and may also be willing to put their business elsewhere during a labor struggle.

A variety of community opponents may exist. One type of community opposition comes directly from the logistics sector, namely, those people and community activists that are concerned with pollution and congestion. We have briefly seen (in chapter 5) how an effective movement was created by the communities surrounding the ports to insist that pollution be kept under some degree of control.

Similarly, as in so many labor struggles, political allies can certainly be found for the kinds of campaigns we are considering here. We have already seen how the Teamsters were able to get cooperation from the California Trucking Association to get legislation passed that would, at least indirectly, help the port truckers. Labor-friendly legislators can also be counted on for support.

The point is that the existence of so many different kinds of enemies created by the big box retailers opens up the possibility of at least temporary or occasional forms of cooperation that could be useful in putting pressure on one of them. True, many of these opponents would rather die than find common cause with organized labor. But there may be ways of working with them on limited reforms that could achieve some of labor's goals.

9. *Strategic Importance of Logistics Workers/Unions.* For a number of the reasons listed above, especially the long supply lines, JIT, seasonality, and nodes, the global transportation and warehousing sector is absolutely vital to the success of global capitalism as we know it. It depends on the constant and unfettered flow of commodities in a timely manner. This opens up the possibility of the workers and unions in this sector to combine with a view to using their potential power to maximum effect.

Of course transportation has always been a critical and vulnerable sector in the economy, and this is undoubtedly the reason why transportation unions, like the IBT and ILWU, have been able to become so powerful. But we have also seen how this power has been undermined by deregulation and the logistics revolution. However, we still believe that considerable potential power resides in this sector—if logistics unions both nationally and around the world could communicate better with each other and find ways to work more effectively together, they would become a formidable force.

Organizing the Logistics Workers in Southern California

Ideally, coordination among logistics workers and unions needs to be developed at the national level, and some of that is occurring. The IBT is pursuing a national campaign to organize port truckers, and the ILWU, along with the ILA on the East Coast, have pledged to support the campaign. The IBT and ILWU also came to an agreement about jurisdictional issues, so that on-dock trucking was left to the ILWU while hauling to and from the docks would be considered IBT work. In addition, the Brotherhood of Locomotive Engineers (BLE) has become part of the Teamsters, a merger that does not address the problem of the warring railroad brotherhoods. Even more significantly, the IBT has joined the newly split-off labor federation Change to Win (CTW), and some of the best thinkers from the new grouping are joining with IBT leaders to help make the ports campaign a winning endeavor.

While we believe that a national-level plan would be ideal, we start with a more modest approach by focusing on Southern California. As we have seen, the ILWU remains a powerful force on the West Coast, including, of course, Southern California, but is under threat by both the shippers and carriers, who would like to tame it. Efforts have been made to organize the port truckers, but so far without success. The railroad workers are stuck in a war of attrition as their jobs are eroded. And the warehouses in the Inland Empire remain largely uncharted territory for the labor movement. What can be done with this diverse set of circumstances? Can these groups of workers and unions find common cause so that they can work together in a drive to organize them all?

Some movement toward cooperation between unions has occurred. Recognizing all the difficulties that lie in the path toward full cooperation, we would like to imagine the possibility. We propose that all of the logistics unions active in Southern California call a convention in which they discuss their common cause. Such a convention would examine the state of organizing among logistics workers, in general, and the need for all the unions involved to coordinate with each other. In particular, the two groups most in need of help are the port truckers and the warehouse workers. The convention could strive to develop an overarching strategic approach to organizing the entire industry complex that makes sure that all groups of workers are included.

How might the groups of workers organize together? Here are a few rudimentary thoughts about it:

1. *Consider where unions already have strength in the system.* The ILWU's position is clearly a tremendous strength, but there are other strong points as well. A list should be made of all the warehouses and DCs that are currently unionized, and with which union. The union LTL trucking companies (including UPS) that operate in this arena need to be identified. The railroad brotherhoods are another union presence. In addition, there are all those shippers that engage in importing, use the ports, have DCs in the region, and are union.

2. *Map the flow of goods.* A major strength of logistics workers and unions is that they intersect with each other in the flow of goods. Truckers, for example, have access to warehouse workers because they deliver containers past the gates, however well guarded, and into the warehouse complex. This allows for communication and coordination across the entire system. Knowing the way goods move and the timing and flow of such movements could allow for coordinated action.

3. *Decide where the campaign should focus.* What part of the logistics system needs to be organized first? For example, should a concerted effort be made to organize the port truckers? Or should the campaign start with a focus on warehouse workers?

4. *Decide on the scope of the effort.* Should they choose a particular company and go after its entire supply chain? Or should they go after a sector, like toys, garments, food, or automotive? Or should the goal be to organize on scale and attempt to unionize the entire logistics system? If a particular company were selected, would it be a good idea to go after a big retailer, like Wal-Mart or Target? Or should one treat the retailers as a sector that needs to be organized as a unit?

5. *Isolate the target's vulnerabilities.* In making these decisions, the coalition would need to figure out the particular weak points of the target. Are its imports highly seasonal? Do they depend on JIT deliveries? Is there a time when a strike would have maximum impact?

Our point is that, in working together, the various logistics unions would multiply their capacity to effect change, not just for themselves, but for other workers in the system. We are not suggesting for a moment that such a plan would be easy to implement. Some of the problems would include: getting diverse organizations with very different structures and philosophies to work together, sharing scarce resources, and deciding on how to carve up the resulting membership. In addition, there would be the danger that shippers might get wind of the campaign and make alternative plans. This raises the issue of bringing in the logistics workers from other ports, both on the West Coast and on the East. Then there is the chance of a fierce government crackdown. The coalition would have to be prepared for it by having aroused community and political support for the campaign so that a crackdown would result in mass protest. In addition, it would be useful to develop consumer support and action at the targeted retailer (or retailers).

Needless to say, this kind of thinking could be spun out endlessly. We simply want to open the possibility that such a thing might be accomplished if a certain kind of leadership came forward and decided to do it. It would require considerable research, let alone organizational work, to become an effective working coalition. And it would require considerable grassroots organizing among workers.

The purpose of organizing all of the logistics workers at the ports into an effective fighting force is not just to gain power and increase the well-being of those workers in the system who are currently unorganized and exploited, like the port truckers—worthy though that goal is in itself. The purpose is ultimately to create among U.S. workers worthy partners for a global struggle. Our vision is one of joining local logistics workers with global production workers in a joint effort to gain power in the global economy. For the U.S. side of this equation to work, the workers must be organized, the unions must be powerful, and they must be able to coordinate effectively with each other.

Interviews

Kay Aguilar, Business Development Manager, Team One (temp agency), 8/23/02 (phone interview)

Jeff Amos, Director of Western Region, Don Breazeale and Associates, 8/4/03

Dave Arian, Head of Harry Bridges Institute and Member of ILWU Local 13

Craig Bagdasar, Member of ILWU Local 94, 5/17/02, 7/19/02

Andy Banks, Instructor at George Meany Center, 5/30/01 (with Fernando Gapasin)

Tracy Bartell, Deputy District Attorney in San Bernardino County, 9/3/02

Rose Bauss, Logistics Manager, Toyota North America Parts

Torben Blichfeld, General Manager, Vessel Coordination, Maersk-Sealand, 11/9/01

Don Breazeale, President, Don Breazeale and Associates, 6/18/03 (phone interview)

Bob Brendza, Director, Facility Development, BNSF, San Bernardino, 6/16/03

Jay Carroll, Vice President of Logistics, Toyo Tires, 7/9/03

Cary Cartwright, Manager of Transportation Planning, POLB, 5/16/01

Maureen Cecil, Customs Broker and Head of Los Angeles Customs Brokers and Freight Forwarders Association, 6/16/01

Chris Chase, Marketing Manager, POLA, 9/17/01

Debby Clerc, Former Inbound Transportation Manager, Pic 'N' Save, Rancho Cucamonga, 9/27/01

Will Collette, Building Trades, AFL-CIO, 9/5/02 (phone interview)

Larry Cottrill, Manager of Master Planning, POLB, 7/10/01

Jon DeCesare, Principal, West Coast Logistics Consulting, 7/15/02, 7/1/04

Juan DeLara, Graduate Student, Ontario, 6/27/02

John DiBernardo, Vice President, SSA Terminals, 5/12/03 (with Peter Hall)

John Dittmer, Inland Empire Economic Partnership, 7/4/02 (phone interview)

Ray Enriquez, Legislative Representative, California State Legislative Board, Brotherhood of Locomotive Engineers Div 660, 6/20/02 (with Gary Smith)

Ray Familathe, ILWU and ITF Representatiive, 3/29/02

John Favor, Marketing Manager, POLB, 2/13/02

Andrew C. Fox, President, Pacific Harbor Line, 6/18/02

Tony Girodo, Manager of Retail Americas, Exel, and Operator of Wal-Mart DC, Mira Loma, 7/24/03 (with Rebecca Giem)

Patricia Goodwin and Joan Acosta, Regional VP and Branch Manager, Preferred Personnel, Riverside, 4/15/03

Kathleen Gordon, VP West Coast Region, Mitsui O.S.K. Lines (MOL), 4/19/02

Peter Hall, Doctoral Student in Regional and City Planning, UC Berkeley, 5/25/01

Steve Harrington, President, Distribution Management Association of Southern California, 8/2/02

Markus Hesse, Professor, Free University of Berlin, 6/4/01

Rob Hickey, Director of Organizing, IBT Local 174 in Seattle, 6/13/02 (phone interview)

Kent Hindes, Cushman and Wakefield Real Estate, Ontario, 9/2/03

Johnny Hodges, Manager of Order Fulfillment, Texas Instruments, 7/19/04, 8/11/04 (phone interviews)

John Husing, Inland Empire Economist, 7/30/02 (phone interview)

Rick Jackson, Logistics Expert, The Limited, 9/8/04 (phone interview)

Gabriel Kahn, Reporter, *Wall Street Journal*, 9/1/04 (phone interview)

Josh Kamensky, Research Assistant, ILWU Organizing, 5/9/01

Lawrence H. Kaufman, Author, Retired, Former Employee of BNSF, Former Vice President for Public Affairs of the Association of American Railroads, *Journal of Commerce*, Transportation Editor, 5/22/02, 2/24/02 (phone interview)

Koko Khiang, Burmese seafarer and union leader, 7/18/02

Norman King, Executive Director, SanBag, 9/4/01 (phone interview)

Bob Kleist, Corporate Adviser, Pacific South West Region, Evergreen American Corp, 6/24/02

George Kuvakis, President, ILWU Local 94, 8/21/01 (with Craig Bagdasar)

Joah Loar, J. B. Hunt Transport Inc., 7/7/03
Tim Mahler, Maersk Logistics USA, 1/30/02
Carolyn Martin, Director of Customer Service, International Transport Service Inc (Terminal Operator and Stevedoring Company), 7/3/01 (with Jill Esbenshade)
Robert McAfee, Manager of Port Operations, BNSF, 3/27/02
Domenick Miretti, ILWU Liaison to CITT, 9/7/01
Bill Mongelluzzo, Reporter, *Journal of Commerce,* 12/20/01
Dave Neumann, Assistant Depot Manager, Costco Depot, Mira Loma, 8/30/04
Ernesto Nevarez, Port trucker activist and leader, 3/15/02, 4/3/02, 4/24/02 (with Manuel Barrajas)
Peter Olney, Director of Organizing, ILWU, various occasions, 2001–2004
Shirley Patrick, York Employment Services Inc., Ontario, 6/10/02, 6/17/02 (with Rebecca Giem)
B. J. Patterson, Western Regional VP, NFI National Distribution Centers, Former Manager of Wal-Mart DC in Mira Loma, 9/30/03
Charles J. (Chuck) Potempa, Director of Pacific South-West Hub Facility Operations (Hobart Railyard) BNSF, 6/5/02, 6/13/02
Wilma Powell, Director of Marketing, POLB, 9/19/02
Chuck Savre, VP, West Coast Ports, Eagle Marine Services Ltd. (APL), 3/21/03 (with Peter Hall)
Kayle Schreiber, Import Transportation Manager, Ontario Import Center T-595, Target Corporation, 6/30/03 (with Rebecca Giem)
Ty Schuiling, SanBag, 6/18/03 (phone interview)
Patty Senecal, Vice President of Sales, Transport Express, Inc., 6/13/01
Glenn Shor, California Division of Labor Standards Enforcement, Division of Workers Compensation, 8/28/02 (phone interview)
Gary Smith, Organizer, Port Trucker Campaign, IBT, various occasions, 2001–2003
Tim Smith, California State Legislative Board, Brotherhood of Locomotive Engineers, 6/11/02, 6/14/02 (phone interviews)
Donald Snyder, Manager, Import and Export Logistics, Mattel, 8/16/01
Dale Stephens, Traffic Manager, Costco, 6/24/04 (phone interview)
Kim Suchomel, Vice President, Costco, 6/30/04 (phone interview)
Mary L. Sullivan, Regional Client Services Manager, Grubb and Ellis Real Estate, Ontario, 6/26/02 (with Rebecca Giem)
Rudy Vanderhider, Southern California ITF Representative and ILWU member, 8/24/02
Marianne Veneiris, Director, CITT, California State University, Long Beach, 7/10/01
John Wall, President, ContainerFreight EIT, 7/28/03, 8/26/03

Chuck Wallace, Vice President for Southern California, PMA, 1/16/02

Harry Wilkes, Director, Logistics Services, Cal Cartage Co., 6/25/02

Jay Winter, Executive Director, Steamship Association of Southern California (SASC), 8/2/01, 12/7/01

John Yettaw, Manager, Intermodal Terminal Operations, Intermodal Container Transfer Facility (ICTF), UP, 8/8/01

Ken Yunger, BNSF, Fort Worth, 8/2/01 (phone interview)

References

Abernathy, Frederick H., John T. Dunlop, Janice Hammond, and David Weil. 1999. *A Stitch in Time: Lean Retailing and the Transformation of Manufacturing—Lessons from the Apparel and Textile Industries.* New York: Oxford.

Amante, Maragtas S. V. 2004. "Industrial Democracy in the Rough Seas: The Case of Philippine Seafarers." *The Industrial Relations Research Association: Proceedings* 2004. Available at www.press.uillinois.edu/journals/irra/proceedings2004/index.html accessed 7/8/05.

Appelbaum, Richard P., and Nelson Lichtenstein. 2007. "A New World of Retail Supremacy: Supply Chains and Workers' Chains in the Age of Wal-Mart." *International Labor and Working-Class History* 70 (Spring).

Armstrong, Philip, Andrew Glyn, and John Harrison. 1991. *Capitalism since 1945.* Oxford: Blackwell.

Association of American Railroads. 2001, 2003, 2004. *Railroad Facts.* Washington, DC: Policy and Economics Department, AAR.

Bank Muñoz, Carolina. 2004. "Mobile Capital, Immobile Labor: Inequality in the Tortilla Industry." *Social Justice: A Journal of Crime, Conflict, and World Order* 31:21–39.

Belzer, Michael H. 2000. *Sweatshops on Wheels: Winners and Losers in Trucking Deregulation.* New York: Oxford University Press.

Bernstein, David E. 2000. "Racism, Railroad Unions, and Labor Regulations." George Mason Law and Economics Research Paper.

Boczek, Boleslaw Adam. 1962. *Flags of Convenience: An International Legal Study.* Cambridge: Harvard University Press.

Bolstorff, Peter, and Robert Rosenbaum. 2003. *Supply Chain Excellence.* New York: American Management Association.

Bonacich, Edna. 2000. "Intense Challenges, Tentative Possibilities: Organizing Immigrant Garment Workers in Los Angeles." In *Immigrants and Union Organizing in California,* ed. Ruth Milkman. Ithaca: Cornell University Press, 130–49.

Bonacich, Edna, and Richard P. Appelbaum. 2000. *Behind the Label: Inequality in the Los Angeles Apparel Industry.* Berkeley: University of California Press.

Bonacich, Edna, and Jake B. Wilson. 2005. "Hoisted by Its Own Petard: Organizing Wal-Mart's Logistics Workers." *New Labor Forum* 14, no. 2: 67–75.

———. 2006. "Global Production and Distribution: Wal-Mart's Global Logistics Empire (with Special Reference to the China/Southern California Connection)." In *Wal-Mart World,* ed. Stanley Brunn. New York: Routledge, 227–42.

Bonacich, Edna, with Khaleelah Hardie. 2006. "Wal-Mart and the Logistics Revolution." In *Wal-Mart: The Face of Twenty-First Century Capitalism,* ed. Nelson Lichtenstein. New York: New Press, 163–87.

Boschken, Herman L. 1988. *Strategic Design and Organizational Change: Pacific Rim Seaports in Transition.* Tuscaloosa: University of Alabama Press.

Bowersox, Donald J., David J. Closs, and M. Bixby Cooper. 2002. *Supply Chain Logistics Management.* New York: McGraw-Hill.

Brooks, Mary. 2000. *Sea Change in Liner Shipping: Regulation and Managerial Decision-Making in a Global Industry.* Oxford: Elsevier Science.

Calix, Robert. 2002. *Southern California Freight Management Case Study (Six County SCAG Region).* Los Angeles: LA County Metropolitan Transportation Authority (MTA), Southern California Association of Governments (SCAG), California Department of Transportation (DOT).

Campbell, Scott. 1993. "Increasing Trade, Declining Port Cities: Port Containerization and the Regional Diffusion of Economic Benefits." In *Trading Industries, Trading Regions: International Trade, American Industry, and Regional Economic Development,* ed. Helzi Noponen, Julie Graham, and Ann R. Markusen. New York: Guilford, 212–55.

Carillo, Eduardo. 2002. "Chinese Onslaught: Pinoys Losing Out to Dragon Seafarers Offering Trouble-Free Service and Accepting Lower Wages in International Vessels." *Tinig ng Marino,* Internet edition, September/October 2002. Available at www.ufs.ph/tinig/sepocto2/09100202.html, accessed 7/9/05.

Cariou, Pierre. 2002. "Strategic Alliances in Liner Shipping: An Analysis of 'Operational Synergies.'" Paper presented at the IAME conference, Panama.

Carre, Francoise, Marianne A. Ferber, Lonnie Golden, and Stephen A. Herzenberg, eds. 2000. *Nonstandard Work: The Nature and Challenges of Changing Employment Arrangements.* Champaign, IL: Industrial Relations Research Association, University of Illinois at Urbana-Champaign.

Castells, Manuel. 1996. *The Rise of the Network Society.* Oxford: Blackwell.

Chilcote, Paul W. 1988. "The Containerization Story: Meeting the Competition in Trade." In *Urban Ports and Harbor Management: Responding to Change Along U.S. Waterfronts,* ed. Marc J. Hershman. New York: Taylor and Francis, 125–45.

Cohen, Shoshanah, and Joseph Roussel. 2005. *Strategic Supply Chain Management: The Five Disciplines of Top Performance.* New York: McGraw-Hill.

Cohen, Stephen S. 2002. "Economic Impact of a West Coast Dock Shutdown." Berkeley: University of California, Department of Regional Planning, January.

Corbett, Kevin S. 1996. "Double or Nothing: The Big Stakes of Hub Ports." *Journal of Urban Technology* 3:1–10.

Cudahy, Brian J. 2006. *Box Boats: How Container Ships Changed the World.* New York: Fordham University Press.

DeBoer, David J., and Lawrence H. Kaufman. 2002. *An American Transportation Story: The Obstacles, the Challenges, the Promise.* Greenbelt, MD: Intermodal Association of North America.

Dicker, John. 2005. *The United States of Wal-Mart.* New York: Jeremy P. Tarcher/Penguin.

Dowd, Thomas J. 1988. "Port Finances and Operations: Understanding the Bottom Line." In *Urban Ports and Harbor Management,* ed. Marc J. Hershman. New York: Taylor and Francis, 217–33.

Ducatel, Ken, and Nicholas Blomley. 1990. "Rethinking Retail Capital." *International Journal of Urban and Regional Research* 14:207–27.

Erie, Steven P. 2004. *Globalizing L.A.: Trade, Infrastructure, and Regional Development.* Stanford: Stanford University Press.

Fairley, Lincoln. 1979. *Facing Mechanization: The West Coast Longshore Plan.* Los Angeles: Institute of Industrial Relations, University of California, Los Angeles.

Featherstone, Liza. 2004. *Selling Women Short: The Landmark Battle for Workers' Rights at Wal-Mart.* New York: Basic Books.

Finlay, William. 1988. *Work on the Waterfront: Worker Power and Technological Change in a West Coast Port.* Philadelphia: Temple University Press.

Fishman, Charles. 2003. "The Wal-Mart You Don't Know: Why Low Prices Have a High Cost." *Fast Company* (December): 68–80.

———. 2006. *The Wal-Mart Effect: How the World's Most Powerful Company Really Works—And How It's Transforming the American Economy.* New York: Penguin.

Foner, Philip S. 1974. *Organized Labor and the Black Worker, 1619–1973.* New York: Praeger.

Forbath, William E. 1991. *Law and the Shaping of the American Labor Movement.* Cambridge: Harvard University Press.

Garnel, Donald. 1972. *The Rise of Teamster Power in the West.* Berkeley: University of California Press.

Gereffi, Gary, and Timothy J. Sturgeon. 2004. "Globalization, Employment, and Economic Development: A Briefing Paper." Sloan Workshop Series in Industry Studies, Rockport, Massachusetts, June 14–16.

Gibson, Andrew, and Arthur Donovan. 2000. *The Abandoned Ocean: A History of United States Maritime Policy.* Columbia: University of South Carolina Press.

Glenn, Evelyn Nakano. 2002. *Unequal Freedom: How Race and Gender Shaped American Citizenship and Labor.* Cambridge, MA: Harvard University Press.

Grimm, Curtis, and Robert J. Windle. 1998. "Regulation and Deregulation in Surface Freight, Airlines, and Telecommunications." In *Regulatory Reform and Labor Markets,* ed. James Peoples. Boston: Kluwer, 15–49.

Gulick, John. 1998. "'It's All about Market Share': Competition among U.S. West Coast Ports for Trans-Pacific Containerized Cargo." In *Space and Transport in the World-System,* ed. Paul S. Ciccantell and Stephen G. Bunker. Westport, CT: Greenwood, 61–83.

———. 2001. *Landside Risks: The Ecological Contradictions of Port of Oakland Globalism.* Ph.D. dissertation, University of California, Santa Cruz.

Hall, Peter Voss. 2002. *The Institution of Infrastructure and the Development of Port-Regions.* Ph.D. dissertation, University of California, Berkeley.

———. 2004. "'We'd Have to Sink the Ships': Impact Studies and the 2002 West Coast Port Lockout." *Economic Development Quarterly* 18, no. 4: 354–367.

Handfield, Robert B., and Ernest L. Nichols Jr. 2002. *Supply Chain Redesign: Transforming Supply Chains into Integrated Value Chains.* Upper Saddle River, NJ: Prentice Hall.

Harrison, Bennett. 1994. *Lean and Mean: The Changing Landscape of Corporate Power in the Age of Flexibility.* New York: Basic Books.

Hartman, Paul T. 1969. *Collective Bargaining and Productivity: The Longshore Mechanization Agreement.* Berkeley and Los Angeles: University of California Press.

Harvey, David. 1990. *The Condition of Postmodernity.* Malden, MA: Blackwell.

———. 1999. *The Limits to Capital*. London: Verso.

Hirsch, Barry T., and David A. Macpherson. 1998. "Earnings and Employment in Trucking: Deregulating a Naturally Competitive Industry." In *Regulatory Reform and Labor Markets*, ed. James Peoples. Boston: Kluwer, 61–112.

Hugos, Michael. 2003. *Essentials of Supply Chain Management*. Hoboken, NJ: John Wiley.

Kendall, Lane C., and James J. Buckley. 2001. *The Business of Shipping*, 7th ed. Centreville, MD: Cornell Maritime Press.

Kimmeldorf, Howard. 1988. *Red or Rackets: The Making of Radical and Conservative Unions on the Waterfront*. Berkeley and Los Angeles: University of California Press.

Kumar, Nirmalya. 1996. "The Power of Trust in Manufacturer-Retailer Relationships." In *Harvard Business Review on Managing the Value Chain*. Boston: Harvard Business School Press, 91–126. Reprinted 2000.

Kyser, Jack. 2006. *International Trade Trends and Impacts: The Southern California Region 2005 Results and 2006 Outlook*. Los Angeles County Economic Development Corporation.

Lane, Tony. 1997. "Globalization, Deregulation, and Crew Competence in World Shipping." In *Transport Regulation Matters*, ed. James McConville. London and Washington, D.C.: Pinter.

Larson, Paul D., and H. Barry Spraggins. 2000. "The American Railroad Industry: Twenty Years after Staggers." *Transportation Quarterly* 54:31–45.

Lee, Ching Kwan. 1998. *Gender and the South China Miracle: Two Worlds of Factory Women*. Berkeley: University of California Press.

Levinson, Marc. 2006. *The Box: How the Shipping Container Made the World Smaller and the World Economy Bigger*. Princeton: Princeton University Press.

Leyshon, Hal. 2001. "Port Drivers Organizing." Unpublished paper.

Lichtenstein, Nelson, ed. 2006. *Wal-Mart: The Face of Twenty-First-Century Capitalism*. New York: New Press.

Lieb, Robert C. 1974. *Labor in the Transportation Industries*. New York: Praeger.

Lieb, Robert, and Michael E. Hickey. 2003a. *The Use of Third Party Logistics Services by Large American Manufacturers, the 2002 Survey*. Chicago: Accenture and Northeastern University College of Business Administration.

———. 2003b. *The Year 2002 Survey: CEO Perspectives on the Current Status and Future Prospects of the Third Party Logistics Industry in the United States*. Chicago: Accenture and Northeastern University College of Business Administration.

Luberoff, David, and Jay Walder. 2000. "U.S. Ports and the Funding of Intermodal Facilities: An Overview of Key Issues." *Transportation Quarterly* 54:23–45.

Mercer Management Consulting, Inc. and Standard and Poor's DRI. *1998. San Pedro Bay Long-Term Cargo Forcast: Final Report.*

Meyer, Mohaddes, and Associates. 2001. *Ports of Long Beach/Los Angeles Transportation Study.* Submitted to the Port of Long Beach and the Port of Los Angeles.

Milkman, Ruth, ed. 2000. *Immigrants and Union Organizing in California.* Ithaca: Cornell University Press, 2000.

Milkman, Ruth, and Kent Wong. 2001. "Organizing Immigrant Workers: Case Studies from Southern California." In *Rekindling the Movement: Labor's Quest for Relevance in the Twenty-First Century,* ed. Lowell Turner, Harry C. Katz, and Richard W. Hurd. Ithaca: Cornell University Press, 99–128.

——. 2006. "Sí, se puede: Union Organizing Strategies and Immigrant Workers." In *L.A. Story: Immigrant Workers and the Future of the U.S. Labor Movement.* New York: Russell Sage, 145–86.

Monaco, Kristen, and Lisa Grobar. 2004. "A Study of Drayage at the Ports of Los Angeles and Long Beach." Long Beach: California State University Long Beach, Department of Economics.

Müller, Gerhardt. 1999. *Intermodal Freight Transportation.* 4th ed. Washington, D.C.: Eno Transportation Foundation and Intermodal Association of North America.

Nelson, Bruce. 1988. *Workers on the Waterfront: Seamen, Longshoremen, and Unionism in the 1930s.* Urbana and Chicago: University of Illinois Press.

——. 1992. "Class and Race in the Crescent City: The ILWU, from San Francisco to New Orleans." In *The CIO's Left-Led Unions,* ed. Steve Rosswurm. New Brunswick, NJ: Rutgers University Press, 19–45.

——. 1998. "The 'Lords of the Docks' Reconsidered: Race Relations among West Coast Longshoremen, 1933–1961." In *Waterfront Workers: New Perspectives on Race and Class,* ed. Calvin Winslow. Urbana: University of Illinois Press, 155–92.

——. 2001. *Divided We Stand: American Workers and the Struggle for Black Equality.* Princeton: Princeton University Press.

Ngai, Pun. 2005. *Made in China: Women Factory Workers in a Global Workplace.* Durham: Duke University Press.

Norman, Al. 1999. *Slam-Dunking Wal-Mart: How You Can Stop Superstore Sprawl in Your Hometown.* Atlantic City, NJ: Raphael Marketing.

Olney, Peter. 2003. "On the Waterfront: Analysis of ILWU Lockout." *New Labor Forum* 12, no. 1 (Summer): 28–37.

Ortega, Bob. 1998. *In Sam We Trust: The Untold Story of Sam Walton and How Wal-Mart is Devouring America.* New York: Times Books.

Overby, Rorie. 2005. "Supply and Demand of Ocean Container Drayage in Southern California." Unpublished paper.

Pacific Maritime Association [PMA]. 2003, 2005, 2006. *Annual Report.*

Peoples, James, ed. 1998. *Regulatory Reform and Labor Markets.* Norwell, MA: Kluwer.

Petrovic, Misha, and Gary G. Hamilton. 2006. "Making Global Markets: Wal-Mart and Its Suppliers." In *Wal-Mart: The Face of Twenty-First Century Capitalism,* ed. Nelson Lichtenstein. New York: New Press, 107–41.

Piore, Michael, and Charles Sabel. 1986. *The Second Industrial Divide: Possibilities for Prosperity.* New York: Basic Books.

Pollin, Robert. 2003. *Contours of Descent: U.S. Economic Fractures and the Landscape of Global Austerity.* London: Verso.

Quam-Wickham, Nancy. 1992. "Who Controls the Hiring Hall? The Struggle for Job Control in the ILWU during World War II." In *The CIO's Left-Led Unions,* ed. Steve Rosswurm. New Brunswick, NJ: Rutgers University Press, 47–67.

Quinn, Bill. 2000. *How Wal-Mart is Destroying America (and the World): And What You Can Do About It.* Berkeley: Ten Speed Press.

Rimmer, Peter J. 1998. "Transport and Telecommunications among World Cities." In *Globalization and the World of Large Cities,* ed. Fu-chen Lo and Yue-man Yeung. Tokyo: United Nations University Press, 431–70.

Salzinger, Leslie. 2003. *Genders in Production: Making Workers in Mexico's Global Factories.* Berkeley: University of California Press.

Santiago, Leo J. 2005. "Seafarers' Groups Hit 'Burdensome' Re-tooling Scheme." OFW Journalism Consortium, Inc., 6/19/05. Available at www.ilocostimes.com/jun06-jun19–05/feature.htm, accessed 7/9/05.

Saxton, Alexander. 1971. *The Indispensable Enemy: Labor and the Anti-Chinese Movement in California.* Berkeley: University of California.

Schechter, Damon. 2002. *Delivering the Goods: The Art of Managing Your Supply Chain.* Hoboken, NJ: John Wiley.

Schneider, Betty V. H., and Abraham Siegel. 1956. "Industrial Relations in the Pacific Coast Longshore Industry." Berkeley: Institute of Industrial Relations, University of California.

Schwartz, Harvey. 1978. *The March Inland: Origins of the ILWU Warehouse Division, 1934–1938.* San Francisco: ILWU. Reprinted 2000.

Seifert, Dirk. 2003. *Collaborative Planning, Forecasting, and Replenishment: How to Create a Supply Chain Advantage.* New York: AMACOM.

Shashikumar, N., and G. L. Schatz. 2000. "The Impact of U.S. Regulatory Changes on International Intermodal Movements." *Transportation Journal* 40:5–14.

Slack, Brian. 1993. "Pawns in the Game: Ports in a Global Transportation System." *Growth and Change* 24:579–88.

Slater, Robert. 2003. *The Wal-Mart Decade: How a New Generation of Leaders Turned Sam Walton's Legacy into the World's #1 Company.* New York: Portfolio.

Sletmo, Gunnar K., and Ernest W. Williams Jr. 1981. *Liner Conferences in the Container Age: U.S. Policy at Sea.* New York: Macmillan.

Stopford, Martin. 1997. *Maritime Economics.* 2nd ed. London: Routledge.

Talley, Wayne K. 2000. "Ocean Container Shipping: Impacts of a Technological Improvement." *Journal of Economic Issues* 34:933–48.

———. 2002. "Wage Differentials of U.S. Ports and Transportation Industries: Deregulation versus Regulation." International Association of Maritime Economists 2002 Conference, Panama.

Talley, Wayne K., and Ann V. Schwarz-Miller. 1998. "Railroad Deregulation and Union Labor Earnings." In *Regulatory Reform and Labor Markets,* ed. James Peoples. Boston: Kluwer, 125–53.

Teske, Paul, Samuel Best, and Michael Mintrom. 1995. *Dergeulating Freight Transportation: Delivering the Goods.* Washington, D.C.: American Enterprise Institute.

Tompkins, James A., and Jerry D. Smith, eds. 1998. *The Warehouse Management Handbook,* 2nd ed. Raleigh, NC: Tompkins Press.

United Nations Conference on Trade and Development [UNCTAD]. 2003. *Review of Maritime Transport 2003.* Geneva: United Nations.

———. 2005. *TNCs and the Removal of Textile and Clothing Quotas.* Geneva: United Nations.

U.S. Census Bureau. Selected years. *Statistical Abstract of the United States.* Washington, D.C.

U.S. General Accounting Office [GAO]. 2003. *Container Security: Expansion of Key Customs Programs Will Require Greater Attention to Critical Success Factors.* Washington, D.C.: Government Printing Office, GAO–03–770.

Varley, Pamela, ed. 1998. *The Sweatshop Quandary: Corporate Responsibility on the Global Frontier.* Washington, D.C.: Investor Responsibility Research Center.

Warehousing Education and Research Council [WERC]. 1994. *The Mass Merchant Distribution Channel: Challenges and Opportunities.* Oak Brook, IL: WERC.

Wellman, David. 1995. *The Union Makes Us Strong: Radical Unionism on the San Francisco Waterfront.* New York: Cambridge University Press.

Willis, Amy, Lisa Gallegos, Eric Schwimmer, Susie Joo, and Francisco Garcia. 2003. "Trucking and Warehouse Sectors: Importance to the Five-County Region and Workforce Implications." Paper prepared for

Urban Planning course taught by Goetz Wolff, University of California, Los Angeles.

Winslow, Calvin, ed. 1998. *Waterfront Workers: New Perspectives on Race and Class*. Urbana and Chicago: University of Illinois Press.

Wood, Donald F., Anthony P. Barone, Paul R. Murphy, and Daniel L. Wardlow. 2002. *International Logistics*. 2nd ed. New York: American Management Association.

World Trade Organization [WTO]. 2005. *World Trade Report*.

Wrigley, Neil, and Michelle Lowe, eds. 1996. *Retailing, Consumption, and Capital: Towards the New Retail Geography*. Harlow, England: Longman.

———. 2002. *Reading Retail: A Geographical Perspective on Retailing and Consumption Spaces*. London: Arnold.

Index